The Irish
Bed & Breakfast
Book

The Irish
Bed & Breakfast Book

FOURTH EDITION

By Frank and Fran Sullivan

PELICAN PUBLISHING COMPANY

GRETNA 2000

First edition, September 1994
Second printing, May 1995
Second edition, July 1996
Third edition, January 1998
Fourth edition, January 2000

---

*The word "Pelican" and the depiction of a pelican are trademarks
of Pelican Publishing Company, Inc., and are registered in the
U.S. Patent and Trademark Office.*

Library of Congress Cataloging-in-Publication Data

Sullivan, Frank.
    The Irish bed and breakfast book : country and tourist homes,
farms, guesthouses, inns / by Frank and Fran Sullivan. — 4th ed.
      p.   cm.
    ISBN 1-56554-684-9 (pbk. : alk. paper)
    1. Bed and breakfast accommodations—Ireland Guidebooks.
2. Ireland Guidebooks.   I. Sullivan, Fran.   II. Title.
TX907.5.I73S85 2000
647.94417'03—dc21

99-39271
CIP

Illustrations by Linda Lewis, Jessica Dominguez, Ellen S. Taylor, and Fran Sullivan

*Front cover: Clover Hill Lodge (Cavan County), border illustration by Ellen Sullivan
Taylor*

Information in this guidebook is based on authoritative data available at the
time of printing. Prices listed are subject to change without notice. Readers
are asked to take this into account when consulting this guide.

Manufactured in the United States of America
Published by Pelican Publishing Company, Inc.
1000 Burmaster Street, Gretna, Louisiana 70053

*We dedicate this book to our great-grandparents
who emigrated to America in the 1800s and
carried with them "a bit of the old sod"—*

*Michael J. and Julia Flannery
and
Michael Patrick and Mary Redden Sullivan*

Contents

Northern Ireland

Acknowledgments

We wish to thank Rebecca Price for her extraordinary work in preparing the new edition and handling the computer/word processing tasks so efficiently. Also, we would like to thank our friends in Ireland who operate B and Bs for their advice on current trends in Ireland. Much of the success of this book is due to their judgment on how the book could better serve the traveling public and be consistent with the realities of operating a bed and breakfast, or other lodgings in Ireland. In addition, we wish to thank Town and Country Home Association Chairman Vera Feeney, in Spiddal, County Galway; the past chairman, Dympna Casey, Mulligar, County Westmeath; Cecilia Kiely, Blarney, County Cork; Helen Sheehan, Kilkenny Town, Carmel O'Gorman, County Cork; and especially Eileen Kelly, Clontarf, County Dublin. Eileen has generously helped us in many ways over the years. All these Irish consultants operate their own bed and breakfasts with the highest standards.

The Irish
Bed & Breakfast
Book

Introduction to the Republic of Ireland

BACKGROUND

Ireland is a land of outstanding beauty, serenity, and mystical charm. Its people and land have been propelled through history by dramatic and devastating events. Yet, the people possess a wonderful personality that is loving, kind, friendly beyond compare, hospitable, devout, infectiously fun-loving, witty, and always ready to tease or crack a joke.

When one decides to travel abroad in a foreign land, one must ask the question—why Ireland? How is it different from Sweden, France, England, or other countries you are considering for a visit, assuming that cost is not a factor? In other words, what's there to see and do?

Ireland is probably one of the most beautiful countries in Europe for scenery; it is one of the best for modern and traditional music, theater, and modern and early Christian art; it has an endless chain of castles and historic sites that date back to 4000-3000 B.C.; and the warm and boundless "welcoming" of its people certainly sets it apart from all other countries.

As Irish-Americans who have recently come to love the land and its people, we would say that beneath the tourist veneer exists a more fascinating land and culture than we had ever imagined or proclaimed by most travel books and brochures. As we worked on this book, we both deepened our understanding of Irish history and culture, and in our writing endeavored to provide the reader with enough information for his or her discovery of the Ireland beneath the surface.

Since Ireland is a relatively small country, you might expect the population to be homogeneous, but this is not so. The people of Donegal and those of the South, like those found in Kerry and Cork, are quite different. The land, many have said before, fashions the character of the people. This is certainly in evidence when you meet the industrious, more serious and somber, yet sincere people of the northwest counties and compare them with the jovial, casual, softer people of the southwest.

This travel book is meant to be a guide for you to design your own itinerary. You should read up on Irish history and the various sights you want to see and then factor in the number of days or weeks you have for your trip, and with the help of a good map, like Michelin's or Bartholemew's, plan an itinerary. Some good references to help you prepare for your trip include:

Rambles in Ireland, by Monie Begley, Devin-Adair Co., Old Greenwich, CT, 1985 (still a great book on Irish culture and history; fascinating writer);

Ireland, World Book Encyclopedia, Field Enterprises Ed. Corp., Chicago and London;

Ireland: A History, by Robert Kee, Abacus Edition, Sphere Books, Ltd., 1982 (excellent but hard to acquire, since it is published in England; published as a result of a special BBC series);

A History of Ireland, by Edmund Curtis, Routledge, 6th Edition, 1961 (the favorite of many historians and general readers).

Francis Bacon's advice still holds true about travel: study the country before you go, read about its culture and history while you're there, and reflect and continue your study when you return.

When planning your trip, a good rule to follow is to allow two nights at each bed and breakfast so you don't get dizzy living out of a suitcase. If you stay only one night at a B&B, it seems like you're on a merry-go-round. You come in at night and leave the next day after breakfast and you get to the point that your days are in the car and the nights in the B&B, without ever getting to know any B&B owners, seeing any local sights, or taking advantage of the many local recreational facilities and special events.

We recommend observing the **Two-Day Rule.** Sometimes you will land at a gem of a place that tickles your fancy and want to stay longer. Don't be so rigid in your plans that you miss the unexpected pleasures of a new town or region like a country fair, a market day, or special musical or dance performance. Have a plan but stay flexible. If you travel in the shoulder season, spring and fall, you won't have to worry so much about booking ahead. But if you travel in the summer, the best B&Bs, those recommended in travel guides, will fill up early.

The Irish Tourist Board, Bord Fáilte, has offices in major cities around the world. In the U.S. it is located at 345 Park Avenue, New York, N.Y., 10154. Telephone: (800) 223-6470 in the U.S., (212) 418-0800, and FAX: (212) 371-9052. In London call, 071-493-3201, and in Sydney,

(02) 232-7177. They offer free guides, maps, and information booklets for almost any travel requirements or interests. Some of their guides are the *Town and Country Homes Association: Guest Accommodation* for the current year, with a B&B listing of homes providing reasonable lodgings; *Farm Holidays in Ireland,* with a listing of farm B&Bs; and the *Hotels and Guesthouses—Illustrated Guide—Be Our Guest,* for the more expensive accommodations. Be forewarned that they are not rated or graded. All that the Irish Tourist Board guides give you are the number of rooms, prices, addresses, facilities available, attractions in the area, etc., but not any rating. One does not really know if they are super places or the run-of-the-mill. Some places have the same prices, but vary enormously in charm and value.

That's where this book comes in handy. It will allow you to stay at the best ones! The places in our book were carefully selected to give you the best lodgings in an area—that is, the ones with ambience, charm, cleanliness, hospitable hosts, good facilities and accommodations, and good value for your travel dollar. They were visited by us after being recommended by other travelers, other B&B operators, and travel agents.

Please remember that B&Bs or guesthouses change hands and owners retire, or the quality of the accommodations changes from when we visited them. Also, the prices may change. We have tried to select only those that have all the qualities above but have staying power as well. You will find descriptions of B&Bs, town and country homes, small hotels, guesthouses, and farm B&Bs. Write us at the publisher's address with your comments—good or bad. We would love to hear from you about our listings and any new ones you could recommend for the next edition.

GUARANTEE OF STANDARDS

Bord Fáilte is the official guarantor of minimum standards for most inns, guesthouses, country homes, farmhouses, and town houses. They establish the maximum allowable rate per person, whether couples or single persons. We chose to publish only nightly rates per person for couples (which in Ireland is called the rate for "sharing"). Unless it is stated to be a double rate or the price of the room, you can determine the double or couple rate by multiplying the rate we list by two. Singles pay a higher rate if they are alone. Travel vouchers you may have obtained in an Aer Lingus package or from a travel agent are good for a standard room, one with shared bath.

Most hosts will charge an additional fee of a few pounds for a private bath, accommodations that the Irish call "a room sharing with shower/toilet en suite." In this book, "private bath" means shower, sink, and toilet unless otherwise indicated. A shared bath, usually larger than the private baths, will often have a tub, shower, sink, and toilet.

Weekend and weekly rates are sometimes available at substantial savings. A weekend rate might include two nights, two breakfasts, and a Saturday-night dinner. Inquire of the host when you make your reservation as to these special arrangements, and always notify the host in advance if you have special dietary requirements for breakfast. Evening dinner is usually reserved by noon. In many locations, the dinner at the B&B is better than you can find at the local restaurant. Those hosts who have won a Galtee Breakfast Award are especially proud of their home-cooked evening meals as well.

B&Bs displaying the green shamrock sign are those that are inspected and approved by the Bord Fáilte. You can be assured of minimum standards. They are contracted to maintain certain standards and rent for approved rates. All B&Bs listed have been inspected by us and the host(s) interviewed, or have been identified by other owners and/or other experienced travelers as outstanding lodgings—usually both. The B&Bs in our *Irish Bed and Breakfast Book* are held to our required high standards. Please write us with your compliments or suggestions, or if you find that any of the lodgings listed here do not meet your expectations.

PRACTICAL MATTERS

Getting There

Flying to Shannon or Dublin airports directly means your choices are narrowed to **Aer Lingus** (1-800-223-6537) from Boston, Chicago, or New York; **Aeroflot** (1-800-867-8774) from Washington, D.C., Miami, and Chicago; or **Delta** (1-800-241-4141) from Atlanta and New York City. You can also book a charter flight contracted by private associations and organizations such as the Ancient Order of Hibernians (AOH), Irish cultural groups, and such. Check to see if a membership fee is added on to the price of the ticket. Check in the telephone directory if you are near a large city that has a large Irish-American population, and make an inquiry about their charters. Otherwise, inquire of your local travel agent. A good travel agent can advise you about the reputation of most charter companies. We traveled American Trans Air (ATA) Charter in 1995. It was cheaper, but the flight was delayed and seats were smaller.

Usually a travel agent's voucher will be good for what the Irish call a "standard" room, one having a shared bath. In some cases you will be asked for a small supplemental fee of a pound or two to cover the cost of the private bath. One package, the Irish Heritage package, includes the services of the Irish Genealogical Research Society.

Genealogical Searches

Millions of Irish were forced to leave their homeland because of the devastation of the famine and other deprivations to seek out a better life in Australia, the United States, or Argentina. You may be descended from the hearty and valiant Irish immigrants who survived those desperate days, and you may return to Ireland in much different circumstances as tourists and travelers. If you do, it is fun and very satisfying to investigate your roots, and possibly find living relatives. In planning your trip you might wish to avail yourself of a registered genealogist to assist you, so that you can set aside time to check archives and records, and visit the appropriate ancestral sites. There are many. We can recommend an excellent one: Mrs. Helen Kelly. Her mailing address is Celtic Heritage, 30 Harlech Crescent, Clonskeagh, Dublin, 14, Ireland. Her e-mail address is kellyfam@iol.ie.

She and Francis Dowling have produced an excellent instructional tape for the more aggressive do-it-yourselfers. It is very informative and leads you step by step through the process of a genealogical search. We found it educational in many ways but particularly in the sense that it explained a great deal about the geopolitical structure of early Ireland. You might want to purchase a tape, *Searching For Your Ancestors in Ireland,* produced by Shoreway Video, Int. Ltd. The tape is playable on Canadian and U.S. videocassette recorders and is available at the same address above.

Using the Internet

You can access the Irish Tourist Board web site at www.ireland.travel.ie. There you will find additional valuable information on getting there, where to stay, and recreational and current cultural events. However, don't expect to find a rating system for bed and breakfasts or as much detail as in our book. It is a good additional tool for planning.

Money and Changing Currency

Traveler's checks are the best way to carry large sums of money. You can get free traveler's checks if you belong to one of the state AAA clubs. Just remember to bring cash to their office when you purchase their American Express checks. Checks or credit cards are not usually accepted.

When you change money in Ireland, do so at a regular commercial bank, like the Bank of Ireland, and you will get the best exchange rate. Avoid the Dublin or Shannon airport branches, as they are usually a little higher than downtown in the nearby city. If you change a little money at the airport to get by for a day or two then do your big exchange in the city branch, you will do better.

B&Bs that accept credit cards are indicated in this book in the full listings. Always ask the host if they accept cards, because we found that credit-card payment is becoming more popular with Irish B&Bs. About a third of town and country home B&Bs use them. Credit-card payment in restaurants and lodgings is a convenient way to handle your money problems. The exchange rate at the date of service is usually quite favorable, and it helps you avoid carrying a lot of cash, especially in Dublin, which has a high incidence of petty theft.

Transportation

Rental Cars

Rent your car before you arrive in Ireland. It is much cheaper. Find a reliable car rental company through your travel agent. The agent will prebook your car with a partial payment to secure the reservation.

Be sure to check with your credit-card company as to the exact insurance coverage they provide when you wave the collision damage (CDW/LDW)—which kind of cars are covered and for what time period. This is extremely important. If you have MasterCard, they will only cover you for 15 days; VISA is currently 30 days. If you rent a car with your MasterCard for 16 days or more, you are not covered at all. Read the fine print in your credit-card brochure describing the services and benefits. If your car is totaled because of this oversight, and you have waived the car company's collision damage, you will pay for a new car replacement out of your pocket. In addition, be forewarned that rental agencies overseas are not regulated by U.S. law, so be sure to rent only from companies that have a reliable track record. Your travel agent can advise you which ones are reputable.

Warning: in Dublin, be careful to read fine print on parking meters, as in many districts they need streets clear for commuter traffic, and if you are still parked there after 4 P.M. you may get towed, as we did, to the tune of a $100 fine.

And another thing: in Ireland you must drive on the left side of the road.

Buses

You can take the train to the major provincial cities, and stay in city B&Bs or inns/guesthouses. However, most of the charming B&Bs are country homes and "using the buses, sometimes you can't get there from here" as they say in Maine. The country bus systems are not very handy due to their odd schedules and frequent stops. If you are lucky to find a main route, they're fine. But check bus schedules carefully. You might take a country bus ride and find that it will be two days before you can catch the return. We had to hitchhike once on the Dingle Peninsula to get to where we were going because of the strange routing and schedules of buses. Fran found bus travel fun and adventurous.

When in the big cities or when tour buses are available in the country, as in the Dingle or Connemara regions, leave your car in the parking garage ("car park") and take the bus. This allows you to take a rest from driving on the left side and to enjoy the ride and sights without aggravation, and your higher perch lets you see over the hedgerows and stone walls. In Dublin and Cork especially, take the bus because the one-way streets and congestion can drive you mad.

City buses are numbered and only pick up at signs marked with their number. Knowing which number bus to catch is a little bit of a hassle, but the drivers are friendly and usually helpful. But move quickly, for bus doors open and close faster that any we've traveled on in Europe.

Weather

The climate in Ireland is like New England, but with a milder winter, not much snow, and the summers are usually cooler. You can count on rain showers whenever you go. Remember this is a small island set in the Atlantic, and ocean storms blow in quickly with intermittent rainstorms. Fortunately, they move out as quickly.

We found that layering clothing is a good technique for such a variable weather pattern. Put on light clothing, and then add a light wool sweater and rainproof jacket or coat. This way you can adjust to the weather as it changes from cool mornings to very mild or warm temperatures at noon.

Booking Ahead

Booking Outside Ireland

Book ahead for the first night after arrival and the first night before departure, preferably within a short drive from the airport. We like the towns of Ennis, Bunratty, and Adare for a Shannon departure, and Malahide, Clontarf, Drumcondra, Swords, or another North Dublin suburb for a Dublin Airport departure. They are close to the airports and also have excellent restaurants nearby, lower rates, and high quality.

You will find many excellent B&Bs in this book that describe how close they are to the international airports. Book these rooms by calling from outside Ireland. In the U.S. dial 1, then 011 (the international code for both MCI and AT&T), then 353 (the country code), then the number listed in our book (but drop the zero (0) in the city/town code). You will be surprised that neither advance payment nor credit-card charge is usually required to hold a room. The Irish are very trusting in this regard, and we urge you to cancel well in advance if your travel plans change.

Booking Inside Ireland

Booking ahead within the country only requires you to call the telephone numbers listed and tell the host when you will be arriving. You may ask directions, although we have provided directions. We find that rehearsing and/or recording the directions over the phone is advisable because some are off in the country, up a maze of rural roads. Many hosts are willing to book ahead for you at no charge if you ask their help. We have found this practice to be quite reliable.

General Information about Lodgings

Rooms

Rooms in private homes are often, but not always, small, though cozy with personal touches and pretty décor. Houses built expressly to run a bed and breakfast have plenty of space in the bedrooms, lounges, and dining rooms. Also, the manor homes have large rooms with high ceilings and afford a special treat not only in spaciousness but also in Old-World ambience. These features are pointed out in this book in the text of the listing. However, in the country homes or older homes we have sought out those whose hosts are especially warm and genuinely friendly. We feel the warmth of the welcome far outweighs the size consideration of the rooms.

Meals

After checking in, you probably will be offered tea or coffee. The Irish tea is better than the coffee because often the coffee is instant. When you arrive, remind the host of any dietary requirements you may have, and whether or not you want dinner, assuming you arrive early in the afternoon. Better yet, if you book ahead, indicate at that time that you would like dinner. This is a good idea if you are staying in a remote area where there aren't any restaurants nearby, or you are driving a good distance and you don't want to get back in the car again after you arrive.

A full *Irish Breakfast* in this book always consists of eggs cooked to order, bacon, sausage, toast or homemade brown bread with farm fresh Irish butter or jam (you have to ask for margarine), juice, dry cereal, and tea or coffee. Extras that might be offered are fresh fruit in season, fruited yogurt, cheeses, porridge or oatmeal, scones and/or other baked goods. Special extras that we are finding more and more are French toast or pancakes with syrup, smoked salmon, or other fish. The portions are generous. Ask when breakfast is served, and ask for a call if you don't have a travel clock. If you have to leave early to catch a plane or train, your host will usually prepare toast and coffee for you upon request. Irish hosts are very accommodating.

If you want a vegetarian or continental breakfast, let them know the night before and they will probably provide you with the fruited yogurt, toast, fresh fruit, hot or cold cereal, muesli, and tea or coffee. The healthy eating pattern recently popular in America is catching on in Ireland, too.

Booking Tours and Events

Your host will help you book plays, Irish football matches (soccer), fishing trips, horseback riding, and all the other recreational activities in the area. If you ask your host's advice, he/she will sometimes call ahead for you. If not, get the telephone number and use the B&B's box phone, which requires 20-30p to get started. In Dublin, get the *Irish Times* or one of the tabloids and you can find advertisements for the plays and musicals. The Abbey Theatre is Ireland's national repertory company, offering plays by Ireland's best. One night at a Dublin pub with music is a special treat, such as the Abbey Tavern in Howth or Slattery's on Capel Street. The show at Jury's Hotel is elaborate and very enjoyable. Your host(s) can direct you.

Telephoning in Ireland

This can be a problem for Americans who are used to easy access and fast service. Telephoning is very different in Ireland.

There are two ways you can call inside Ireland: with coins, or with a CALLCARD (or Phonecard). CALLCARDS are purchased in local shops and post offices. They are available with so many calling units for so many Irish pounds. We used 20-unit cards and found them far superior to paying with coins. You use the CALLCARD at a telephone booth marked with a yellow band and with the *Card Phone* sign. You just put your card in the slot as indicated and dial the number. The decreasing units are indicated on a digital monitor. One unit is equal to about 20p. When you call long distance, your units will decrease much more rapidly then for local calls. Don't be surprised at the number of phone booths out of order, especially in the countryside.

When you call from your B&B, inn, or guesthouse, you can make local calls for 20 or 30p. The amount for an initial call is indicated in the digital window. Many B&Bs now have coin box telephones near the front door. You dial the number, listen for the dial tone to change when the person answers, then you put in the coin. The remaining time is indicated on a digital clock, and you put more coins in, 10p or better, when time runs out.

Phone calls from hotel rooms have a 200-300 percent surcharge. Be forewarned!

Laundry

We find packing clothes for five days and taking dirty clothes to the laundry is the best way to avoid a lot of heavy luggage.

Except for two B&Bs in our book (Vera Feeney's in Spiddal and Maeve Walsh's in Tubbercurry), you need to take your laundry to a local laundromat to wash and dry your clothes. Because time is of a premium, we leave our clothes and pay to have them to be washed, dried, and folded. There is only a small additional charge for this. In inns and large guesthouses, they will send them out for you and put the charge on your bill. You send out one day and usually get them back the next. We like to deliver our clothes directly, as it speeds up the process and is less expensive.

Northern Ireland

Information on practical matters for Northern Ireland can be found in that section, later in the book.

Having visited the Irish Republic and Northern Ireland, we found the people in both countries to be open, generous, intelligent, and interested in other people. Many have innate wisdom. Other enduring qualities are their humility and kindness. Seldom will you meet an arrogant Irishman or one who would hurt your feelings knowingly. They like to know about your life, your story, and tell you about theirs, spiced with a little humor, and they'll go way back to ancestors.

Security

In the larger cities, such as Cork, Galway, and especially Dublin, be sure to leave nothing of value that can be seen inside your car while it is parked on the street. Lock cameras, suitcases, and shopping bags in your trunk out of view. Those B&Bs that have a locked car park off the street are much preferred in Dublin. Unfortunately, in Dublin, as in other big cities where tourists congregate, there has been a high incidence of thefts. So be careful to keep wallets in your deeper front pockets, and wear no pocketbook slung over your shoulder but carry it in front with one arm over it. One option is to buy a waist purse or fanny pack that straps around your body. Travel in pairs or larger groups if possible.

Country Carlow

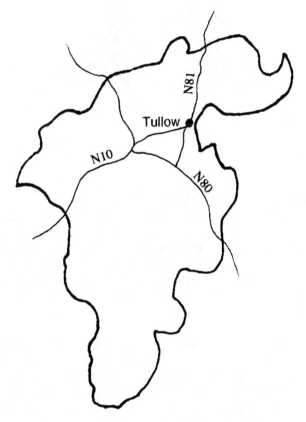

County Carlow presents you with soft rolling hills and lush pastureland. Two important rivers run through it, the Barrow and the Slaney, which give great opportunities for avid anglers. Fish to your heart's content for pike, trout, or salmon or do "coarse" fishing. The lovely Mount Leinster is good for hiking; it is part of the Blackstairs Mountain Range along the southeast border. Near the center of the county is Ballymoon Castle. Peaceful Carlow is only an hour away from busy Dublin for a getaway vacation. It is close to Glendalough in County Wicklow, and only 10 to 15 miles away from exciting Kilkenny.

Laburnum Lodge
Anne Byrne
Bunclody Road N81
Tullow, County Carlow
Telephone: 0503-51718
Bedrooms: 6, all with private baths.
Rates: £18 p.p. with bath; £24 for a single; 25 percent discount for children under 12. Vouchers accepted. £11 dinner. **Credit cards:** None.
Open: March to November. **Children:** All ages. **Pets:** No. **Smoking:** In tea rooms only. **Provision for handicapped:** Yes. 2 rooms on ground floor. **Directions:** There are signs posted. From the bridge in Tullow, take the N81 towards Dublin and Laburnum Lodge will be 1 mile up on the right.

This lovely new Georgian home is in the beautiful Tullow Valley surrounded by mountains. Anne is cheerful and outgoing and like a breath of fresh air. There is a feeling of bringing the outside in as there are lots of large windows, and the sliding-glass doors in her dining room open onto her award-winning gardens. The handsomely decorated sitting room has bold, dark-blue drapes and cream walls and the bedrooms have unusual colors such as lemon, pink, and rose. Her Irish Breakfast includes choice of eggs or French toast, and fruit, yogurt, and cheeses. We can attest to her very tasty fresh scones, which we smelled baking as we entered. On a getaway weekend here you'll have access to fishing, golf (18 holes at Mount Wolseley), hunting, river cruising, signposted walks, and visits to Altamount Gardens. You may visit the historic Ring Rath or Brown's Hill Dolmen Stones or even go hang gliding nearby. Anne's brother, Jim O'Toole, wrote a book on manor houses in County Carlow.

County Cavan

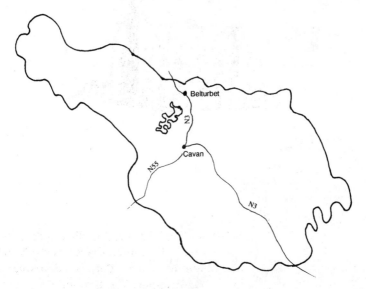

County Cavan has an odd shape, like a paramecium. The tail is sandwiched between Fermanagh and Leitrim, the head towards Monaghan, the Meaths, and Longford. It is a county of picturesque farms, lakes, and the Erne and Analee rivers. There are many good lakes for fishing, especially Lough Erne and Lough Oughter above Cavan and Butlers Bridge. This is a particularly pretty area to see. The Derragarra Inn, an award-winning pub at Butlers Bridge, has good, reasonable meals. There is a Folk Museum just across the street from it. Cavan is a bustling town with Cavan Crystal and several singing pubs. Visit Killysheen Forest Park not far from Cavan, with the ruins of Lough Oughter Castle and nature trails, swimming, and fishing. You can rent a forest chalet here by the week.

In the south of Cavan is the lovely, quiet town of Virginia, amidst miles of rolling green hills, much resembling our state of Virginia. Flowers and farms abound, and it borders on Lough Ramor, with its 22 islands. The lake is part of the town and adds much to its special beauty. North of Virginia is another small town known for its mention in a well-known Irish ditty. This town, Ballyjamesduff, is worth a visit. County Cavan is known for its golf and for being a crossroads.

Hilltop Farm B&B
Philomena O'Connor
Belturbet, County Cavan
Telephone: 049-22114
Bedrooms: 10, all with private baths.
Rates: £18 p.p. with bath; Single £23; 20 percent discount for children under 12. Vouchers accepted. Four-course evening meal £10. **Credit cards:** VISA, MasterCard, Eurocard. **Open:** All year. **Children:** All ages. **Pets:** Yes. **Smoking:** Yes, but not in dining room. **Provision for handicapped:** Yes, through the kitchen. **Directions:** From Cavan take the N3; farm is exactly three miles from Butlers Bridge on the right.

This fairly new house is an actual farmhouse. Philomena, the gracious hostess, will greet you with tea. This bed and breakfast has clean comfortable rooms, all with pink and beige covers and cream or lilac walls. All baths are carpeted. There are sinks in every room, and the halls are stenciled. The living room has a marble fireplace, and the dining room is huge, with views of the lake, which is famous for fishing. People come from all over Europe to fish here. Philomena packs a lunch, serves fantastic evening meals, and is always ready with a cup of tea for travelers. Her Irish Breakfast includes a selection of cereals, yogurt, or a bowl of fruit. You may have pancakes if you like. They serve freshly ground coffee. There are also activities like golf, river cruising, cycling, and walking tours right in the town of Belturbet.

Lisnamandra
Iris Neill
Crossdoney
Cavan, County Cavan
Telephone: 049-4337196; **FAX:** 049-4337111; **E-mail:** neolneill@tinet.ie
Bedrooms: 4; 3 with private baths, 1 with shared bath.
Rates: £18 p.p. private bath; £16 p.p. shared bath. Discount for children on a sliding scale. Vouchers accepted. Dinner is offered for £14 p.p. **Credit cards:** VISA, MasterCard. **Open:** April 1 to November 1. **Children:** Yes, all ages. **Pets:** No. **Smoking:** Restricted. **Provision for Handicapped:** None. **Directions:** From Cavantown, take the R198 (Killeshandra Road) via hospital and golf club. Lisnamandra is 4.5 miles on left, i.e. 1 mile before Crossdoney Village.

This very large three-story farmhouse has spacious rooms and high ceilings. The rooms are modern, comfortable, and pretty, with hair dryers and tea/coffee facilities. Two rooms have safety deposit boxes. Set on a dairy farm, part of the house dates back to the seventeenth century, and the main block is from the eighteenth century. The latest addition dates back to the mid-nineteenth century. It is surrounded by scenic gardens, overlooked by a majestic pillar spruce tree, and has an ancient ring fort on the property. Two couples from Massachusetts called it "the best B&B in the world." A letter from a Northern Irish guest states she hasn't had as great a breakfast in all her travels to guesthouses and hotels. Many folks from all over Europe praise Iris's warm hospitality. Children enjoy watching the milking of cows on the farm. Iris won a Galtee Award for her varied breakfasts. There is a golf course and beautiful forest nearby, as well as horseback riding, tennis, and coarse angling.

Halcyon
Brid and Walter Myles
Drumalee
Cavan, County Cavan
Telephone: 049-4331809; **FAX:** 049-4362531
Bedrooms: 5; 4 with private baths, 1 shared.
Rates: £18 p.p. with bath; £16 p.p. shared bath; 20 percent discount
for children under 12. £12 dinner on request. **Credit cards:** Access,
VISA, MasterCard. **Open:** January 8 to December 18. **Children:** All
ages. **Pets:** No. **Smoking:** Yes, but not in dining room. **Provision for
handicapped:** None. **Directions:** Immediately after the Roman Catholic
Cathedral on the N3 take a right onto the Cootehill Road. At first crossroads, turn right and Halcyon is 100 yards up that road on the left side.

This cozy bungalow is family run and Walt and Brid will greet you;
they are very personable and helpful. Their genealogical library and
books on Irish history are in the lounge. This is where you get your
welcome tea and share the family TV. They'll give you lots of guid-
ance on ancestral tracing, hiking in the area, and trips around Ireland.
We really enjoyed their conversation. The lounge has many lovely original Irish paintings. The large garden and conservatory is for guest use
and has coffee/tea facilities. The dining room is spacious and Walt
does the cooking. The bedrooms are well organized, with huge towels and facecloths. One room is decorated in antique white linen and
lace, one is cream and pale green, another is cream with navy-striped
duvets. The front room is rose and white. Tea and coffee facilities are
also available. The bungalow's good central location puts you very
close to the Cavan Sports Centre, the Equestrian Centre, an 18-hole
golf club with special fees available, and fishing. The hosts have discounts for Cavan Crystal. Dinner is available on request.

ALSO RECOMMENDED

Cavan Town, *Oakdene,* Ann and Paddy Gaffney, 29 Cathedral Rd. Telephone: 049-31698. Bedrooms: 4, all with shared baths. Recommended by Brid Myles of Cavan Town.

COUNTY CLARE

County Clare

County Clare's most important feature is that it contains Shannon Airport, where everyone who wants to see the west coast enters the Irish Republic. So that will be our starting place. If you head south toward Limerick, you'll have to see the Bunratty Castle and Folk Park. If you make reservations for the Medieval Banquet at Bunratty Castle, you'll encounter quite a wild party. If you'd like to see bright costumes, music, performers, and storytellers, try some genuine mead, and try eating a big meal with only a knife—all amidst a huge hall full of people from every country you can imagine—then you'll have a jolly, even hilarious evening. Durty Nelly's, a pub next door, is a fun place to do your first Irish singing, but it's a bit seedy.

Lough Derg and the River Shannon form the eastern edge of the county. The lengthy river finally meets the sea at the southern edge, forming a narrow bay. Killaloe, a town at the base of Lough Derg, has water-skiing, sailing, and a riverboat tour of the lake. Also, visit the twelfth-century St. Flannan's Cathedral and Ogham Stone there.

If you head northwest, you'll come to Ennis, a busy little town with a marketplace, good B&Bs, restaurants, and many singing pubs. There is a castle at Knappogue in Quin, and the Dromoland Castle is almost into Ennis. Surrounding Ennis are pretty, peaceful farmlands. From Ennis, travel north to Lahinch via the N85, which passes through Ennistymon, or go by the R476 and visit Corofin first, a good freshwater fishing spot. Here you will find the Clare Heritage Centre with lots of information for Clare genealogy seekers.

Lahinch is an interesting seaside resort with shops, quaint cafés, beaches, and lovely sea views. Horses graze on the green cliffs above the beach. To the south of here, you'll find surfing beaches at Spanish Point and the spot where ships of the Spanish Armada were wrecked. Farther south on the sea is Kilkee, with some gorgeous cliff scenery.

The most fascinating steep cliffs of fame are the Cliffs of Moher, dropping down to the sea just outside Liscannor. The cliffs are worth a look in all kinds of weather except thick fog. They are hauntingly dramatic, moss green in summer and gold-brown in fall. From the Cliffs, travel north to Doolin on the coast, where you may catch a ferry to the Aran Islands. There used to be an old custom for Aran Island boys to row over to Doolin on a specified day each year to seek a bride. Next you'll want to see the Burren, a natural geological wonder of stark, rocky hills that holds unique wildflowers, animal life, and mystical springs. You can take a walk through with a guide if you book ahead. Ask at Lisdoonvarna or Ballyvaughn. See the Aillwee Caves, too, with many stalactites and a tearoom for a snack.

Bunratty Lodge
Mary Browne
Bunratty, County Clare.
Telephone: 061-369402; **FAX:** 061-369363
E-mail: bunrattylodge@tinet.ie
Bedrooms: 6, all with private baths.
Rates: £19 p.p.; Single £34; 20 percent discount for children under 12. Vouchers not accepted. **Credit cards:** VISA and MasterCard. **Open:** Mid-March to November 1. **Children:** Yes, 7 years and older. **Pets:** No. **Smoking:** No. **Provision for handicapped:** None. **Directions:** Coming from Shannon Airport (on the N18), after about 4 miles take side road to Bunratty Castle, sign on left. Then take road on left between Bunratty Castle and Durty Nelly's Pub. Go 1.5 miles to intersection. Bunratty Lodge is the two-story blue home across the intersection in country setting.

Bunratty Lodge is stunning inside and out, a stately neo-Georgian modern home painted blue and trimmed in white, surrounded by a well-kept garden and gated entrance. The living room is spacious and elegant with a blue rug, white fireplace, and beautiful flowered drapes. The bedrooms are pink and grey or green and pink, with a myriad of flowered designs and all with thick, fluffy quilts. All the spacious bedrooms have color TVs and large tiled baths with towel heaters. Besides the full Irish Breakfast, your gracious hostess, Mary Browne, serves a choice of eggs and potatoes, fruit, yogurt and cheeses, and an option of French toast. She has received the Galtee County award for her breakfasts. The dining room is comfortable and well lighted, with large windows to the garden, and choice of large table or separates. Medieval banquets at the nearby Bunratty Castle can be arranged, along with other advice on touring this area. Golf, horseback riding, swimming in the heated pool at Shannon-Shamrock Hotel, fishing, or a visit to the Folk Park behind the Castle, followed by a pint at the famous Durty Nelly's pub, are some of the local features.

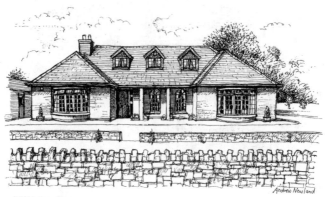

Andrew Newland

Clover Hill Lodge
Anne Nash
Low Road
Bunratty, County Clare
Telephone: 061-369039; **FAX:** 061-360520; **E-Mail:** clover@tinet.ie
Bedrooms: 4, all with private baths.
Rates: £18 p.p.; £26 single; 20 percent discount for children. Vouchers accepted. **Credit cards:** VISA and MasterCard. **Open:** April 1 to October 31. **Children:** Yes. **Pets:** No. **Smoking:** No. **Provision for handicapped:** Yes. **Directions:** Coming from Shannon Airport, take the N18 for 4 miles. Take the side road to Bunratty Castle, sign on the left. At Bunratty Castle, follow a sign for Low Road in front of Durty Nelly's Pub. Pass the entrance to Bunratty Folk Park, and drive up signposted road for about 1¼ miles. House is on left.

This modern, red-brick, dormered house is situated right between Bunratty Castle and Durty Nelly's, so it is easy to find. Anne will be very helpful to you in finding the airport, only 10 minutes away, as well as other places of interest. Her rooms are beautifully decorated and all have orthopedic mattresses, TVs, and hair dryers. Anne gives you a choice of breakfasts from a menu. They include juice, cereal, all-Irish fresh fruit with low-fat organic yogurt, ham slices with Irish cheese and fruit, poached or scrambled eggs, and pancakes and maple syrup, along with filtered coffee, herb teas, or hot chocolate. Try the medieval dinner and show at Bunratty Castle. It is lots of fun—you'll get a glass of mead, and you will be served very good period-style food while being entertained by a beautiful group of young people in period costumes. Durty Nelly's is a good pub for singing and trying Guinness stout, or a good pub snack. This area gives you an early rest after your flight, and easy access to the Cliffs of Moher and coast or south to County Kerry. There is also golf, horseback riding, and fishing nearby.

Headley Court
Kathleen Browne
Deerpark, Bunratty
County Clare
Telephone: 061-369768
Bedrooms: 5, all with private baths.
Rates: £19 p.p.; 20 percent discount for children. Vouchers not accepted. **Credit cards:** VISA and MasterCard. **Open:** January to December. **Children:** Yes, all ages. **Pets:** No. **Smoking:** No. **Provision for handicapped:** Yes. **Directions:** From Shannon Airport, after approximately 4 miles, take left turn to Bunratty. Take Low Road between Bunratty Castle and Durty Nellie's Pub. Go 1½ miles to intersection. Turn right. Headley Court is the first house.

This attractive, modern, two-story home is painted with burgundy and white trim, and set among mature trees, new shrubs, and flowers. The bedrooms are bright and airy, each with its own color scheme. Some doubles have romantic canopies over them. All fabrics are coordinated, such as navy and pink, blue and cream, or pink and white. All rooms have spacious bathrooms, tea/coffee facilities, alarm clocks, hair dryers, and color TV. The furniture is eclectic, with modern and antiques mixed. The living room has a maple floor with apricot-colored walls and modern swag and tail curtains. The lounge is unique and handsome with its terra cotta tiles. Kathleen is an attentive host and will serve you a delicious and varied breakfast. There are the usual choices of eggs, bacon, and sausage, waffle fries, or cereal. Fruit and yogurt are also served, along with tea and coffee. Nearby, horseback riding, golf, fishing, and swimming are available. Banquet tickets can be arranged by the Brownes for Bunratty Castle.

Rockfield House
Margaret Garry
Hill Road
Bunratty, County Clare
Telephone and **FAX:** 061-364391
Bedrooms: 6, all with private baths.
Rates: £18 p.p.; Single £27; 20 percent discount for children under 12.
Vouchers accepted. **Credit cards:** VISA and MasterCard. **Open:** January
1 to December 22. **Children:** All ages. **Pets:** No. **Smoking:** No. **Provision
for handicapped:** None. **Directions:** As you approach Bunratty Village,
make a left turn after Avoca Handweavers, just before Fitzpatrick
Bunratty Shamrock Hotel. You will find Rockfield House about 300 yards
up that windy road on the right-hand side. There are two white eagles on
the entrance gates. Note: Avoca Handweavers has since closed.

Besides being in the midst of all the Bunratty sights and activities,
this is also a very pleasant and modern home hosted by a very friendly
and warm Mrs. Garry. One bedroom has a balcony and view of River
Shannon. All bedrooms are pink and green and have TVs, tea and coffee, hair dryers, and electric blankets. A trouser press is in the hallway.
With its modern décor and perched on a peaceful hillside, Rockfield
House reminds one of California and commands a panoramic view of
the River Shannon. However, the Irish wit and charm, bright and cheery
rooms, and the tasty breakfast will let you know you are enjoying the
best of the Irish Republic. Great brewed coffee is served along with your
tasty cooked breakfast. You may also choose a delicious continental or
vegetarian one. All are served in a beautiful dining room that has a light
green theme with lace tablecloths. A lounge with TV can be enjoyed,
with coffee or tea upon request. Fishing at Six-Mile Bridge, golf, swimming at the nearby hotel, or visits to nearby Bunratty Castle and Folk
Park and Durty Nelly's can be arranged by Mrs. Garry. Let her prebook
your night at the castle banquet.

Massabielle
Monica O'Loughlin
Quinn Road
Ennis, County Clare
Telephone: 065-6829363
Bedrooms: 5; 4 with private baths, 1 shared.
Rates: £18 p.p. private bath; £16 p.p. shared bath; Single £18; 20 percent discount for children under 12. Vouchers accepted. **Credit cards:** Yes, VISA and Master Card. **Open:** April 1 to October 15. **Children:** All ages. **Pets:** No. **Smoking:** No. **Provision for handicapped:** Yes, rooms on first floor. **Directions:** At Ennis railway station, travel out the Quinn Road for 1 mile to sign for Massabielle. The road to the B&B is on the left. In Ennis, at first light go right at roundabout to Old Ground Hotel, right out O'Connell Street toward Quinn. After about 2 miles, go left at the sign for Massabielle, Quinn Road, and out the winding country road for about ½ mile. Massabielle is on the left.

Massabielle is a lovely modern house with landscaped gardens in a peaceful country setting just out of the center of Ennis town. It is a good stop (30 minutes) from Shannon Airport for people heading north. The Irish setter, Ross, may greet you, and you may see cows nearby. Monica is kind and sweet, as are all her children, who help her. Their warmth and sense of humor pervade the house. The rooms are prettily decorated in soft pastel colors and antique wardrobes and dressers. The pleasant living room has a piano, fireplace, and TV and opens to the handsome dining room. Expect a delightful visit from younger children—James, Roisin, Edel, or Claire. Breakfast is typical, with additions of fruit and yogurt and homemade muffins. An all-weather tennis court is right on the premises. Bunratty Castle and Folk Park are 20 minutes away. The Burren is 20 minutes north and the beaches of Lahinch are 30 minutes away. Ennis is a bustling county seat and older city and a fun place to visit on Market Day. Golf, fishing, sailing, cycling, swimming, horseback riding, and tennis are offered in the area.

Harbor Lodge

Patsy Flanagan
6 Marine Parade (N67)
Kilkee, County Clare
Telephone: 065-9056090
Bedrooms: 4; 3 with private baths.
Rates: £18 p.p.; Single £23. Vouchers accepted. **Credit cards:** None.
Open: March to October. **Children:** Yes. **Pets:** No. **Smoking:** Yes.
Provision for handicapped: None. **Directions:** Proceed down Main
Street (O'Curry Street) to traffic roundabout. Take third exit, then
along sea front. Harbor Lodge is the second B&B on the sea front.

This is an old-style, single-storied terraced town home, across the
road from the beach in a scenic area. The garden is available for
guests' use. Off-street parking is also provided. A welcoming tea and
coffee with biscuits is offered upon arrival. Breakfasts are cooked to
order, from the full Irish one to vegetarian cheese and yogurt or beans
and toast. Patsy cooks whatever guests want from their order the night
before. The dining room has a bay window in front to view the sea.
The pretty décor is cream and green throughout, with a TV and fireplace in the sitting room. Bedroom selection is one with two double
beds, one with double and single, and two with double beds, so families can be accommodated nicely. Across the street, a walk on the
beach or the promenade can be a delightful way to end the evening.
Fishing, horseback riding, golf, pitch and putt, and scuba diving are
available nearby.

Moher Lodge
Mary Considine
Cliffs of Moher
Liscannor, County Clare
Telephone: 065-7081269, 065-7081589; **E-Mail:** moherlodge@tinet.ie.
Bedrooms: 5, all with private baths.
Rates: £18-19 p.p. Discount for children negotiable. Vouchers accepted. **Credit cards:** None. **Open:** April 1 to October 31. **Children:** Yes, all ages. **Pets:** No. **Smoking:** In lounge only. **Provision for handicapped:** Yes, as far as possible. **Directions:** 3 km from Liscannor village on the R478. 1.5 km from the Cliffs of Moher.

This is a beautiful seaside dormer-style modern home with pretty front garden, part of a mixed working farm with comfortable en suite triple and twin/double rooms, and a lounge with warm peat fire and TV. Breathtaking views and fresh air found in this seacoast region will renew your spirits. A breakfast menu is offered to guests. Nearby is the renowned golf course at Lahinlir. Also, a pitch and putt course is available for less ambitious golfers. Additionally, there is horseback riding and pony-trekking. Of course a trip to the Cliffs of Moher for spectacular views is a must. That first step is a long way down. For the side trippers, go farther north a short distance and investigate the unusual geological formation of the Burren (Burren National Park) and its unique ecology, a must for the naturalist, plus include a visit to the megalithic tombs. Mary can direct you. After your late afternoon walk or hike, a stop at a local pub will cap the day's pleasure. Don't forget to bring your camera, for the scenery of this region is outstanding!

Sea Haven
James and Sheila Lees
Road to Cliffs of Moher
Liscannor, County Clare
Telephone: 065-81385; **FAX:** 065-81474
Bedrooms: 6, all with private baths.
Rates: £18 p.p.; Single £24; 12 percent discount for children under 12. Vouchers are accepted. £14 reserved dinner. **Credit cards:** None. **Open:** January to November. **Children:** Over 10. **Pets:** Yes, in garage. **Smoking:** Restricted. **Provision for handicapped:** Yes. **Directions:** From Lahinch, take the road to the Cliffs of Moher. Sea Haven is a white-gabled bungalow on a hill on the right. A big B&B sign is on a gable.

Sea Haven is a lovely house, sitting high enough to have a gorgeous panoramic view of Liscannor Bay and surrounding farms. The Lees' good service and the tranquil surroundings make this a special place to stay. Most of the rooms are large, with a floral theme; all have wardrobes, coffee and tea service, and a view of walled meadows or the bay. The rooms are peach and pastel, with antiques for ambience. The bathrooms are tiled. The handsomely decorated sitting room has a fireplace and TV; the dining room is pretty, too, and both have views of the water. For breakfast, served buffet style, you can have Full Irish, choice of fruit or juice, brewed coffee, choice of eggs—scrambled, boiled, fried, or poached—local cheeses, and mackerel or herring in summer. Nearby features are the Cliffs of Moher, all watersports, golf, fishing, horseback riding, caving, and cliff walks.

ALSO RECOMMENDED

Corofin, *Burren Lodge,* Rita Kierce, Kilnaboy. Telephone: 065-6837143. 3 Bedrooms, 2 en suite. Spacious house with Burren countryside views on R476. Convenient to Lake District and Burren National Park. Dinner available. Recommended by Mary Considine of Liscannor, County Clare.

Doolin, *Churchfield,* Maeve Fitzgerald. Telephone: 065-707420; Fax: 065-7074622; E-Mail: churchfield@tinet.ie. Bedrooms: 6, 5 en suite, 1 shared. Panoramic view of Cliffs of Moher, sea, and countryside. At bus stop in Doolin. Recommended by Carmel O'Halloran of Galway. Member Town and Country Home Association.

Ennis, *Hazeldene House,* Mrs. Ina Troy, Barefields. Telephone: 065-27212. Bedrooms: 4, all en suite with TV. Private parking. Evening meals available. Modern country home on Ennis-Galway road (N18). It's 5 minutes from Ennis Center. Ideal touring base for the Burren, Cliffs of Moher, and Aillwee Caves.

Ennis, *Villa Nova,* Mrs. Mareaid O'Connor, 1 Woodlawn, Lahinch Road. Telephone: 065-28570. Bedrooms: 5, 3 with private baths. Vouchers accepted. Bungalow on N85. Restaurant and pub with music are a 2 minutes' walk.

Lahinch, *Mulcarr House,* Mrs. Brid Fawl, Ennistymon Road. Telephone: 065-81123. Bedrooms: 4, 3 private baths. Walking distance to golf and beach. Vouchers accepted. Smoke-free home.

Lisdoonvarna, *Fernhill Farmhouse,* Tessie Linnane and family, Doolin Road. Telephone: 065-74040. Bedrooms: 6, 4 with private baths. A comfortable 300-year-old farmhouse 2 miles from Doolin village and 2 miles from Lisdoonvarna. Traditional Irish music nightly in Doolin. Recommended by Tim and Chris-Ann Kane of New York.

Shannon, *Moloney's B&B,* Kay Moloney. Telephone: 061-364185. Bedrooms: 4, 2 en suite. Five minutes from airport terminal. 21 Coil Mhara. Very nice modern home.

COUNTY CORK

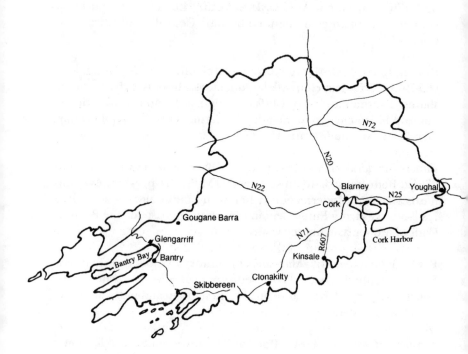

County Cork

County Cork makes up almost half of southwest Ireland, so as you can guess, there are vast differences in the terrain. In the north, around Mallow, the pastureland is flat and broad with dark-green, low shrubs separating the sheep enclosures. Purple mountains can be seen to the north and west.

Moving south you will come to the town of Blarney first, with its famed Blarney Woolen Mills and the Blarney Castle, which contains the celebrated Blarney Stone. The Blarney Park Hotel nearly always has some kind of Irish music, modern or traditional, along with step-dancing or set dancing to watch. Just five or six miles southeast you may visit the largest city of the southwest, which is Cork City. Most of it sits between the north and south channels of the split Lee River, with its numerous bridges.

Here you may want to take the traditional walk along Patrick Street to the Grand Parade or wander to the edges of the city to catch glimpses of St. Mary's Pro-Cathedral or St. Finn Barre's Cathedral, the Church of St. Peter and St. Paul, or Father Matthew Memorial Church. Peruse the many art galleries and craft centers, museums, and the Cork Opera House, which offers delightful plays, musicals, and operas. We had an excellent meal in the dining room of the Moore's Hotel on Morrison's Island, at the south end of town. One memorable night we walked into a small, dark, well-visited pub called An Bodhran, and found a well-loved young fiddler playing his heart out with other musicians. He played for hours, to our joy. In September and October, look for the famous Cork Film Festival and the Jazz Festival.

Due west of Cork City on the N22, headed towards Killarney and just before a mountain pass, is the beautiful medieval town of Macroom, set out in the country. Flowered window boxes abound, and an old stone fort graces the town center.

About 16 miles southwest of Cork is the happy seaside town of Kinsale, labeled the "Gourmet Capital of Ireland." We just missed a big gourmet competition among the many fine restaurants there on our last visit. It has the good gift shops and coffee shops of a tourist town, but a small place where we had the best soup and sandwich by a peat fire is Mother Hubbard's on Pearse Street.

From here you might want to head out to West Cork on winding little roads along tiny bays that cut into the whole of the southwest. You'll pass beautiful small villages like Courtmacsherry, Clonakilty, Rosscarberry, and Baltimore, tucked around harbors full of sailboats. On the N71 is the classy town of Skibbereen, which booms in summer; farther west, then north, is Bantry, with more formality and sophistication, and a commanding view from its hills of Bantry Bay and the wonderful mountains of the Beara Peninsula beyond.

To the east of Cork city, you'll want to see the charming port of Cobh (pronounced "Cove"), from which most emigrants had to leave by boat in the 1800s for the foreign shores of America. Imposing St. Colman's Cathedral reigns on a hill overlooking the town with its multicolored buildings fronting the harbor. Farther east is the medieval town of Youghal, with remnants of an old town gate and walls, and ancient buildings where Cromwell hid his arms. It has a pretty old lighthouse and farms that stretch out with views of the sea.

Dunauley
Rosemary McAuley
Seskin
Bantry, County Cork
Telephone: 027-50290
Bedrooms: 5, all with private baths. 1 self-catering suite.
Rates: £20 to £30 p.p. private bath; £25 suite; Single £25 to £30. 20 percent discount for children. Vouchers not accepted. **Credit cards:** None. **Open:** May 1 to September 30. **Children:** Yes, 12 or older. **Pets:** No. **Smoking:** Restricted. **Provision for handicapped:** Yes. **Directions:** From the center of Bantry follow the signs to the hospital. Take the one-way street up the hill. Pass the Bank of Ireland, post office, and large church on the right. Take the second right. Continue up the hillside road to the Dunauley sign. The B&B is the third house on the right. The main entry door is at the back, but car parking is provided in front once unloaded.

This modern country home is elegant, and the large, comfortable living room/dining room with fireplace has wraparound bay windows with a most extraordinary panoramic view of all of Bantry Bay and the Beara Peninsula from high atop the hill. The bedrooms are very pretty and spacious. One suite of rooms downstairs is available for self-catering or long rental. All are tastefully decorated in blue, pink and green, or apricot. One of the downstairs rooms is the honeymoon bedroom. All rooms have tea- and coffee-making facilities. The breakfast menu almost defies description as it excels in most categories, from fresh-squeezed orange juice or grapefruit decorated with kiwi fruit, to a trolley of cereals with toppings of raisins and fruit, to omelets with four fillings, or smoked salmon and scrambled eggs. Brewed coffee and a variety of teas complement the entrées, not to mention the scones and homemade breads. Extraordinary! Fishing, sailing, golf, walks, and Bantry House are in town 5 minutes away.

Larchwood House
Sheila Vaughan
Pearsons Bridge
Bantry, County Cork
Telephone: 027-66181
Bedrooms: 4, all private baths.
Rates: £25 p.p. Vouchers not accepted. £20-25 dinner. **Credit cards:** Yes. **Open:** All year. **Children:** Yes, all ages. **Pets:** No. **Smoking:** Limited. **Provision for handicapped:** None. **Directions:** On the N71 at Ballylickey, take Kealkill Road for 2 miles, north of Bantry. At Pearsons Bridge on Kealkill Road, take a sharp right. The house is 300 yards on the right.

A rare find is this enchanting "restaurant with rooms." The B&B is part of a small, intimate gourmet restaurant with cooking that has flair and originality. The bedrooms are luxurious, spacious, and beautifully decorated. The dining room overlooks their grand gardens and a small river. For those who like exquisite dining and then a peaceful evening in an elegant bedroom upstairs—instead of a lot of driving—this is the place. The gardens are the handiwork of the husband, Aiden Vaughan, a professional photographer, who has transformed the surroundings, using stone and plants, into an extraordinary, enchanting six acres of beauty. Sheila matches his artistry in the culinary department. Breakfast is ordered off a menu and features fresh fruit; eggs any style, some with smoked salmon (typically Irish) or grilled kippered herring; baked fresh haddock; and a local cheese plate. She has been a super chef at the Dromoland Castle. The small lounge provides drinks in a homey atmosphere, or you can take a stroll through the garden down the "39 Steps" to a place where the local salmon river becomes a pool. The Vaughans are gracious and will make this an idyllic treat off the beaten path. Golf and horseback riding are also nearby.

Shangri-la
Ursula Schiesser
Glengarriff Road
Bantry, County Cork
Telephone: 027-50244; **FAX:** 027-50244
Bedrooms: 6, all with private baths.
Rates: £18 p.p. private bath; Single £24; 20 percent discount for children under 10. Vouchers accepted. **Credit cards:** All major ones.
Open: March 15 to November 15. **Children:** All ages. **Pets:** No.
Smoking: Restricted. **Provision for handicapped:** No, hillside lot.
Directions: Coming from Cork on the N71, the Glengarriff Road, take the first right after ROWA Pharmaceuticals and then the first left to enter the car park at the back of the property.

The view from the living room and sun porch is panoramic and beautiful. The rooms are handsomely decorated: one in green and aqua flowers, one with a pink and white canopy, another with an orange and lace canopy. All are fashionable, charming, and comfortable, with coffee- and tea-making facilities. Ms. Schiesser is a delightful host and will make your stay in Bantry a pleasant one. We were enchanted with the story of the first settlers in Ireland, who came ashore in Bantry, led by Cessera, a woman captaining the crew of 53. Ask Ms. Schiesser about the soup field across the street. There is a choice of menu for breakfast. Some different choices are coddled eggs and pancakes, as well as cheeses, fruits, and yogurts. The full Irish Breakfast is served in the pretty dining room adjoining the well-appointed living room. All common rooms have views of the water and the garden. Many rooms also have a view of the water. This B&B maintains high standards! Bantry House and Gardens and fishing, sailing, walks, and golf are in the area. In 1996, there was a bicentennial celebration of the French Armada in Bantry Bay.

Brehon House
Adrian and Mary Spillett
Killowen
Blarney, County Cork
Telephone: 021-385047
Bedrooms: 3, all with private baths.
Rates: £18 p.p.; Single £25. Vouchers accepted. Ten percent discount for children under 12. **Credit cards:** Yes. **Open:** April to September. **Children:** All ages. **Pets:** No. **Smoking:** Restricted to sun room or conservatory. **Provision for handicapped:** None. **Directions:** Pass the Blarney Park Hotel, leaving Blarney. Take second turn on right and keep right for 2 miles. Note the sign to Brehon House with the shamrock 300 yards on the right, near Killowen Garden Centre.

This charming couple will make you feel right at home at this modern house in a quiet, farm-country setting. You will receive welcoming tea and scones. Their guest book overflows with glowing and superlative comments. The dining room has oval tables and fresh flowers. The breakfast is the full Irish Breakfast with homemade sausages and fresh free-range eggs, fruit, yogurt, and cheeses. The dinner is prepared with vegetables from the large garden beside the house. Rooms are cheery and bright, decorated in pretty pinks, blue-greys, and whites, with white dressing tables. Two rooms have TV. Bathrooms are modern and tiled. The lounge is comfortable and adequate for this size B&B. The ambience and the hosts make this a great place to stay. Golf and a riding center are nearby, as is Blarney Castle. This is an ideal base for touring the south.

Claragh Bed and Breakfast
Cecilia Kiely
Waterloo Road, Garrycloyne
Blarney, County Cork
Telephone and **FAX:** 021-886308; **E-Mail:** claraghbandb@tinet.ie
Bedrooms: 4; 3 with private baths, 1 with shared bath.
Rates: £18 p.p. private bath; £16 p.p. shared bath. 10 percent discount
for children. Vouchers accepted. **Credit cards:** None. **Open:** April 1 to
October 31. **Children:** Yes, ages 6 to 12. **Pets:** No. **Smoking:** No.
Provision for handicapped: Yes, all rooms on ground level. **Directions:**
Follow signs on Waterloo Road out of Blarney Village to Claragh.
About 2 miles out, you'll find the house on the left. Waterloo Road is
200 yards past Blarney Woolen Mills on left (going towards Cork city).

Cecilia Kiely will surely lighten your visit to the Irish Republic with
her boundless energy and special Irish humor. You are always greeted
with tea and hot scones on your arrival. But the hostess makes your visit
especially warm and friendly with her care in directing you to the sights
and sounds of Blarney and Cork City. Electric blankets are turned on
before you retire. The lovely lounge offers tea and coffee facilities and
has a fireplace, and the dining room allows for separate tables. The bedrooms are decorated in pink and green, and peach and green with floral accents. The baths have modern showers with sinks and toilets.
Breakfast has fresh homemade brown bread, fruit, and yogurts, along
with a choice of cooked Irish Breakfast. Cecilia features a French toast
with syrup that is delicious. The quiet of the countryside will be restful
and relaxing after a hard day on the road. It is ideal for relaxing walks or
invigorating jogs. This home is near Blarney Woolen Mills and other
shops. You can kiss the Blarney Stone at the castle, hear Irish music,
dance traditional Irish set dances, or swim at Blarney Park Hotel. You
may want to try to catch the big salmon, as Frank did (tried, that is).
Check out Christie's Restaurant. It's great!

Inchavara House
Breda O'Dwyer
Stoneview
Blarney, County Cork
Telephone: 021-385549; **E-Mail:** stainlessservices@tinet.ie.
Bedrooms: 4, all with private baths.
Rates: £19 p.p. private bath; Single £30. Vouchers not accepted. **Credit cards:** None. **Open:** May 1 to November 1. **Children:** Yes. **Pets:** No. **Smoking:** No. **Provision for handicapped:** None. **Directions:** It is 2 km outside of Blarney Village off R617. Off the N20 from Mallow, take the first right turn to Blarney, go half a mile, and take the second right. Inchavara House is on your right.

This lovely country home was recommended to us by a guest in Dublin, and again by another B&B owner in Blarney, and we are thrilled to include it. What a delightful home, with a beautiful dining room and a spacious lounge, both opening to a large conservatory or sun room with floor-to-ceiling glass, overlooking the beautiful garden in front and hills and Blarney Castle beyond. It is a great place for having a before-dinner drink or playing cards. The bedrooms are decorated in blues and pinks. There are various room accommodations. One bedroom with a huge bath is very large, fitted with a double and a single brass bed. Mrs. O'Dwyer is a congenial and welcoming host. The breakfast is regular or continental. The regular breakfast includes a choice of eggs, black pudding, and hot scones, to name a few extras. The buffet of cereals, yogurts, and fruits makes a nice continental one. The coffee is brewed! In fact tea and coffee facilities are available in the sun room during the day. Horseback riding and golf can be found nearby in Blarney, and there are lovely walks in this area.

Knockawn Wood
Ita and Fergus O'Donovan
Curraleigh
Inniscarra
Blarney, County Cork
Telephone and **FAX:** 021-870284; **E-Mail:** odknkwd@iol.ie.
Bedrooms: 4; 3 with private baths, 1 with shared bath.
Rates: £18 p.p. private bath, £16 p.p. with shared bath. Discount for children 50 percent. Vouchers accepted. Dinner £12 p.p. **Credit cards:** VISA and MasterCard. **Open:** January 1 to December 31. **Children:** Yes, all ages. **Pets:** No. **Smoking:** Restricted. **Provision for handicapped:** None. **Directions:** From Blarney (4 miles away) follow Killarney signs on R618. From Cork take N22 for 3 miles, then turn right onto R618 for 5 miles.

If you need a lodging easily accessible to Cork City and Blarney, this is a good choice. Ita and Fergus will make your stay in the area a pleasant one. Tea and scones are offered on arrival. You can also request a delicious dinner for the evening meal while you're settling in. Their quiet, picturesque setting in the country and their experience in the hospitality profession (Ita managed hotels) will take care of your every need. Even babysitting is provided. Bedrooms are done in blues, pinks, and green and cream combinations. A comfortable lounge with bright lemon décor has a sparkling chandelier and corniced ceiling. The breakfast menu is quite extensive, starting with juices and fresh fruit, followed by a variety of hot and cold cereals. The main course has a full Irish plate plus extras like tomatoes, mushrooms, and beans, or pancakes with syrup. Nearby is salmon fishing on the Lee River and course angling on Inniscarra Lakes. Cork airport and ferry are 30 minutes away.

Hillside Farm
Bella Helen
Kilgarriffe
Clonakilty, County Cork
Telephone: 023-33139
Bedrooms: 4; 2 with private baths, 2 with shared.
Rates: £18 p.p. private bath; £16 shared bath; Single £18; 50 percent discount for children. Vouchers accepted. £14 dinner. **Credit cards:** None. **Open:** April to October. **Children:** All ages. **Pets:** Yes. **Smoking:** No. **Provision for handicapped:** None. **Directions:** To the northwest from Cork, turn right at the Shell station onto Enniskean Road (R588). The farm is 2 miles on the left.

When we were there, pups were being born in the hayloft, new calves were suckling their mothers, and chickens, geese, and rare fowl were clucking and calling in the barnyard. This is a 150-acre, living, vibrant dairy farm, with all the noises and smells one would expect at a rural homestead. Mrs. Helen served us fresh scones with her own crab apple jelly (just made) on the side shelf of her old-style kitchen. She gives baking demonstrations. Although rustic, this pink farmhouse B&B has appeal for those who like to visit a working farm. There are fine views from beautifully furnished rooms. The comfortable lounge has antique furniture, and the dining room is attractive. Dinner features four courses, with a roast such as leg of lamb or salmon, potato, fresh brown bread, two vegetables from the garden, and berry pie. Yum! Breakfast is likewise scrumptious and generous, with homemade white pudding, jams, and jellies. It is a great place for young children to learn about farm life. They would never want to leave. This farm is within 45 minutes' drive of Cork Airport and Ringaskiddy Ferryport. There is good bird watching along the estuary. Look for the ancient Temple Bryan and the Lisnagun Stone.

Belvedere Lodge
Tim and Marie McGrath
Tivoli
Cork City, County Cork
Telephone and **FAX:** 021-501682
Bedrooms: 11, all with private baths.
Rates: £25; Single £33. Vouchers not accepted. 50 percent discount for children. **Credit cards:** All major ones. **Open:** All year, except December 20-30. **Children:** Yes, all ages. **Pets:** Small. **Smoking:** Yes. **Provision for handicapped:** Yes. **Directions:** One mile east of Cork City on Rosslare/Dublin road, just 100 yards past service stations on left. Belvedere is opposite Silver Springs Hotel.

This lovely Victorian guesthouse with a unique wrought-iron veranda has spacious and beautifully decorated bedrooms. There are elegant curtains and quilts and wall-to-wall carpeting in the bedrooms. All are beautifully decorated in two-tone rose, apricot, or turquoise. One room has a bay window with seats and one has a sliding-glass door to the garden. All rooms have TVs, telephones, and tea and coffee makers. The beautiful lounge is light cranberry and has a Victorian floral decor with marble fireplace and accompanying period furniture. The equally handsome dining room is rose with green carpeting with separate tables, all adjoining the patio with a view of the garden. An elaborate breakfast menu includes selection of fresh fruits, fresh-squeezed orange juice, cereals, fresh fish and grills, and scrambled eggs with smoked salmon. There is a private, secure car park. The Belvedere Lodge offers a good base for visiting the sights in Cork, Blarney, and Kinsale, and many historical and cultural sights. The McGraths can direct you to the recreational facilities and restaurants.

Victoria Lodge
Brendan Long
Victoria Cross
Cork City, County Cork
Telephone: 021-542233; **FAX:** 021-542572
Bedrooms: 30, all with private baths.
Rates: £25 p.p.; Single £35. 75 percent discount for children.
Vouchers accepted. **Credit cards:** Yes. **Open:** December 28 to
December 24. **Children:** All ages. **Pets:** Yes. **Smoking:** Nonsmoking
rooms available. **Provision for handicapped:** Yes, one room.
Directions: At the city tourist office, facing north, drive to first traffic
lights. Turn left onto N22. Drive straight through toward Killarney, but
after crossing river turn left just before Crow's Nest pub. Victoria Cross
is 10 meters (almost 33 feet) on your right.

This four-star Irish Tourist Board-rated luxury guesthouse is situated in a peaceful garden on the west side of Cork city. This former
monastery, newly renovated, offers great accommodations for visiting
the sights in Cork, just minutes away from the City Center and convenient to Tennis Village. It offers guests color TV, semi-orthopedic
beds, lifts to each floor, direct-dial telephone, tea-making facilities,
and a secure car park—a modern lodging in all regards. Breakfast is
the full Irish Breakfast, and/or delicious menu items. The warmth of
welcome is unsurpassed. Golf clubs, museums, and fishing facilities
are not too far away. Frank tried his hand at catching salmon on the
Lee River, but the big ones got away.

Cois Collie
Rita Barry-Murphy
Glengariff, County Cork
Telephone: 027-63202
Bedrooms: 6, all with private baths.
Rates: £18 p.p. 20 percent discount for children. Vouchers not accepted.
Credit cards: None. **Open:** April 1 to October 31. **Children:** Yes, all ages. **Pets:** No. **Smoking:** No. **Provision for handicapped:** None.
Directions: Sign posted on Bantry Road, 100 meters from the Eccles Hotel, overlooking Glengariff Harbor.

Cois Coille is a lovely, modern, dormered home in an award-winning riverside garden on a hill overlooking Bantry Bay. It is a comfortable country home in a quiet neighborhood. The rooms are beautifully decorated and designed to be pleasant to the eye. Rita offers an extensive breakfast menu, featuring her homemade breads and preserves. Golfing, boating, fishing, scenic walks, and horseback riding are available in the area. Public and private gardens are also open for your inspection. Tour the famous Beara Peninsula with ferries to Clear Island. Irish is spoken here.

The Lighthouse

Carmel Kelly-O'Gorman
The Rock
Kinsale, County Cork
Telephone: 021-772734; **FAX:** 021-773283
Bedrooms: 6, all with private baths.
Rates: £25 p.p.; £35 p.p. (private suite); Single £38; discount for children. Vouchers not accepted. **Credit cards:** VISA, MasterCard/Access, Eurocard. **Open:** All year. **Children:** Yes, 12 and older. **Pets:** No. **Smoking:** Restricted. **Provision for handicapped:** None. **Directions:** Take R600 to town. At the White House Hotel, bear left, follow the white line for 2 minutes (⅛ mile) until you reach the sign for the community school. Go right and follow the white line to the top of the road. You'll see a signpost for a lighthouse. The home is up a short, steep hill on the right. It is a Tudor house with an old inn sign.

This elegant bed and breakfast was built on the site of the old Kinsale Beacon. It has been completely renovated since the fire of 1993. Carmel, an interior decorator, among other things, fashioned a B&B with a touch of class and refinement. Every room is appointed with antiques. One private suite has its own sitting room. The four-poster and canopy beds in the Georgian suite and the Empire room are beautiful. The Victorian dining room is in Regency style, with old prints of London that provide a perfect match for the period décor. Breakfast features a choice of juices or raspberries in champagne, cereals (including honey muesli), yogurts, fancy teas, smoked salmon and scrambled eggs, Irish cheddar and other cheeses, black and white puddings, mushrooms, kippers with lemon butter, and so on. You will certainly have your fill of Irish delicacies. Carmel, with her professional approach to hospitality, will lead you to the best restaurants and make your visit to Kinsale a highlight of your trip to the Irish Republic. Her B&B is within easy reach of shark fishing, yacht rental, world championship Old Head golf links, and three horseback riding stables.

Rivermount House
Claire O'Sullivan
Knocknabinny, Barrells Cross
Kinsale, County Cork
Telephone: 021-778033; **FAX:** 021-778225
Bedrooms: 6, all with private baths.
Rates: £21; 10 percent discount for children. Vouchers accepted.
Dinner offered. **Credit cards:** None. **Open:** February 1 to December 1.
Children: All ages. **Pets:** No. **Smoking:** No. **Provision for handicapped:**
None. **Directions:** Continue on R600 through Kinsale to the Old
Head. Go over bridge and turn right. Continue on 1.5 km to large
crossroad. Turn right; Rivermount is the 4th house on right. It is 4
km from Kinsale on road to Ballinspittle.

This large, lovely, modern country home, situated on a four-acre
lot in a quiet setting with spectacular views of the Brandon River, has
a great deal of charm and character. There are many amenities such as
babysitting, TVs, tea- and coffee-making facilities, telephones, radios,
hair dryers, and private off-street parking. The bedrooms are pink
with matching fabrics, the large lounge has warm red walls and green
carpeting, and the bright and airy conservatory is yellow and green.
A luxurious décor exists throughout the whole house and is obvious
the minute you enter. The breakfast is varied from traditional to
salmon or pancakes; the emphasis is on home produce. Nearby there
is sailing (Kinsale is one of the largest recreational sailing centers in all
of Ireland), fishing, beaches, and horseback riding. Also, Kinsale hosts
a gourmet restaurant festival in the fall, but you will find good eating
here any time of the year. There are many quaint and extraordinary
restaurants where you find gourmet and country fare served in varied ambiences. The Old Head golf club is nearby.

Walyunga
Myrtle Levis
Sandycove
Kinsale, County Cork
Telephone and **FAX:** 021-774126
Bedrooms: 5; 4 with private baths, 1 with shared.
Rates: £22 p.p. private; £20 p.p. shared; Single £24; 20 percent discount for children under 12. **Credit cards:** None. **Open:** March to end of October. **Children:** Yes, 5 or older. **Pets:** No. **Smoking:** No. **Provision for handicapped:** None. **Directions:** From the Trident Hotel in Kinsale follow the Sandycove signs across the long bridge. As you approach Sandy Cove signs, you will see the Walyunga sign. Follow that. Walyunga is about 2 miles from trident. Take the first right, then the first left, and then the next immediate right. Travel a short distance to the Walyunga sign and then go up the hill. At the top of the hill, take a sharp left and Walyunga is on the left. Parking is at the rear.

This pleasant couple offers a modern country home with hanging plants and a feeling of openness to nature by a creative use of glass and skylights. There are grand views of the Atlantic Ocean with a lighthouse in the distance through large picture windows. A sliding-glass door in front opens to a garden and meadow. Mr. Levis, an elementary-school teacher, knows the natural history of the region, and gives advice on genealogical quests. They had spent many years in Australia, thus the name Walyunga. All rooms are modern and spacious with fluffy quilts. One is a front corner room with a large bed and spacious bath that we took to be the "honeymoon suite." The pastel colors in the rooms with fine furniture and woodwork make this an attractive home. The sun was brilliant when we were there, and the delicious breakfast with brewed coffee and a view out the front was memorable. They offer a variety of cereals, porridge, fruit salad, yogurt, smoked salmon, and scrambled eggs in addition to an Irish Breakfast. Nearby are sandy beaches, fishing, and scenic coastal walks. Walyunga is en route to the internationally acclaimed Old Head of Kinsale Golf Links.

Ballymakeigh House
Margaret Browne
Killeagh
Youghal, County Cork
Telephone: 024-95184; **FAX:** 024-95370; **E-Mail:** ballymakeigh@tinet.ie
Bedrooms: 6, all with private baths.
Rates: £30-40 p.p.; Single £5 extra. Vouchers not accepted. £22.50 for
dinner. **Credit cards:** All major ones. **Open:** February to November.
Children: All ages. **Pets:** Negotiable. **Smoking:** Restricted. **Provision
for handicapped:** None. **Directions:** House is 22 miles east of Cork
City, off the N25. Go straight between Old Thatch Pub (where there
is a sign for Ballymakeigh House) and the church in Killeagh when
turning off the N25. Their driveway is on the right, about ½ mile.

This stately and refined eighteenth-century farmhouse, elegantly
decorated by Mrs. Browne, is a showpiece for décor and colors. The
Brownes were the 1992 winners of the A.I.B./I.F.J. Agri-Tourism
National Award for Best Farmhouse B&B. In 1999 Ballymakeigh
House won the Farm Guesthouse of the Year Award. There is a
glassed-in conservatory for lounging and teas. The bedrooms are spacious, with charming views of the meadows. They have extras like
French soap, facecloths, hair dryers, and suitcase racks. All bedrooms
are newly decorated in pastel shades. The dining room is done in
green and red with an antique piano. Fresh flowers abound. Gourmet
cooking by your host will delight your palate both at breakfast and at
dinner. For breakfast you get a choice of free-range eggs, porridge,
fresh orange juice, grapefruit, or apple juice. Kippers are offered too.
Tennis courts are on the grounds. They also have a game room and
play area. Ballymakeigh has opened its equestrian centre for all levels
of riders. Three golf courses are nearby and the house is convenient to
Midleton Heritage Park, Fota, Trabolgan, Vee, Blarney, Cork Airport
and Ferryport, Ballymaloe, and sandy beaches.

ALSO RECOMMENDED

Blarney, *Ashlee Lodge Tower,* Anne and John O'Leary, on the Blarney Kilarney Road (R617) 3 km out of town. Telephone: 021-385346; FAX: 021-385726; E-Mail: ashlee@iol.ie. Bedrooms: 6, 5 en suite, 1 shared. Superbly appointed luxury bungalow. Prize-winning garden. Excellent cuisine. French and German spoken.

Blarney, *Emerald House,* Bridget Murphy, The Square. Telephone: 021-385148. Bedrooms: 4, all with private baths. Vouchers accepted. Period house nearest to castle entrance overlooking the town common. Walking distance to Blarney Woolen Mills, restaurants, and Blarney Park Hotel, where there is music, dancing, and swimming. Tea/coffee facilities. Color TVs in rooms.

Blarney, *St. Anthony's,* Mr. Pat O'Flynn, Sunset Place, Killeens. Common's Road, on N617. Telephone: 021-385151. Bedrooms: 6, 3 with private baths. 5 minutes to Cork City. Country home in scenic surroundings.

Blarney, *The White House,* Pat and Regina Coughlin, Blarney Town. Telephone: 021-385338. Bedrooms: 6, 4 with private baths. ½ mile from Blarney Center on the Mallow road.

Clonakilty, *Ard Na Griene,* Norma Walsh, Ballinascarthy. Telephone: 023-39104; FAX: 023-39397. Bedrooms: 6, 4 en suite. Farm B&B. 6 km from Clonakilty on N71. Dinner available. Won Galtee Breakfast award. Recommended by many travel guides. Spectacular view of countryside.

Clonakilty, *Inchydoney Hotel,* Colette and Denis Murphy, managers, Inchydoney. Telephone: 023-33143. Bedrooms: 29, 23 with private baths. Family-owned and -operated hotel that has the feel of a country home B&B. Apartments also available. Two beaches nearby, tennis, fishing, golf, and indoor and outdoor playgrounds. Recommended by Betty Ann and John Callanan of Hampton, N.H.

Gougane Barra, *Gougane Barra Hotel,* Christopher and Breda Lucey, Ballingeary. Telephone: 026-47069/47223; FAX: 026-47226. Bedrooms: 28, all with private baths. Lovely guesthouse on its own grounds tucked away in beautiful mountains of West Cork. Inland from Glengarriff overlooking Gougane Barra Lake, the source of the Lee

River. Family-owned and -operated hotel. The favorite of Dan Callanan of Beverly Cove, Mass.

Kinsale, *Griffin's Hillside House,* Margaret Griffin, Camp-Hill, on the hill above Kinsale Town. Telephone: 021-772315. Bedrooms: 6, 3 with private baths. Open all year. Beautiful sea view.

Kinsale, *The Moorings Guesthouse,* Pat & Irene Jones, Scilly. Telephone: 021-772376. Bedrooms: 8 (luxury), all with private baths. Breakfast served in elegant conservatory overlooking the estuary, forts, and yacht marina.

Kinsale, *The Old Presbytery,* Ken and Cathleen Buggy, Cork Street, Kinsale Town. Bedrooms: 6, 4 with private baths. Unusual B&B, an old Victorian house tastefully decorated with antiques both decorative and functional.

Skibbereen, *Glencar,* Josephine Griffin, Cork Road, in suburbs of Skibbereen on N71. Telephone: 028-21638. Bedrooms: 5, 3 with private baths. 2 single bedrooms. Spacious house overlooking open countryside.

COUNTY DONEGAL

County Donegal

County Donegal, way up in the northwest corner of Ireland, has a definite rugged character all its own. Settlers came here in 7000 B.C. It doesn't seem to suffer from being almost entirely bordered on the east by Northern Ireland. You could spend a week or two there and not see all the wonderful and varied sights. To the northwest, it is very mountainous, and the N56 takes you on a grand tour of the seacoast, with its hundreds of inlets and wonderful fishing villages on the Atlantic Ocean. You'll find great rock formations and fine sandy beaches for swimming and surfing.

If you decide to travel up the eastern side of Lough Swilly to see the ancient ruins and castles of the spectacular Inishowen Peninsula, the R38 makes a circular tour. This area was settled by Normans in the tenth century.

Letterkenny seems to be the most central city for all these trips, and it's a fun town to visit on its own. Tourist Information is on Derry Road and open June to September. The majestic St. Euman's Cathedral is especially pretty lit up at night. Visit the Donegal County Museum on High Road, and choose from a number of good pubs downtown almost any night in summer for singalongs and traditional Irish music. Two good restaurants are the Gleneany House and the Silver Tassie in Letterkenny. Golf, fishing, and swimming are very close at hand. From here it's only 30 minutes northwest to the unspoiled wildness of Glenveagh National Park, with its Castle and Gardens on 25,000 acres and beautiful, dramatic views of mountains, rivers, and vales. Letterkenny is a good home base for a trip around to the Antrim coast, with the peculiar, enormous, step-rock formation called the Giant's Causeway. It's a quick ride to the thriving, exciting town of Derry, too. Try the excellent DaVinci's Restaurant for atmosphere and great choices. On the way, through Carrigans, in eastern Donegal, you'll find charming country scenes and vistas, a photographer's dream.

To the south is the lovely Lough Eske and Donegal, a small town with charm, great for shopping and trying dinners in good hotels and restaurants. You'll find handcrafted woolen goods and Donegal tweeds for sale in the shops. Donegal Castle is a walk from the Diamond in the center of town. Ask where the good Irish music is playing in lounges and pubs. It's very popular there. Hyland Central Hotel has a good Sunday buffet.

Travel out west of Donegal on the N15 to Killybegs, with its fishing fleet. When we were in County Wexford, clear across the country, we met a man who said he traveled every week to fish on his boat out of Killybegs, as the fishing is so good there. It's a pleasant drive north to the fishing villages of Portnoo, Ardara, and Glencolumbkille, with its Folk Park, all on the Atlantic Ocean.

Ballyshannon is the southern gateway to Donegal County. It has a musical Folk Festival every July or August. Visit Beleek with its delicate pottery, just a few miles away on the Fermanagh border and visit the neat beaches of Rossnowlagh, where you can surf or water-ski.

Cavangarden House
Agnes McCaffrey
Ballyshannon, County Donegal
Telephone: 072-51365; **E-Mail:** cghouse@iol.ie
Bedrooms: 6, all with private baths
Rates: £18 p.p.; Single £22; 50 percent discount for children.
Vouchers accepted. £12 dinner on request. **Credit cards:** All major
ones. **Open:** March 1 to November 1. **Children:** All ages. **Pets:** No.
Smoking: No. **Provision for handicapped:** None. **Other features:**
Plenty of parking. **Directions:** The house is 11 miles south of Donegal
Town on the N15 on the right, or 3 miles north of Ballyshannon on
the left.

We drove down a country lane with sheep and cows grazing on
either side and came to a stately 1750 stucco manor house. Mrs.
McCaffrey graciously served us tea in the classically decorated, high-
ceilinged living room, by the marble fireplace. Antique gold-framed
mirrors and pictures graced the walls, and a conversation piece was a
fancy lounge couch covered in caramel-colored velvet. The rooms
were a surprise, with oversized antique mahogany beds, comfy quilts,
and handsome dark bureaus and tables. Walls all have large-floral-
printed paper, Victorian style. The two rooms on the third floor are
more modern and sunny, with skylights. Pastoral scenes and bright
green hills can be seen from each room. Cavangarden House
reminded us of a grand old house we stayed at in Limoges, France.
The castle-sized dining room has a very long, dark, wood table and
carved-back chairs. Beside the Irish Breakfast, Mrs. McCaffrey serves
yogurt and fruit and features delicious homemade scones.
Rossnowlagh Beach is three miles away, with swimming and windsurfing, and the house is quite near to Donegal Town.

Mount Royd
Josephine Martin
Carrigans (near Derry), County Donegal
Telephone: 074-40163
Bedrooms: 4, all with private baths.
Rates: £17 p.p.; Single £19; 50 percent discount for children under 12. Vouchers accepted. £12 dinner; £6.50 high tea. **Credit cards:** None.
Open: March to November. **Children:** Yes. **Pets:** Yes. **Smoking:** Restricted. **Provision for handicapped:** None. **Directions:** Carrigans has signs posted on the N13 and N14. From Derry City, take Letterkenny Road (A40) and stay on A40 to Carrigans. Mount Royd is on left. From Letterkenny, take N13 until you see signs for Carrigans.

This elegant 50-year-old Georgian country home is one of our favorites because of the pastoral setting and the extraordinary care that Mrs. Martin has taken in decorating and furnishing her spacious home. It was a farmhouse and they still have sheep grazing in the meadows of their 12 acres. Your hostess greets you with tea and her special apricot or nut scones, and shows you a video of the highlights of the region in the cozy living room in front of the fire. Recently she has won the Galtee Irish Breakfast Award and is now AA [Automobile Association of the UK] recommended, with a 4-Qs rating. The guest rooms are all large and very lovely with lots of ruffles in varying shades of pink, blue, or peach. The breakfast is served in her handsome dining room with a trolley of apricots, grapefruit, and mandarin oranges, fresh fluffy scones, and home-baked currant bread, in addition to a choice of omelet or fried eggs, bacon and sausage, or yogurt, cheese, and cereal. The Martins love to tell of Agatha Christie living and writing her mysteries in a big house just across the road. Derry is only five miles away, with excellent restaurants like DaVinci's, to name one good one we favor. This is a good base for touring the Inishowen Peninsula, Londonderry, and the fascinating Giant's Causeway on the coast of Antrim. Also five miles away is the Cavanacor Historic House and Craft Center, the ancestral home of former U.S. president, James Polk. A historic fort, Grianin of Aileach, is nearby, too.

Ardeevin
Mary McGinty
Lough Eske, Barnesmore
Donegal Town, County Donegal
Telephone and **FAX:** 073-21790; **E-Mail:** seanmcginty@tinet.ie.
Bedrooms: 5; 4 with private baths, 1 private not in room.
Rates: £20 p.p.; 20 percent discount for children under 12. Vouchers accepted. **Credit cards:** None. **Open:** March to November. **Children:** All ages. **Pets:** No. **Smoking:** No. **Provision for handicapped:** None.
Directions: Going south from Letterkenny on the N15, 2 miles after Biddy O'Barnes' Pub on the right, turn right. Follow the signs down the winding country road for about l mile. Out of Donegal Town, follow Derry Road (N15) for 5 km until you come to a fork in the road. Turn left, follow the signs to Lough Eske, then follow the Ardeevin signs the rest of the way.

Mary McGinty and her husband, a charming and hospitable couple, run the nicest B&B country home, which is newly renovated. The bedrooms are pretty, with flowered duvets in pinks and blues and handsome mahogany wood headboards. All rooms, including the dining room, have an exquisite view of Lough Eske. Tea- and coffee-making facilities are in each room. You are close to Donegal Town with its restaurants and shops. Visit McGinty's knitting shop for some real bargains. This place is a delight because of its beautiful rooms, the spacious dining room with lake views, and genuinely friendly hosts. The buffet-style breakfast has a full array of delicious offerings like kippers and seafood crêpes, but we were thrilled with the pancakes and syrup. Other offerings were fresh fruit, yogurt, cheese and scones, and of course the Irish Breakfast. O'Donnell Castle in town is restored and open to the public. Harvey's Point restaurant across the lake is great. The area is ideal for horseback riding, fishing, hiking nearby, and golf, eight miles away at Rossnowlagh.

Lismolin Country Home
Bernie Cahill
Fintra Road
Killybegs, County Donegal
Telephone: 073-31035; **FAX:** 073-32310
Bedrooms: 6, all with private baths.
Rates: £18 p.p.; Singles £24.50; 30 percent discount for children. Vouchers accepted. £14 dinner. **Credit cards:** VISA, MasterCard, Access. **Open:** All year, except 3 days of Christmas. **Children:** All ages. **Pets:** On request. **Smoking:** Restricted. **Provision for handicapped:** Can take wheelchairs. **Directions:** Go west through Killybegs Town toward Glencolumbkille; 1 km west of Killybegs, take the street on the left. The B&B is the first house on the left; a single-level ranch with a tile roof.

The turf fire was burning during our visit, and Bernie's hospitality was captivating. This lovely modern home is situated beside a verdant forest and has a picturesque view of Cronard Mountain across the road. All rooms are redecorated each year, but you will find trebles, doubles, and singles—all kinds of accommodations—in pretty floral patterns (dark blue and white or peach, or green and pink) with baths to match. There are electric blankets on all beds. All have TVs and hair dryers. Being off the street, the house is quiet. The car park in front makes it convenient for getting in and out for your day trips. The spacious dining room has five separate tables with royal blue table-cloths. The red and violet hydrangea in the garden outside can be seen from the sliding-glass door in the fireplaced dining room. This is a pleasant place to have one of Bernie's delicious cooked break-fasts accompanied by porridge and homemade soda and brown breads, slathered with her own black currant, gooseberry, or rhubarb jelly. Broiled fish is also featured. Pleasure boat and deep-sea-fishing trips are offered. Killybegs is Ireland's largest fishing port. Try the Blue Haven Restaurant nearby for good, reasonably priced food. Traditional Irish dance music can be heard nearby.

Ardglas

Breid and Paddy Kelly
Lurgybrack, Sligo Road
Letterkenny, County Donegal
Telephone: 074-22516/25140
Bedrooms: 6; 5 with private baths, 1 with shared bath.
Rates: £18 p.p. private bath; £16 shared bath; Single £21; 30 percent discount for children under 12. Vouchers are accepted. **Credit cards:** None. **Open:** April 1 to September 30. **Children:** All ages. **Pets:** No. **Smoking:** Restricted. **Provision for handicapped:** Yes. **Directions:** Take N14 out of Letterkenny, take Derry Road to Dry Arch Roundabout to the N13 (Sligo Road). Go 1 mile—the house is on the left.

This beautiful, spacious Georgian bungalow with many windows is high on a hill and some of the rooms look out onto grazing sheep and mountain views. The Kellys have dogs and cats. Breid is most gracious as a hostess. The modern living room is large, with a TV, flagstone fireplace, and soft cocoa-colored chairs. All the rooms are large and attractive and have matching duvets in flowered prints of quiet colors such as beiges, pinks, and browns. The upstairs rooms are larger. All of the rooms have TVs, hair dryers, and tea-making facilities. Breid has four family rooms. Her Irish Breakfast includes fresh fruit, yogurt, and cereal, boiled or poached eggs, or porridge. Paddy and his son both teach woodworking in secondary schools. It is an ideal place for visiting North Donegal, Derryveigh, and Northern Ireland's wonderful seacoast. It is close to golf, fishing, bowling, and horseback riding, and you'll find three cinemas as well as a leisure center in town.

Glencairn House
Maureen McCleary
Ramelton Road
Letterkenny, County Donegal
Telephone: 074-24393/25242
Bedrooms: 6; 5 with private baths, 1 private not in room.
Rates: £18 p.p.; £16 shared bath; Single £22; ⅓ discount for children under 12. Vouchers accepted. **Credit cards:** All major ones. **Open:** All year, except Christmas week. **Children:** All ages. **Pets:** No. **Smoking:** Restricted to lounge. **Provision for handicapped:** Rooms on ground floor. **Directions:** Coming into Letterkenny take Ramelton Road (R245) to the right. As you climb the hill, Glencairn House is on your right. Drop down into the large car park. It is near Mount Errigul Hotel.

This modern suburban home on a hillside is gorgeous. From the etching on the front door, to the large gold and beige bathroom, to the spacious room with a spectacular view of the whole valley—all is beautiful! You may see the Swilly River valley from the side patio, which has lounge chairs. The pink and green, beige and pale apricot, and grey and pink in the bedrooms give them a soft and elegant look. All headboards are covered in velvet. Rooms have tea- and coffee-making facilities and TV. The family room on the right is Frank's favorite. It has a double and single bed, dressing table or desk, and large bath in the back. The large lounge with a fireplace will be where you are greeted with tea or coffee on your arrival. A full Irish Breakfast is served with fruit, yogurt, cheese, cereal, and porridge in the large dining room, which has separate tables and a view. This place is a great bargain! Golf, bowling, and three cinemas are in the area. Ask for directions to good salmon fishing, too.

Hill Crest House
Larry and Margaret Maguire
Lurgybrack
Letterkenny, County Donegal
Telephone: 074-22300/25137
Bedrooms: 6; 5 with private baths, 1 private not in room.
Rates: £18 p.p. private bath en suite; £16 p.p. unattached bath; Single £20-£25. 33 percent discount for children under 12. Vouchers are accepted. Dinner offered. **Credit cards:** Yes, all but Diners. **Open:** All year. **Children:** All ages. **Pets:** No. **Smoking:** Restricted. **Provision for handicapped:** Yes, if they are with help. **Directions:** From Letterkenny, take the N14 towards Derry; at Dry Arch Roundabout, take the N13 (Sligo Road). The house is 1 km up the road on the right, past the school at the top of the hill.

This modern house with a car park sits on a hill, so some of the rooms have a grand view of the town and river. The very cozy guest lounge has a TV, VCR, and fireplace; a neat rack there contains many brochures of all the nearby places to visit. The bedrooms are blue, pink, beige, and orange, all with TVs, orthopedic beds, and electric blankets. The two upstairs rooms have terrific views. Margaret and Larry were just unpacking their new delftware with wildflowers and matching napkins when we arrived. They served us tea, scones, and tarts in their large kitchen, where we met three of their five children. The dining room has lace tablecloths and Margaret serves a routine full Irish Breakfast along with fruit, yogurt, and choices of eggs. The Maguires conceived and published a brochure that shows different tour routes to Glencolumbkille to the south, with 5,000 years of history; Inishowen Peninsula in northern Donegal; Fanad and Rosguill circuits; and the Gaelacht Heritage trail, including Glenveagh Castle and Gardens. Golf, swimming, and horseback riding are nearby.

Radharc Na Giuise
Jennie and Jim Bradley
Kilmacrennan Road
Letterkenny, County Donegal
Telephone: 074-22090; **FAX:** 074-25139
Bedrooms: 6, all with private baths.
Rates: £18 p.p., single person £25. Children 33 percent discount.
Vouchers accepted. **Credit cards:** VISA, Eurocard, MasterCard. **Open:**
January 6th to December 18th. **Children:** Yes, all ages. **Pets:** No.
Smoking: Restricted. **Provision for Handicapped.** None. **Directions:**
Situated on the main Glenveagh National Park Road overlooking
town on the N56 to Dunfanaghy. 0.5 km above hospital roundabout.
Look for modern grey stone and white home with two-windowed
dormer, garden with shrubs in front and driveway on the right.

This attractive dormered bungalow overlooking the town, with
pretty gardens in front and back garden for visitor's use, is convenient to local shops and restaurants. Jennie will give you a warm and
friendly Irish welcome when you arrive, and describe the tourist highlights of Donegal if requested. The lounge is cozily decorated with a
fireplace for postcard writing or card playing. You have a selection of
six beautifully decorated bedrooms with soft-colored curtains and
throwovers. One is done in white, cream, and brown, two in champagne with green and gold curtains and green patterned rug, and all
have throwovers to match the décor. Each room has a TV, hair dryer,
tea/coffee facilities, tissues, and a small flower arrangement.
Recreation in the area gives you a choice of golfing, horseback riding, and fishing. Letterkenny also has a leisure center. Jennie's bed
and breakfast was a "Tidy Towns" award winner last year. She can also
tell you about *Riverdance,* as her daughter has been a member of the
troupe the last four years.

Town View B&B
May and Danny Herrity
Leck Road
Letterkenny, County Donegal
Telephone: 074-21570/25138
Bedrooms: 6, all with private baths.
Rates: £18 p.p.; Single £23; Vouchers accepted. Dinner offered, £14 p.p. **Credit cards:** None. **Open:** All year. **Children:** Yes, 5 or older. **Pets:** No. **Smoking:** Restricted. **Provision for handicapped:** Yes. **Directions:** From the center of town, take Main Street to the foot of the hill to Dunnes Store, go left, cross over the bridge, and stay left for ½ mile; follow the signs to the B&B, or call owner from town.

A modern, white-stucco bungalow, this B&B has pleasantly comfortable rooms all decorated in pastel blues and greens. May is a great hostess, serving you tea on arrival and leading you on a good tour around the area. The view of the whole town from her sitting room is spectacular by day or night. Beautiful lamps and antiques adorn the house and the dining room is spacious with views also. Breakfast is a gourmet delight with a buffet of lots of fruits, cereals, yogurts, and cheeses in addition to her full cooked Irish Breakfast. She has won a Galtee award for her good breakfasts. Danny and her son and daughter help with the work; Dan has a horse of his own in a little barn. A large car park is available, and golf, ten-pin bowling, and a swimming pool are open to visitors of Letterkenny town. They are close to the famous Glenveagh Castle and Gardens, and Rathmullen Beach. One night we drove to Derry for an excellent dinner. Horseback riding is nearby.

Thalassa Country Home
Eva Friel
Narin
Portnoo, County Donegal
Telephone: 075-45151
Bedrooms: 4, all with private baths.
Rates: £18 p.p.; Single £18.50; 25 percent discount for children under 12. Vouchers accepted. £13 dinner; £8 high tea. **Credit cards:** VISA.
Open: February to December 1. **Children:** All ages. **Pets:** No. **Smoking:** Restricted. **Provision for handicapped:** None. **Directions:** Take the N56 to Ardara, then R261 to Portnoo-Narin, about 5 km. Follow the sign for Portnoo. The house is on the coast road overlooking the ocean and golf course. Look for "Thalassa" signs.

If ocean views are your choice, this modern country home will provide you with plenty of breathtaking scenery in this beautiful part of Donegal. Mrs. Friel keeps a nice bed and breakfast and comes highly recommended by other B&B owners. She serves a home-cooked Irish breakfast, yogurt, fruit, and a choice of cereals. The house has bay windows in front for ocean views. A beautiful garden graces the front yard with folding chairs to lounge in during the off hours. The rooms are well decorated and furnished and there is a comfortable lounge with a TV. You will receive an especially warm welcome of tea or coffee, and babysitting can be arranged while you play golf at the nearby 18-hole course or go out for a pint at the local pub. This quiet location has forest and cliff walks and trips to historic monuments. Visit gorgeous Gweebara Bay, with a long stretch of sandy beaches, just a 10-minute walk away. The water is safe for bathing.

ALSO RECOMMENDED

Ardara, *The Green Gate,* Paul Chatenoud, Ardvally. Telephone: 075-41546. 2 miles from Ardara on Ardara-Donegal Road. Unique cottage off the beaten path. Delightful French host who charms the guests with a wonderful ambience.

Bruckless, *Bruckless House,* Clive and Joan Evans. Telephone: 073-37071; FAX: 073-37070. Bedrooms: 5, 2 with private baths. Clive breeds traditional Irish draft horses and Connemara ponies. Home handsomely decorated and appointed. On N56 towards Killybegs. Bruckless House on left in the village of Bruckless.

Donegal, *Eske View,* Mary and Keith Pearson, Lough Eske, Barnesmore. Telephone: 073-22087. Bedrooms: 3, 2 with private baths.

Donegal, *Woodlands,* Mrs. Bernie McGonigle, Coast Road, Doonan. Telephone: 073-21453. Bedrooms: 5, all with private baths. 1 km west of Donegal Town. Recommended by Brid and Walter Myles of Cavan Town.

Killybegs, *Glenlee House,* Mrs. Ellen O'Keeney, Fintra Road. Telephone: 073-31026. Bedrooms: 5, all with private baths. Very nice. Recommended by Mary McGinty of Lough Eske, Donegal.

Killybegs, *Lough Head House,* Mrs. Sadie McKeever, Donegal Road. Telephone: 073-31088. Bedrooms: 3, 2 with private baths. Vouchers accepted. Panoramic view of Killybegs Harbor. Smoke-free home.

Letterkenny, *Pennsylvania House,* Nuala and Michael Duddy, Curraghleas, Mountain Top. Telephone 074-26808; Fax: 074-28905. Bedrooms: 4, 3 en suite. Exceptionally beautiful home with a warm touch of elegance and hospitality. Panoramic views of hills, valleys, and mountains of Donegal. Offers bedroom telephones, facsimile, and photocopying. 4 minutes from Letterkenny.

Rossnowlagh, *Ardeelen Manor,* Mrs. Fun Britton. Telephone: 072-51578. Bedrooms: 4. Recommended by Walter and Brid Myles of Cavan Town.

COUNTY DUBLIN

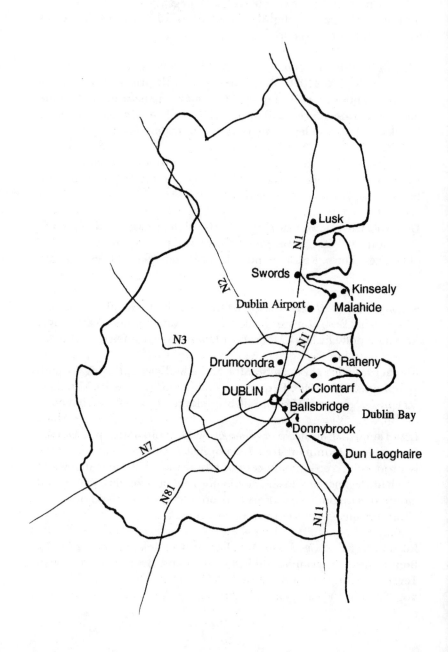

County Dublin

County Dublin is nearly the smallest county in Ireland, but by no means the least important. The capital city of Dublin dominates the area, taking up about one-fifth of the county. Besides the city center, suburban areas such as Clontarf, Drumcondra, Raheny, and Fairview to the north, and Ballsbridge, Donnybrook, Rathmines, and Sandymount to the south are all considered part of Dublin City.

Dublin Center is a very exciting visit with all its history and culture. The best way to get a sense of it all is to ride a tour bus from O'Connell Street, with colorful commentary, all around, and see the museums, theaters, cathedrals, Trinity College with its famed *Book of Kells*, Saint Stephen's Green, the Liffey River with its "humpy" bridges, well-known Grafton Street (no traffic) for shopping and buskers playing sweet music, the National Gallery and Government buildings, and the Post Office, still with marks of the Easter Rebellion of 1916. For genealogical study, stop at the National Library on Kildare Street and the General Register Office of Births, Marriages, and Deaths at Joyce House, 8/10 Lombard Street East. You may get off at any stop and pick up where you left off in an hour or two and continue the tour.

Dublin City spawned and is very proud of great writers such as James Joyce, Jonathan Swift, Samuel Beckett, Sean O'Casey, Brendan Behan, Kate O'Brien, Oscar Wilde, Mary Lavin, George Bernard Shaw, Brian Friel, Maeve Binchy, Christy Brown, and many others. Visit the James Joyce Cultural Centre at 35 North Great George's Street. There is a whole walking tour you may take of the spots visited by Leopold Bloom, the hero of *Ulysses*. Dublin even celebrates "Bloomsday" on June 16 each year.

Be sure to visit the Dublin Zoo; Phoenix Park; the Bewleys Cafe on Grafton Street, with its delicious fresh coffee and food and its delightful James Joyce Room; and many of the old and charming pubs, some with traditional music. Scan the papers for current plays at the Abbey, the Peacock, and the Gate Theaters. We found them very enjoyable. The original Abbey Theater was started by William Yeats and Lady Gregory.

Outlying districts have beautiful old Dublin homes; go east to Howth on a point of land that has the lighthouse called "The Eye of Ireland," and visit the restaurants and the Abbey Tavern in Howth, where a show of traditional Irish music is played nightly. In Clontarf, there is St. Anne's Rose Garden to visit and an excellent restaurant, The Yacht, on Clontarf Road, with super choices and good prices, especially at noon. Of course, Dublin Airport is just 20 minutes from Clontarf, Drumcondra, or Raheny. North and near the airport is the town of Malahide, with its smart castle and grounds and lovely old buildings downtown. To the south, Ballsbridge flaunts the R.D.S. Arena with its famous horse shows and other events, and the Jury's Hotel with its nightly cabaret show, which is an extravaganza. Sandymount and Merrion have great beaches. Farther south is Bray Head, a wonderful place to climb, with ocean views, and the lovely seaport of Dun Laoghaire with its beaches and ferries to Holyhead, England. Dun Laoghaire also has the famed Joyce Tower to visit.

The DART, a very efficient electrical railway system, operates to outlying areas as far as Howth to the north and Dun Laoghaire to the south. It begins at 6:30 A.M. and ends at 11:30 P.M. There is very extensive bus service to all areas. The Tourist Information Office (Tel. 01-747733) at 14 Upper O'Connell Street is open weekdays from 9 to 5:30 and Saturdays 9 to 1. The Irish Tourist Board (Tel. 01-765872), at Baggot Street Bridge, is open weekdays only, 9 to 6.

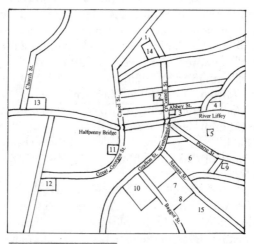

PLACES OF GENERAL PUBLIC INTEREST

1. Writer's Museum	6. Trinity College	11. Dublin Castle
2. General Post Office	7. National Museum	12. St. Patrick's Cathedral
3. Abbey Theatre	8. National Library	13. Four Courts of Justice
4. Central Bus Station	9. Pearse Station	14. Parnell Square
5. Tara St. Station	10. St. Stephen's Green	15. Merrion Square

Aisling House
Frances and Robert English
19/20 St. Lawrence Road
Clontarf, Dublin 3, County Dublin
Telephone: 01-8339097; **FAX:** 01-8338400
Bedrooms: 6, all with private baths.
Rates: £25 p.p. private bath; Single £30-£40; Vouchers not accepted.
Credit cards: None. **Open:** All year, except Christmas week. **Children:**
All ages. **Pets:** No. **Smoking:** Restricted to the lounge. **Provision for handicapped:** None. **Directions:** From Dublin, stay left of the Liffey River, go left before the Custom House and left after the bus station to Amiens Street, follow to North Strand to Fairview to Clontarf Road, and take a left at the Methodist Church onto St. Lawrence Road. Aisling House is on the left.

The Aisling House is two elegant Victorian houses combined and fronted by a lovely rose garden, with a fruit tree orchard and children's area to the rear. The location gives it easy access to the airport, ferry, and city center, and other amenities. It is beautifully restored, with some very large bedrooms to accommodate families. A cozy new sitting room with glass doors is very appealing. All floors are newly polished. Bedrooms vary in style from old Victorian floral to fresh, bold colors, and luxurious throw quilts on each bed. Each room has a remote-control TV. In the dining room, each breakfast table has a different pottery milk jug, preserve bowl, and white and brown sugar bowls. Irish pottery by Stephen Pierce, Stonewall Jackson, and Nichalas Moss is on display here, and two stunning still-life oil paintings adorn the walls. Frances and Robert want guests to enjoy the fine décor and furnishings, but yet feel at home and relaxed as well. Breakfast consists of homemade compote of fruit, homemade muesli, scones, and breads, all of which compliment a typical cooked Irish Breakfast. Guests may serve themselves with fruit juice, whole grapefruit segments, and fresh fruits with an assortment of cereals on the side buffet before the main course.

Torc House
Eileen Kelly
17 Seacourt, St. Gabriels Road
Clontarf, Dublin 3, County Dublin
Telephone: 01-8332547
Bedrooms: 3; 2 with private baths, 1 with shared.
Rates: £23 p.p. private bath; £20 p.p. shared bath; Single £28.
Vouchers not accepted. **Credit cards:** None. **Open:** May to October.
Children: Yes, 12 or older. **Pets:** No. **Smoking:** Restricted to lounge.
Provision for handicapped: None. **Directions:** From Dublin, go left on
Amiens Street to North Strand and Clontarf Road to Seafield and go
left. The first right is St. Gabriels Road, opposite the church.

We have stayed here a number of times and Eileen is a wonderful
host, always helpful with a cup of tea at the ready in the comfortable
lounge with a TV. Her interior-decoration skills show in all her pretty
rooms and baths; one room is newly and exotically decorated with
red and gold with cream rolled pillows; one has butterscotch flowered duvets with matching print wallpaper; her other is lovely pink,
green, and rose. She uses dried bouquets of flowers, and embroidery
and lace on her towels. Besides her regular Irish Breakfast, she offers
special food for people on low-fat diets, yogurt, lots of fruit and cereal,
and sometimes porridge or French toast. The dining room looks out
onto a garden terrace and is set with elegant fine china. They can park
five cars safely off the street. Eileen has a great grasp of Dublin entertainment and will help with your itinerary. Walk to the beautiful St.
Ann's Rose Garden, where there is tennis, or to the Dollymount
Restaurant. You'll be 10 minutes from Howth and the beach, 20 minutes from the airport, and a walk to a bus for Dublin and all of its great
culture and history.

Clonliffe Bed and Breakfast
Larry and Mary Weathermon
94 Clonliffe Road
Clontarf, Dublin 3, County Dublin
Telephone: 01-837-9656; **FAX:** 01-837-9656
E-mail: Clonliffe@clubie.ie
Bedroooms: 4; 3 with private baths, 1 with shared.
Rates: £18 p.p. for private bath; £16 p.p. for shared bath. £20 discount for children. **Credit cards:** VISA and Western. **Open:** All year. **Children:** From 5 and up. **Pets:** No. **Smoking:** Yes. **Provision for handicapped:** None. **Directions:** From airport toward city, turn left at "Guinness Welcome to Dublin" sign. Go over railway bridge. House is on left, halfway down Clonliffe Road—an off license (liquor store) is across the street.

This attractive 1940s country-style town house is only 15 minutes from the airport and 5 minutes from the city center by car or by bus. The Weathermons will give you care and attention, and they will suggest the best ways to enjoy Dublin. Besides the Irish Breakfast, Mary will serve you vegan or vegetarian breakfasts, including organic yogurt and fruit. The rooms are simple and tastefully decorated with bright and cheerful colors of peach and yellow and have polished wood floors. All rooms offer tea/coffee facilities and hair dryers. You will notice fresh flowers and lovely polished wood floors in the common areas. There is a beach 5 minutes away, and tennis, golf, and bowling are only a 10-minute drive. The exciting city of Dublin with its historic castles, structures, shopping, and wonderful choices of plays to see is only 15 minutes away.

The Villa
Nualla Betson
150 Howth Road
Clontarf, Dublin 3, County Dublin
Telephone and **FAX:** 01-833-2377/833-0905
E-Mail: thevillabb@tinet.ie
Bedrooms: 5; 4 with private baths, 1 with shared.
Rates: £20 p.p. private, Single £23, Single in Double £28. Children's discount 20 percent. Vouchers not accepted. **Credit cards:** None.
Open: All year, except four days at Christmas. **Children:** Yes. **Pets:** No.
Smoking: Restricted to porch. **Provision for handicapped:** None.
Directions: From Dublin Airport take Motorway (M1). Turn left at Red Church onto Collins Street. Continue on through the residential area to the end and turn right on Howth Road. It is the eighth house on right, Number 150.

This delightful Tudor home is a period piece that shows a refined Edwardian décor with flocked burgundy wallpaper in the hallway, a seventeenth-century antique clock, beautiful prints and paintings, a crystal chandelier, and many other antiques, but not overbearingly so. The solarium outside the lounge is perfect for letter writing and reading. The dining room looks out on the front garden and lawn. The bedrooms are rose and pink with floral decorations. All are neat as a pin. Even the single room is quite large. The bus stops at the Beachcomber across the street. The Hollybrook Hotel has become our favorite for the pub lunch with carvery; it is super! The Villa is operated by two very welcoming sisters who make you feel comfortable from the start. The breakfast is Full Irish, or vegetarian if required. The brewed coffee is a hit with American visitors. In the afternoon, guests can sit in the rear garden and be surrounded by roses, other flowers, and songbirds at the feeder. There is plenty of parking.

Willowbrook
Mary Mooney
14 Strandville Avenue East
Clontarf, Dublin 3, County Dublin
Telephone: 01-8333115
Bedrooms: 3, all with private baths.
Rates: £25 p.p.; £40 single. No discount for children. Dinner is offered. Vouchers not accepted. **Credit cards:** None. **Open:** From December 31 to December 20. **Children:** No. **Pets:** No. **Smoking:** No. **Provision for handicapped:** None. **Directions:** From airport, head towards city on motorway. After the red-brick church on left, turn left at the next set of lights, Collins Avenue. Then turn right onto Howth Road. At the end of Howth Road go left onto Clontarf Road. Take the first left onto Strandville Avenue East.

This large brick house was built by a builder for himself, so it has beautiful cornices in each room, and solid-mahogany doors and windows. The rooms are spacious and have cream walls with very fresh pink, turquoise, and green curtains and bed covers. All rooms have orthopedic mattresses and electric blankets, coffee/tea facilities, and safes. Mary provides fresh fruit and flowers each day. She offers a traditional Irish Breakfast and a varied menu. The beautiful dining room has cream walls, royal blue carpeting, a Waterford Crystal chandelier, and antique furniture. This house is close to Dublin City and closer to Howth with its lighthouse, walks, and great restaurants.

Calderwood House
Mary and Barry Memery
2 Calderwood Road
Drumcondra, Dublin 9, County Dublin
Telephone: 01-8379568; **FAX:** 01-8379568; **E-Mail:** bmemery@tinet.ie
Bedrooms: 4; 3 with private baths, 1 with shared.
Rates: £20 p.p. private bath; £18 p.p. shared bath; Single £23-28.50; 50 percent discount for children 2-12 years; babies free. Vouchers not accepted. **Credit cards:** VISA and MasterCard. **Open:** All year, except 2 weeks at Christmas. **Children:** All ages. **Pets:** No. **Smoking:** Restricted. **Provision for handicapped:** Yes. **Directions:** From the airport, take the N1 to the red-brick church (Whitehall). Go to the fourth set of lights, turn left onto Griffith Avenue, then take your second left. The first two-story building on the right is Calderwood House.

This tall brick building is 15 minutes from the airport or city center. Mary and Barry are very congenial and will help you plan tours through Dublin. Their rooms are decorated in yellows, green, and olives, and are all different, neat, and attractive; three are on the ground floor and one is upstairs. The en-suite one downstairs is all pale pinks and has a garden view. The upstairs room has a high ceiling with a lovely stained-glass window facing west, left over from when the house was a convent. The living and dining rooms have handsome original pine floors. Mary is proud of her freshly brewed coffee served at the Irish Breakfast with a choice of fruit and yogurt. In the pretty townhouse area near Griffith Avenue, the house is close to many colleges and institutions. It is 10 minutes to the city by bus, and beaches, golf, and tennis are within 15 minutes' drive.

Parknasilla
Teresa Ryan
15 Iona Drive
Drumcondra, Dublin 9, County Dublin
Telephone: 01-8305724
Bedrooms: 4; 2 with private baths, 2 with shared.
Rates: £20 p.p. private bath; £18 p.p. shared bath; Single £22; 20 percent discount for children under 12. **Credit cards:** None. **Open:** All year, except December 21 to January 31. **Children:** 3 and over. **Pets:** Only guide dogs. **Smoking:** No. **Provision for handicapped:** None.
Directions: From airport follow signs for City Centre on M1 as far as Guinness Railway Bridge, then turn right onto St. Alphonsus Road. The third right after the church is Iona Drive.

A beautiful Edwardian red-brick home in a quiet residential area close to Dublin, this is an "Old Dublin"-style house built in 1908. The dining room has a rich red-marble fireplace and there is colored glass inside and outside of this elegant home. It combines old-world charm and modern conveniences. The rooms are pretty, spacious, and have high ceilings. Teresa Ryan is pleasant and very helpful to travelers. Her full Irish Breakfast is augmented with yogurt, fruit, and a continental breakfast. They are near the Botanical Gardens, 5 minutes from the B&I Ferry, 15 minutes from the airport or downtown, and near buses. Book ahead, as they are often full.

Ashbrook House
Mrs. Eve Mitchell
River Road
Ashtown, Castleknock
Dublin15, County Dublin
Telephone and **FAX:** 01-8385660
Bedrooms: 4, all with private baths.
Rates: £35 to £40 p.p.; single £50 to £60. Discounts for children.
Vouchers not accepted. **Credit cards:** All except American Express.
Open: January 14 to December 19. **Children:** All ages. **Pets:** No.
Smoking: Lounge only. **Provision for handicapped:** None. **Directions:**
Take the M50 motorway from the Dublin Airport. Exit at the N3
turnoff for Blanchardstown/Castleknock. Turn left at the roundabout,
and onto another roundabout. Then go straight until the next round-
about, where there is a pub on the left called the Halfway House Pub.
Turn left at the pub, and go over a railway crossing to a crossroads.
Turn left. Ashbrook House is the second gate on the left.

This attractive, large, 1897 Georgian home is just 10 minutes from
the airport and 10 minutes from Dublin center. The bedrooms are
all rather large with large baths, and one room has a marble fireplace.
Eve has used pinkish salmon, blues, blue-and-yellow, and pink-and-
white color schemes in her rooms. Some furniture is pine and one
new room is knotty pine in tea, orange, and green colors, and another
room is decorated with cranberry and white. All look onto handsome
gardens and countryside views. Eve serves a buffet breakfast of cereals,
fruit, and juices, besides poached or boiled eggs, bacon, mushroom,
and tomato. There is a grass tennis court on the premises and golf
courses and horseback riding areas are available. A good place to eat
is the Halfway House Pub, which is very close by.

Annesgrove
Anne D'Alton
28 Rosmeen Gardens
Dún Laoghaire, County Dublin
Telephone: 01-2809801
Bedrooms: 4; 2 with private baths, 2 with shared.
Rates: £22 p.p. private bath; £20 p.p. shared bath; Single £25-35; 25 percent discount for children under 12. Vouchers not accepted.
Credit cards: None. **Open:** January 1 to December 15. **Children:** Ages 4 and up. **Pets:** No. **Smoking:** Restricted. **Provision for handicapped:** None. **Directions:** From town center, take Georges Street south. The first right after the stoplight is Rosmeen Gardens, opposite People's Park. The house is number 28, a few houses up on the left.

This attractive brick and stucco house was built in 1932. Your hostess, Anne D'Alton, exudes a pleasant, professional charm and is always close at hand to look after special requests. The rooms are neat and peaceful, tastefully decorated in greens and beiges with wall trims, duvets, and curtains that match. Mrs. D'Alton has graced her walls with her husband's delicate watercolor landscapes, and they certainly add a lot to the rooms. All rooms have sinks and plenty of heat and hot water. The sitting room has a TV and is quite cozy. The dining room, where you'll be served an Irish Breakfast and a choice of fruit or yogurt or porridge, cereal, and juice, looks out onto delightfully landscaped gardens a few steps down on a lower level. If you must leave before breakfast, Mrs. D'Alton offers a special rate. They are very close to People's Park, the waterfront and ferry terminal, buses, and the DART into Dublin. Visit the many fine restaurants in town, swim at Sandy Cove Beach, and play golf or tennis very nearby. The D'Altons will tell you where. And the DART ride into Dublin is only 20 minutes. Dún Laoghaire is an ideal location to start or finish a holiday in the Irish Republic.

Park View House
Helen Callanan
1 Rosmeen Gardens
Dún Laoghaire, County Dublin
Telephone: 01-2806083
Bedrooms: 4; 2 with private baths, 2 with shared.
Rates: £22.50 p.p. private bath; £20 shared bath; Single £25-30; 20 percent discount for children under 12. Vouchers not accepted. **Credit cards:** None. **Open:** All year, except Christmas. **Children:** All ages. **Pets:** No. **Smoking:** Restricted. **Provision for handicapped:** None. **Directions:** From town center, go south on Georges Street. Rosmeen Gardens is 2 streets after the bus depot on the right, and Park View House is the first house on the right.

This 1890s red-brick Victorian is right across the street from a large park with lovely gardens, and all the rooms have a view of the harbor. You may walk to the center of this charming village, to the port where ferries arrive from Holyhead and Liverpool, England. The ferry terminal is only three blocks from the house. Mrs. Callanan is entertaining and helpful. Her pale-green living room, with a fireplace and attractive antiques, is elegant. You may want to choose the cool, light-green rooms with gorgeous duvets or a large luscious raspberry room with a bay view. The full Irish Breakfast will be served in the pretty dining room with lots of glass windows for a view of Mrs. Callanan's prize rose garden to the back and side. Breakfast options include choice of eggs, fresh fish or smoked salmon some days, and yogurt and fresh fruit. Frank enjoyed the smoked salmon with scrambled eggs. Sandy Cove Beach is 15 minutes away, and tennis and golf, walks in the People's Park, and many good restaurants are right in town. The DART gets you to the center of Dublin in only 30 minutes.

Liscara
Jane Kiernan
Malahide Road
Kinsealy, County Dublin
Telephone: 01-8483751 **FAX:** 01-8483751
Bedrooms: 6, all with private baths.
Rates: £20.; Single £30; 25 percent discount for children. Vouchers not accepted. **Credit cards:** None. **Open:** February 1 to November 30. **Children:** Over 5. **Pets:** No. **Smoking:** No. **Provision for handicapped:** Yes, one ground-floor room can take w/c. **Directions:** Drive to Fairview, then turn left on Malahide Road at end of park. Liscara is one mile on right after third roundabout.

This brand-new, red-brick manor house is a treat. On one acre, there are cabbage fields and a nursery to the back of it. Jane Kiernan is very attentive. Her husband is newly retired. The rooms are all large and elegant; one is dark lavender, white, and pink; one double has a spectacular view of fields and way out to the water and Howth. Another room is robin's-egg blue. There is a room on the first floor with wide bathroom access for the handicapped. The handsome dining room has three tables, a flowered white wall, and a teal rug. In addition to her standard full Irish Breakfast, Jane serves fresh fruit and yogurt and cheese or kippered herrings. There is babysitting available here by their daughter. They are close to golf courses, fishing, boating, bowling, horseback riding, swimming pools, and fine restaurants. There is a Cinema 10 nearby and they are only six minutes away from the airport. Charming Malahide town and Castle are two minutes away.

Pebble Mill B&B
Monica Fitzsimons
Off Malahide Road
Kinsealy, County Dublin
Telephone and **FAX:** 01-8461792
Bedrooms: 3, all with private baths.
Rates: £20 p.p.; Single £25; 50 percent discount for children. Vouchers not accepted. **Credit cards:** None. **Open:** February to October. **Children:** All ages. **Pets:** No. **Smoking:** Lounge only. **Provision for handicapped:** None. **Directions:** From the airport, take the N1 to the first roundabout, go all around, head back, and take the first left at Coachman's Inn. Go over a humpy bridge, then drive approximately ¾ km, and take the first left marked "Kinsealy." Drive for 1 km and at T-junction go right onto Malahide Road; watch for the sign on the right for Pebble Mill. Turn left opposite the sign. The house is on the left.

This stately neo-Georgian house sits on 4 acres in a farm area. The long driveway winds up with flower baskets hanging from posts on either side. The family ponies are in a corral next to the house. The décor in the large living room with TV is modern and creative. It has a white-marble fireplace, very comfortable chairs, a carved horse, and a green rug. Monica, very kind and personable, puts you at ease from the start. All the rooms are large and well lighted, with big windows and views of gardens and have TVs and hair dryers. One room has rainbow colors, one has rosebud designs, and there is one extra bath with a tub. The dining room is red and white, with a sliding glass door to the outside. Along with a full Irish Breakfast you may have fruit or yogurt. The beach is 5 minutes away, and horseback riding, tennis, and golf are 10 minutes away, as well as Malahide Castle and town. It is only 6 minutes from the airport.

ALSO RECOMMENDED

Donnybrook, *Hazelhurst,* Joan Donnellan, 166 Stillorgan Rd. Telephone: 01-2838509. 5 rooms, all with private baths. Modern townhouse right on the N11, across from University College Dublin. Extralarge living room with fireplace for reading and writing. Major credit cards accepted. Accessible to City Center and Dún Laoghaire ferry.

Dublin, *The Georgian House Guest House,* Annette O'Sullivan, 20 Lower Baggot Street. Telephone: 01-8618832; FAX: 01-8618834. Bedrooms: 26, all with private baths. Discounts for children. Credit cards accepted. Lunch and dinner available. Restored Georgian town house located near St. Stephen's Green. Off-street parking. Recommended by Jean and Richard Higgins, Seattle, Washington.

Dún Laoghaire, *Duncree,* Mrs. C. O'Sullivan, 16 Northumberland. Telephone: 01-2806118. Bedrooms: 4, all shared bath but with sink and mirror in rooms. Modest home but very nice hostess. Within walking distance of shops and restaurants.

Dún Laoghaire, *Stoneview House,* Patrick and Della Lynch, 5 Clarinda Park East. Telephone: 01-2800433. Bedrooms: 4, all en suite. Recommended by Jeremy Barlow, London, England.

Lusk, *Carriage House,* Curtin Family. Telephone: 01-8438857; FAX: 01-8438933. Bedrooms: 5, all with private baths. "Purpose-built" house, which means it was built to be a B&B. Lots of amenities. In a town north of Dublin, 10 minutes to airport.

Malahide, *Lynfar,* Mrs. Margaret Farrelly, Kinsealy Lane. Telephone: 01-8463897. Bedrooms: 5, 1 with private bath. Vouchers accepted. Close to Dublin Airport, beside Malahide Castle, 2 km to Malahide, home set in private grounds.

Rathgar, *Roslyn House,* John and Benita Ryan, 63 Tenure Road East, Dublin 6. Telephone: 01-4925807/4925809/4929349; Fax: 01-4929378. E-Mail: roslyn@iol.ie. Lovely 4-star, 4-story brownstone Victorian guesthouse. Fluent Italian and French spoken.

Sutton, *Dun Aoibhinn,* Mary McDonnell, 30 Sutton Park, Dublin 13 (North County). Telephone/FAX: 01-9325456. Bedrooms: 3, all en suite. Luxurious detached home in quiet residential area. Adjacent coast road. Five-minute walk to bus and DART. Recommended by John and Sue Ley, Harrowgate, Yorkshire, UK.

COUNTY GALWAY

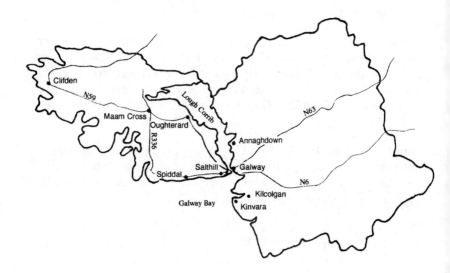

County Galway

County Galway is one of the largest counties in Ireland and Galway City is known as the capital of the west of Ireland. This county has a ruggedness of terrain that differs from the soft greens of the south. Galway, with its rivers, mountains, bays, lakes, and seacoast, is very photogenic. In north Galway, have a look at the peaceful Killary Harbor, which separates Mayo and Galway. The fields of green sweeping down to blue water and gentle hills beyond are a sight to behold. Between tiny Leenane on the border and Letterfrack, visit the Kylemore Abbey. Although Letterfrack seems to be in the boondocks, there is a lovely woolen craft shop there with a tearoom with sandwiches and scones. Stay along the N59 to reach the stunning town of Clifden, called the capital of Connemara, sitting high on a hill. It has marvelous views of bays and high mountains, such as the Twelve Bens, which change colors with the light and the season.

Clifden has joys of its own—pretty B&Bs with views, excellent restaurants, and traditional Irish music right into October. We tried Mitchell's Restaurant and D'Arcy Inn; both were quite good. It's fun to shop and browse through the art galleries, too. When you tear yourself away from the specialness of Clifden, drive around along the coast and visit the pretty fishing towns of Roundstone and Cashel. For a shorter drive, go down the N59 through rough and rocky Connemara country (look for ponies and donkeys grazing) to Oughterard. This pretty town is right on Lake Corrib, which reportedly has the best fishing in Ireland.

Salthill and Galway town are tied together and are noted for their beaches, called strands, and boardwalks. Salthill has the very large Leisureland Amusement Park, with a swimming pool and rides, and an 18-hole golf course. It's a refreshing walk along the beach just outside of Galway. Look for the Galway "hookers," special fishing boats with very rounded sides and sails.

Galway City is old, with one-way streets and many, many shops and eating places. There are art galleries and two theaters, the An Tarbhdhearc on Middle Street and the Druid on Chapel Lane. Catch an Irish music session any evening in summer at one of the many pubs. At the end of July or the beginning of August, the famous Galway Races run for six days, with much music and festivities. Book way ahead, for the Irish fill the rooms for this event. Another event you might enjoy is the Oyster Festival the third or fourth weekend in September.

We spent some time in Spiddal, west of Galway, where a lot of Gaelic is spoken in the pubs, the accents are strong and melodious, and the spontaneous fiddling and singing is good. From Galway City, the N6 takes you straight across the midsection of the country to Dublin. Visit the starkly beautiful Aran Islands at the opening of Galway Bay. It's a happy trip back in time.

South of Galway you'll find the sweet town of Kilcolgan, with its fishing rivers, and a bit farther there is the important, pretty, small town of Kinvara. This town has farms and horseback riding, Dunguaire Castle with a feast and costumes, and a little port with pastel buildings looking out on fishing boats sitting at the docks. We couldn't resist painting some of these scenes. Eat at Partners Restaurant: good food, good prices.

From Galway City, the N6 takes you straight across the midsection of the country to the N4 and on to Dublin. The town of Athenry, just to the east of Galway City, is noted in the song "Fields of Athenry," an Irish favorite. Visit the castle there. In October, the largest horse and cattle fair in Europe (called the Great October Fair) is held farther on at Ballinasloe, out on the eastern border of the county.

Corrib View Farm
Mary Scott-Furey
Annaghdown, County Galway
Telephone: 091-791114
Bedrooms: 5; 3 with private bath, 2 with shared bath
Rates: £20 p.p. with private bath; £18 p.p. for shared bath; £25-29 for single person. Dinner £18 (organically grown fruit and vegetables).
Credit cards: None. **Open:** April to October 1. **Children:** Yes, 4 years and up. **Pets:** No. **Smoking:** Sitting room only. **Provision for handicapped:** None. **Directions:** 10 minutes north of Galway city. 3 km off Galway-Headford-Castlebar road (N84 road). Sign posted at Cloonboo Cross near Regan's Bar-Restaurant.

This award-winning, one-hundred-year-old family farm bed and breakfast, surrounded by pretty lawns and landscaped gardens, is located in a scenic setting alongside Lough Corrib. It has a bright and airy dining room in soft pink with matching tablecloths and china at each separate table. The sitting room is tastefully decorated in peach and brown, with an accompanying writing area. All the bedrooms are in varying shades of orchid and white. Tea- and coffee-making facilities are in bedrooms. Homemade breads and jams are included in their delicious full Irish farm breakfast, and top off the day with a fantastic home-cooked evening meal. The location midway between Galway and Headford is ideal for touring Connemara. Mary, with her vast knowledge of the region, will help you plan day trips to Connemara and the Aran Islands, or locally, trips to Annaghdown Pier and Abbey ruins, or hiring a boat on Lough Corrib. There is also a horseback riding center nearby. The less adventurous can relax in the leisure garden at the farm.

Beach View House
Bridie Conneely
Oatquarter, Kilronan
Aran Islands (Inis Mór), County Galway
Telephone and **FAX:** 099-61141
Bedrooms: 6; 3 with private baths.
Rates: £17 p.p.; £23 single; 25 percent discount for children under 12.
Vouchers accepted. **Credit cards:** None. **Open:** May 1 to September
30. **Children:** All ages. **Pets:** Yes. **Smoking:** Only in lounge. **Provision
for handicapped:** None. **Directions:** Take a ferry to Inis Mór from
Galway or Rossaveal; the bus to Rossaveal is provided with the ferry
ticket. From the port on the island, take a bus, pony trap, bike, or walk
6 km to the B&B.

Beach View is a large, family-run home with a sitting area in the
front yard. It is situated in a tranquil spot in the center of the island.
Bridie Conneely is charming and friendly. The six bedrooms are neat
and delightfully furnished in pleasing colors. Bridie includes scones
with her full Irish Breakfast. Recreational features in the area are
horseback riding, fishing, cycling, and swimming just two miles away
on the safe, sandy beach. The house is within walking distance of
famous Fort Dun Aengus, and convenient to a restaurant and pub.
Inis Mór, "The Big Island," has the only harbor suitable for steamer
docking. You may take a jaunting car ride around the island to see ring
forts or Dun Aengus, perched on a three-hundred-foot cliff above
the sea. Bikes are for rent, too. You may take ferries to other fascinating and unique Aran Islands during your stay. Gaelic is the everyday
language, but polite islanders will speak English.

Mallmore Country House

Kathleen Hardman
Ballyconneely Road
Clifden, County Galway
Telephone: 095-21460
Bedrooms: 6, all with private baths, plus separate full bath with tub.
Rates: £18-20 p.p.; 20 percent discount for children under 12.
Vouchers not accepted. **Credit cards:** None. **Open:** March 1 to
November 1. **Children:** All ages. **Pets:** No. **Smoking:** Restricted.
Provision for handicapped: Four steps in front, but after that all on
one floor. **Directions:** Outside Clifden 1 mile on Ballyconneely Road,
look for Mallmore House sign on the right. Turn right at Connemara
Pottery. Go up a narrow country road to their gate.

This is a beautiful 1790s manor house that was built by a John
Darcy, lord of this region. It reminds you of a French country home
because of its rich flocked walls, arched doorways, and pretty hall
lights. It has been completely renovated by the Hardmans. The dining
room is luxurious, with red wallpaper, antique vases and side tables, six
to eight separate meal tables covered with linens, ballooned curtains
at all windows with shutters, and a fireplace. Award-winning breakfasts
include pancakes, omelets, and smoked salmon. The spacious bedrooms are also handsomely decorated with armoires and velvet
boudoir chairs, and some have bowed windows viewing the cheery garden and the scenic harbor beyond. Our room was more of a suite, with
two antique chairs in the bowed window where we enjoyed reading
and even watercolor painting. Rooms are individually decorated in
soft pastels. The sitting room with a fire is ideal for curling up with a
good book. The Hardmans are genuinely nice. They take special care
of their guests and run the inn with a steady, gentle touch.

High Tide
Pal Greaney
9 Grattan Park
Galway City, County Galway
Telephone: 091-584324/589470; **FAX:** 091-584324; **E-Mail:** high-tide@iol.ie **Bedrooms:** 4, all with private baths.
Rates: £18 p.p.; Single: £25. 25 percent discount for children. Vouchers accepted. **Credit cards:** VISA and MasterCard. **Open:** February 1 to December 1. **Children:** Yes, all ages. **Pets:** No. **Smoking:** Yes. **Provision for handicapped:** Yes. **Directions:** Take the coast road from City Center toward Salthill. The house is midway between the two.

High Tide is a modern two-story home overlooking Galway Bay, with panoramic views of the ocean and Clare Hill. A small flower garden graces its front. The bedrooms are well decorated in soft pastel shadows with all conveniences. Pal will serve you a wonderful Irish Breakfast or other choices of eggs, cereals, and fruits. This B&B is close to the fishing village of Claddagh, home of the world-famous Claddagh Betrothal Ring. It is a 10-minute walk from the city of Tribes (Galway). The old Anglo-Norman town sits side by side with the new University city. Galway, a young vibrant city, boasts excellent theaters and music. It is the gateway to Connemara and the Aran Islands. Pal will arrange tours on bus rides to these areas.

Castle View
Anne and Martin Kerins
Weir Road
Kilcolgan, County Galway
Telephone: 091-796172
Bedrooms: 4; 2 with private bath, 2 with shared.
Rates: £15 p.p. shared bath, £17 p.p. private bath; Single £22.50 to 24.50; ⅓ discount for children under 12. Vouchers accepted. **Credit cards:** None. **Open:** All year. **Children:** All ages. **Pets:** Yes. **Smoking:** Restricted to lounge. **Provision for handicapped:** Yes, rooms on first floor. **Directions:** In the village of Kilcolgan, note the sign for Castle View and Moran's Seafood. Go down the road 500 yards from the Village.

When the three daughters danced into the room in their step-dance costumes on a Sunday afternoon, we knew we were in a special place. You might not see the dance, but you'll have a jovial time with the Kerins family. This modern country home not only overlooks the peaceful Kilcolgan River, but also has a view of Dunguaire Castle, where medieval banquets are served. The rooms, decorated in pink, rose, and lavender, are comfortable and modern; some have a view of the river. Breakfast is full Irish with added fruit, brown bread, porridge, and yogurts. The hearty breakfast is served at a large family table. The lounge with a TV and fire is comfortable and has pleasant views from large bay windows. Martin can put you onto some fine fishing trips. There are salmon and trout in the river. The welcome is warm and genuine, and they proudly point out that Maureen O'Hara stayed there in 1993. The country setting is pretty enough to paint. One of Ireland's best seafood restaurants is down the road—it's called Moran's. Galway Bay golf is next door, and sailing and horseback riding are nearby. A babysitter can be provided, and Irish is spoken.

Clareview House
Brenda McTigue
Kinvara, County Galway
Telephone: 091-637170
Bedrooms: 5, all with private baths.
Rates: £18 p.p.; Single £5 extra; 25 percent discounts for children.
Vouchers accepted. £15 dinner. **Credit cards:** None. **Open:** March 1 to
November 2. **Children:** All ages. **Pets:** Small. **Smoking:** No. **Provision
for handicapped:** None. **Directions:** From the town of Kinvara, go
north to Dunguaire Castle, then take the road on the right, and go 3
km. The farm is on the left.

This 1890s, two-story white farmhouse is set back behind gates on
lovely grounds with flower gardens. It is a 120-acre dairy and beef
farm. Brenda and her shepherd will greet you and offer you a relaxing
tea by the fire in the black marble fireplace. The lounge has a special
antique buffet. The rooms are very neat and pretty, done in cream and
pink, pale green and cream, and turquoise and off-white, and all the
bathrooms are large. All rooms have a great view of the countryside
and garden. Brenda's full Irish Breakfast includes homemade black
and white pudding. You may have dinner of salmon, trout, or lamb
roast. Relax after dinner in the large new conservatory. Since the farm
is centrally located, you may go 3 km to the charming town of Kinvara,
with its nature walks, shops, colored buildings, nice little restaurants,
and fishing boats in the harbor; or to the Dunguaire Castle, where
there is a very popular medieval banquet and show, all reserved. There
is a nine-hole golf course 10 miles south in Gort; Coole Park with
wildlife in Gort; the Burren and Ailwee Caves just south of Kinvara;
boat trips, fishing, and swimming at Traught Beach just north; and
you'll be only 15 miles from Galway City and 30 miles from Lahinch
and Cliffs of Moher.

RONCALLI HOUSE 1st March '99

Roncalli House
Tim and Carmel O'Halloran
24 Whitestrand Avenue
Lower Salthill, County Galway
Telephone and **FAX:** 091-584159
Bedrooms: 6, all with private baths.
Rates: £18 p.p.; 20 percent discount for children. Vouchers accepted.
Credit cards: VISA and MasterCard. **Open:** All year. **Children:** Yes.
Pets: No. **Smoking:** No. **Provision for handicapped:** none. **Directions:**
From Tourist Office follow signs for Salthill, over Wolfe Tone bridge,
through three lights onto "Y" junction. Turn left. The house is on the
right, on the corner of 336.

The O'Hallorans have a lovely modern and comfortable two-story
home beside Galway Bay, within walking distance of the city center.
Warm Irish hospitality greets you as you have your welcoming tea by
the fireplace. There are two ground-floor bedrooms and four others
upstairs, all done in soft pastel colors with sinks and built-in
wardrobes. There is a sunny front lounge and two outdoor patios for
guest use. There is central heating and good parking in front. Carmel
is proud of the fact that Chelsea Clinton, the president's daughter,
stayed here with her entourage for two nights.

Nearby there is a large swimming complex, golf, tennis, and horseback riding. Salthill is a popular Irish tourist spot. Many excellent
restaurants/pubs are available locally, in town or on the road going
out to Spiddal.

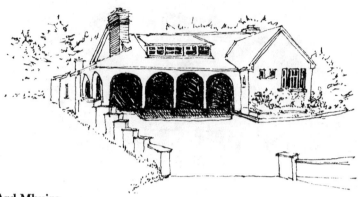

Ard Mhuire
Pat and Teresa McDonagh
Knocknacarra Road
Salthill, County Galway
Telephone: 091-522344; **FAX:** 091-529629
Bedrooms: 6, all with private baths, plus separate full bath.
Rates: £18 p.p.; Single £25; 25 percent discount for children under 12.
Vouchers accepted. **Credit cards:** Yes. **Open:** All year, except Christmas
week. **Children:** Yes. **Pets:** No. **Smoking:** No. **Provision for handi-
capped:** Yes. **Directions:** Go out along the water from city center, along
Promenade, where Leisureland is located on your right, toward Barna.
When you get to Spinnaker House Hotel on the left, the next right is
Knocknacarra Road. Ard Mhuire is in the second block on the left, a
white home with Spanish arches in front and a white wall surrounding
the car park.

This charming modern home has a nice ambience. Rooms are spacious and nicely decorated. Floral grey and white, pale apricot and
green, and pink rose are used in an elegant manner. You don't feel
crowded in this home as in some B&Bs. The tiled baths are extra large
in four of the rooms; some have tubs and showers. All combinations of
beds are available, from twins to doubles to triples, so if you reserve
early you should get the right accommodations. The gorgeous honeymoon suite with a view of the sea has a king-sized bed with an inset
classic archway above, a bright floral-print bedcover, and blue-green
walls—very nice! The breakfast menu is a full Irish Breakfast served
at a large, antique, hand-carved table and chairs or at separate small
side tables. The large lounge adjoins the dining area. Mrs. McDonagh
is a pleasant hostess who makes you feel right at home and whom we
enjoyed chatting with over tea and homemade scones.

Carraig Beag
Catherine Lydon
1 Burren View Heights
Salthill, County Galway
Telephone: 091-521696
Bedrooms: 4, all with private baths.
Rates: £18-20 p.p. (race week—£18); Single £25-32; ⅓ discount for children. Vouchers not accepted. **Credit cards:** None. **Open:** All year, except Christmas week. **Children:** Yes. **Pets:** No. **Smoking:** Restricted. **Provision for handicapped:** Rooms available on first floor. **Directions:** Past the golf course, take the second road on the right across from Spinnaker. The Cottage Shop is at the corner. Go up Knocknacarra to the corner of Burren View Heights; the house is the first on the right.

Pretty flowers adorn the front of this modern brick home, with its look of a stately manor house. It is even more attractive inside, with its handsome wood doors, broad staircase, and elegant large dining room with crystal chandelier, adjoining a large living room with marble fireplace for relaxing. Guests have a cozy separate lounge with a TV. The spacious rooms are handsomely decorated in pinks and whites, green and greys, and wine colors, all with tea/coffee facilities and TV. Some have views. Breakfast is served on a large lace-covered table where you can even view the water through the living room. Breakfast is a full Irish cooked one with home-baked goods and fruit. Catherine Lydon is gracious and dignified, yet a charming and friendly hostess who will make your stay in Galway a pleasant and memorable one. She will be quite willing to guide you to the best places for walks, golfing, horseback riding, fishing, or short trips, such as to the Aran Islands, Connemara, or the Burren. She will even tell you about the special sights and traditional music in Galway.

The Connaught
Colette and Tom Keaveney
Barna Road
Salthill, County Galway
Telephone: 091-525865; **FAX:** 091-525865
E-Mail: tconnaught@tinet.ie
Bedrooms: 6; 5 with private baths, 1 with shared.
Rates: £18-20 p.p. private bath; £16-18 shared bath; Single £20; 20 percent discount for children under 12. Vouchers accepted. **Credit cards:** None. **Open:** April 1 to October 31. **Children:** All ages. **Pets:** No. **Smoking:** No. **Provision for handicapped:** No. **Directions:** Drive west along the water from Galway town and continue on Salthill until you pass the golf club. Turn left at Knocknacarra Cross onto Barna Road. The Connaught is 600 yards on the right.

This is a bright and cheerful Georgian home, probably made so by the Keaveneys. It has a modern exterior and handsome interior. Good-sized bedrooms, all on the second floor, are done in soft pastel colors and are furnished with twin or double beds (some triples), electric blankets, and nice mirrors. There is access to a large balcony facing Rusheen Bay from two of the rooms. This is nice for lounging in the sun. Downstairs is a cozy, pink and brown guest lounge with a TV and stone fireplace. Breakfast is a full Irish cooked one with homemade brown bread and possibly some other pastries, fruit on the buffet, and freshly brewed coffee, served at separate tables. Tom teaches baking and confectionery at a local college, so he provides some added treats to the menu, such as his famous croissants. After this hearty breakfast, you can play golf at a nearby championship 18-hole course or go for some water fun at the indoor pool down the road at Leisureland. This young couple is very likeable.

Marian Lodge

Mrs. Celine Molloy
Knocknacarra Road
Salthill, County Galway
Telephone: 091-521678; FAX: 091-528103
E-mail: celine@iol.ie
Bedrooms: 6, all with private baths.
Rates: £19-22 p.p.; Single £30-40; ⅓ discount for children. Vouchers not accepted. **Credit cards:** All major ones. **Open:** All year except Christmas. **Children:** Yes. **Pets:** No. **Smoking:** Restricted. **Provision for handicapped:** None. **Directions:** Go along the water from Galway to Salthill; pass Leisureland on the right. Across from Spinnaker turn right on Knocknacarra Road. The home is on the left, with a sign above the wall, to the right of the driveway.

The smell of fresh baked goods greets you as you enter Marian Lodge. You will receive an especially warm welcome from Celine when you arrive. She and her husband, Pat, are very friendly and most anxious to please. This is a cozy and restful place, with lots of good food and comfortable rooms with orthopedic beds, TVs, and tea- and coffee-making facilities. Rooms are decorated in blues, greens, and pinks, with reading lights over the beds and many combinations of beds to suit the traveling public. Some rooms have showers and large tubs in the bathrooms. The living room, or "lounge," has a TV and a brick fireplace with old antique pots and a barrel of peat for burning. Celine tells how her house was built quite recently with solid concrete walls so as to keep it quiet inside. Breakfast is the traditional Irish one and includes fresh-baked scones and soda bread. They have tickets here for deep-sea fishing and windsurfing. They are close to a 22-hole golf course, swimming at Leisureland, horseback riding, and a bus to the Aran Islands. They have private car parking.

Marless House
Mary Geraghty
Threadneedle Road
Salthill, County Galway
Telephone: 091-523931; **FAX:** 091-529810
Bedrooms: 6, all with private baths.
Rates: £20 p.p.; Single £30; 25 percent discount for children under 12.
Vouchers accepted. **Credit cards:** All major ones. **Open:** All year,
except Christmas week. **Children:** Yes. **Pets:** No. **Smoking:** No.
Provision for handicapped: None. **Directions:** Take the street along
the water from Galway, past Leisureland. About 2 km from Galway,
turn right on Threadneedle Road. The B&B is on the right, a pretty,
Georgian 2-story, with a brick front, white pedimented entrance, and
white sides.

This beautiful modern Georgian brick home is spacious and decorated with fine woodwork and bright colors. Mary is a generous and
kind hostess and spends a lot of time with guests. Her attention to
details and good management results in a pleasant stay. She jokes
that her husband, Tom, who cooks on weekends, is her "honeydew"
husband: "Honey, do this, and Honey, do that." We were impressed
with the comfort, size, and décor of our bedroom and bathroom. Our
room was a bright cheery yellow and white. You can have your breakfast on the large dining-room table, if you like to chat with fellow travelers, or at separate tables, if you want privacy. The juice, fruit, cereal,
and yogurt are self-service on the side buffet. Delicious hot entrées
and beverage orders are brought to your table. The living room is
warmly decorated in apricot and blue-green, with a white fireplace.
Mary encourages guests to walk the Promenade along the beautiful
Galway Bay, or indulge in the many recreational activities such as golf,
swimming, or tennis.

Ardmore Country House
Vera Feeney
Greenhill
Spiddal, County Galway
Telephone: 091-553145; **FAX:** 091-553596
Bedrooms: 7, all with private baths.
Rates: £18-20 p.p.; Single £24-26.50; discount for children. Vouchers accepted. **Credit cards:** All major ones. **Open:** March through December. **Children:** All ages. **Pets:** No. **Smoking:** Restricted. **Provision for handicapped:** Yes, in "Guide to Handicapped." **Directions:** Go out to Spiddal from Galway, through Barna on R336. It is 8 miles to Spiddal (10 miles from city center). The house is ½ mile west of Spiddal town on the left.

This lovely, modern home, surrounded by a beautifully landscaped garden, boasts a panoramic view of the bay and the Burren beyond. Vera Feeney is a very well-organized, experienced, and gracious hostess who runs one of our favorite B&Bs. She will even arrange a trip to the Aran Islands from Rossaveel. The laundry facilities for weary guests are very popular. The blue or pink bedrooms are very trim and comfortable. Each has two or three beds with a vanity and sink in separate alcoves, in addition to a private, tiled bathroom. We enjoyed the huge dining/living room with a fireplace for Vera's award-winning breakfasts, and the delightful chats with other guests on the comfy sofas. Rollicking traditional music can be heard in Spiddal at Hughes Pub almost every night, but be prepared for cramped quarters and lots of smoke. There are plenty of good restaurants in Spiddal, so you don't have to go into Galway. Budget-priced and very good meals are available in the Bridge House Hotel. We enjoyed the Bolvisce restaurant for its coziness and great seafood. Activities available here are fishing, riding, golf, watersports, and swimming at safe sandy beaches within walking distance, and bus tours to Connemara. Excellent bargains can be found at Standum Handcraft Shop in Spiddal.

ALSO RECOMMENDED

Aran Islands, *Cois Cuain,* Martin Faherty, Innis Meain, 100 yards from pier. Telephone: 099-73097. Sister Brid: 01-8382132. Sleeps 20. Bed and breakfast or self-catering accommodations all year.

Aran Islands, *Pier House,* Inishmore, Lower Kilronan. Telephone: 099-61416; FAX: 099-61122. Bedrooms: 12, all en suite. Nice 3-star guesthouse with all the amenities.

Clifden, *Failte B&B,* Maureen Kelly, Ardbear. Telephone: 095-21159. Bedrooms: 5, 2 en suite. 2 km from town, off Ballyconneely Road.

Clifden, *Winnowing Hill,* Mrs. Margaret Kelly, Ballyconneely Road. Telephone: 095-21281. Bedrooms: 6, 2 with private baths. Pretty modern country home with views of Clifden village and the Twelve Needles Mountains.

Gort, *Teac Seamus,* Una McCotter, Galway Road. Telephone: 091-31884. Bedrooms: 4, 3 en suite. Quaint thatched-roof cottage on N18, just outside town. Convenient to travelers to and from Galway town.

Maam Cross (Connemara area), *Tullaboy House,* Mrs. Iris Joyce. Telephone: 091-82305. Bedrooms: 4, all with private baths. Home cooking and hospitality their specialty. Peacocks Restaurant here used in filming of *The Quiet Man.*

Oughterard, *Ashlawn House,* Mrs. Mary C. Flaherty, Ardvarna, on N59, near lake. Telephone: 091-82349. Bedrooms: 3, 2 with private baths. Vouchers accepted. Open April to September. Modern home with beautiful gardens.

Oughterard, *Avondale House,* Mrs. Brid Kelly, Portacaron, near Lough Corrib (turn left off the N59 going south at the edge of town). Telephone: 091-82398. Bedrooms: 5, 4 with private baths. Open April to November. Comfortable modern bungalow on quiet country lane. Fishing and boating available.

Oughterard, *Cashel Rock Farmhouse,* Sheila Walsh, Raha. Telephone: 091-550213. Bedrooms: 5, all en suite. National award winning farmhouse for 1997. Suckler and sheep farming. 2 km off N59, Galway side of Oughterard.

Oughterard, *Corrib Wave House,* Maria and Michael Healy, Connemara (located 2 miles east of Oughterard off the N59). Telephone: 091-82147. Bedrooms: 8, 6 with private baths. Lakeside farmhouse with panoramic view. Boats, engines, and boatmen available for hire.

COUNTY KERRY

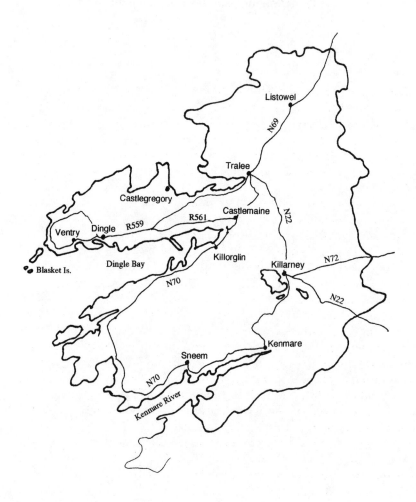

County Kerry

County Kerry is a wonderful blend of purple mountains, green pastures, sea cliffs, smooth beaches, old castles, ancient ruins, and history. Dingle, our favorite town in Ireland, still retains the flavor of a small traditional town, in spite of all the tourists who flock there in summer. You'll hear Gaelic spoken in shops and pubs, and all street signs are in both Gaelic and English. Gaelic sounds like Danish or Norwegian.

The beauty and serenity of blue Dingle Bay dominates the town. It is still a fishing village, so you may go to the docks of Dingle and watch them unload fish. In summer, you'll note young folks rowing or racing black *curraghs* (boats made of treated skins). The Slieve Mish Mountains in the background are impressive. Buildings, all a different color, stairstepping up the hilly main street, make a beguiling scene.

We found some good sales in the shops, and we were satisfied each time we visited the Forge Restaurant. A favorite lunch place is An Cafe Litearta, a bookstore with a café in the rear that serves everything, including decaf coffee, great soups, and hot scones. O'Flaherty's Pub is where you go for music. Some summer nights the walls bend in and out with the rollicking crowds. Try the beach in Ventry or travel down the road to the beach at Inch for swimming and sunning. Conor Pass is a wonder to the eye—you feel like you're on top of a magical green world, with wonderful water views on each side.

Be sure and take the ride out to Slea Head to see the Blasket Islands, where fishermen lived until 1953. Read the book called *Peig*, by the last woman to live there. It tells of the hardship of their lives. Take the steep walk down to the boat ramp; it's invigorating. Notice the miles of stonewalled sheep pens right down to the sea. Go inland a bit and visit some of the ancient beehive houses made of stones, and the old stone church, St. Malcathair, built in the 600s. The stones are all pale lavender, green, blue, pink, and gold.

Tralee is a charming town. It has a show called "Siamsa Tire," put on by the National Folk Theatre of Ireland, that is a winner. The show is full of colorful music, dancing, and mime, so it doesn't matter that it's in Gaelic—you'll understand it all. There is a festival every September that features a "Rose of Tralee," chosen from any country in the world.

Killarney is the biggest tourist town of Kerry, and it has plenty to offer. Visit the soft Lakes of Killarney; take a jaunting-car ride to Muckross House or Abbey. The funny drivers have surely kissed the Blarney Stone. Don't forget to see the Gap of Dunloe. The hotels have great Irish musical shows and there are many good Irish singing pubs. Northwest of Killarney, if you hit it just right in August, you'll catch the Puck Fair in Killorglan with plenty of stepdancing and horse trading. Supposedly it's the oldest fair in Ireland. The Mill Inn in Ballvourney has the best lunch between Killarney and Macroon.

The Ring of Kerry in the south provides a thrilling ride around the outer rim of the Iveragh Peninsula. You'll see lovely farms and breathtaking sea views from high cliffs.

Beenoskee Bed and Breakfast
Mary and Michael Ferriter
Cappateige, Conor Pass Rd.
Castlegregory, County Kerry
Telephone: 066-7139263; **FAX:** 066-7139263
Bedrooms: 4; 3 with private baths, 1 with shared.
Rates: £16 to 18 p.p.; 50 percent discount for children. Vouchers accepted. £13 dinner. **Credit cards:** Yes. **Open:** All year. **Children:** All ages. **Pets:** No. **Smoking:** Ask owner. **Provision for handicapped:** None. **Directions:** From Tralee, take the Conor Pass Road. Beenoskee is one mile west of Stradbally Village, overlooking Brandon Bay Beach.

This luxurious, spacious, yellow bungalow sits on a hill overlooking Brandon Bay and unspoiled beaches. It is surrounded by beautiful mountains. Mary will treat you with warm hospitality and will serve you complimentary tea or coffee and homemade Guinness cake. The rooms are nicely situated and decorated, and they have a spectacular view of the seafront, beaches, and mountains. Mary serves an extensive breakfast menu, including Traditional Irish, in her elegant dining room that overlooks the sea. Delicious evening meals are offered, with fresh vegetables and delicious home baking. In the area, there are archeological sites, a heritage center, and museums to visit. There are tranquil walks, surfing, golf, horseback riding, mountain climbing, fishing, windsurfing, and swimming nearby. This home is centrally located between Tralee and Dingle, on the beautiful Conor Pass Road. Visit the Blennerville Windmill, Crag Caves, beehive huts of Dingle, and Tralee's Siamsa Tire Theater.

The Shores Country House
Annette O'Mahoney
Cappatigue, Conor Pass Rd.
Castlegregory, County Kerry
Telephone: 066-7139196
Bedrooms: 3, all with private baths.
Rates: £17 to 20 p.p.; Single £5 extra. 33 percent discount for children under 12. Vouchers accepted. £16 dinner. **Credit cards:** VISA, MasterCard, Eurocard. **Open:** March 17 to November 30. **Children:** All ages. **Pets:** No. **Smoking:** No. **Provision for handicapped:** Yes.
Directions: From Tralee , follow Dingle Road for about 10 miles to a junction, take turn to Dingle via Conor Pass. Pass through Stradbally Village and in approx. 1 mile you will see The Shores Country House. If you need further directions, please call the owner.

This family-run inn off in the country is a great getaway for city folks. Overlooking the longest beach in Ireland, it has landscaped gardens, and Mount Brandon is in the mountain range just behind the house. The oak, pine, and blue rooms all have wonderful sea views and handsome antiques. There are beautifully extended new Victorian-style rooms in creamy gold and white, all with sea views. There is a superb dining nook with an open fire and a library for guests. Annette greets you with tea and homemade porter cake. Her breakfasts are full Irish, or scrambled eggs and smoked salmon, fresh fruit and yogurt, waffles, croissants, and Irish farmhouse cheese. Annette will pack a lunch for you. Her gourmet dinners, featuring fresh salmon, chicken, lamb, or cod, and great desserts, are on a menu. Mountain walks are near and the beach is only 10 minutes away. Watersports and horseback riding are available.

Murphy's Farmhouse
The Murphy Family
Boolteens
Castlemaine, County Kerry
Telephone: 066-9767337; **FAX:** 066-9767839
Bedrooms: 14; 13 with private baths, 1 with shared.
Rates: £17 p.p.; Single £18; 25 percent discount for children under 12, under 2 free. Vouchers accepted. £12 dinner. **Credit cards:** None.
Open: All year except Christmas Day. **Children:** Yes. **Pets:** No.
Smoking: Yes. **Provision for handicapped:** No. **Directions:** The farmhouse is 2 miles from Castlemaine town. Take the Dingle road west to Boolteens. A sign will be on the right. Follow the road to the end. There are signs in Castlemaine and Brackhill Cross.

This lovely farm B&B situated on the south flank of the Slieve Mish Mountains was first discovered by us in 1984, and is still a great place to stay. It has been in the family since 1847. When we were at Murphy's, we went to the Puck Fair in Killorglin, originally a pagan country fair where a goat rules as king, and we enjoyed swimming at nearby Inch Beach. At the farm the meals are delicious. The full Irish Breakfast, augmented with kippers and various cheeses, as well as the tasty farm dinners, are served in the newly decorated dining room. All the bedrooms have been redecorated with flowered wallpaper and new bedcovers, and now have tea/coffee makers, electric blankets, and electric heaters. The roses and ivy in front, set against the pink house with white trim, make it look like a picture postcard. The cozy and spacious lounge, with a fireplace and TV, provides a good opportunity to visit with the many other guests. We found many Irish guests here who come every year. The Murphy family all pitches in to make your stay here at their ancestral dairy farm a pleasant one. There are golf courses nearby, and walking is very popular in this area.

Ard Na Greine House
Mary and Michael Houlihan
Spa Road
Dingle, County Kerry
Telephone: 066-9151113; **FAX:** 066-9151898
Bedrooms: 4, all with private baths
Rates: £18-20 p.p. No discount for children. Vouchers accepted.
Credit Cards: VISA, MasterCard, and Eurocard. **Open:** Jan.1 to Dec. 20. **Children:** Yes, 7 years and older. **Pets:** No. **Smoking:** No. **Provision for handicapped:** None. **Directions:** When entering Dingle from Tralee or Killarney turn right at roundabout onto The Mall road. Continue straight on at the next intersection. This is Spa Road. Stay to the left at the Hill Grove Hotel. Ard Na Greine is the third house on the left.

This attractive pink bungalow, in a quiet location within walking distance of the village center, is highly recommended by many other B&Bs and the British AA and RAC. All bedrooms have TV with satellite channels, refrigerator, direct-dial telephones, electric blankets, tea/coffee makers, iron, and an ironing board. So you can see you will be fully equipped to enjoy this popular town in comfort and style. Breakfast features the smoked salmon or herring, and homemade breads with the full Irish Breakfast. The advantage to this B&B is that you receive a quality bed and breakfast, and you will be within walking distances to pubs with excellent traditional music and the great restaurants of Dingle. Up the road is Connor Pass, and of course, a trip around Slea Head is a must.

Ard-na-Mara Country House
Mrs. Ann Murphy
Ballymore, Ventry
Dingle, County Kerry
Telephone: 066-9159072
Bedrooms: 4, all with private baths.
Rates: £18 p.p.; Single £18.; 50 percent discount for children under 12. Vouchers accepted. **Credit cards:** Yes. **Open:** March 1 to October 31. **Children:** All ages. **Pets:** No. **Smoking:** Restricted. **Provision for handicapped:** None. **Directions:** From Dingle, go by the harbor, continue to the bridge, and then go left toward Slea Head Drive. On the left, 2 miles from the bridge, look for the sign. Turn left toward the water.

This modern home overlooking scenic Ventry Harbor is nicely situated on the R559 for your tour of the Dingle Peninsula. Ann gives you a warm welcome with tea and cookies when you arrive. All the rooms have duvets with tiny green prints and matching curtains. Doubles, twins, and triples are available. All rooms have tea and coffee makers, hair dryers, and alarm/clock radios. The lounge is a large living room with a fireplace, TV, and piano, so if you'd like an Irish singalong, this is your place. A breakfast menu is provided. We noted that French toast, yogurt, fruit and cheese, and other tasty items were included, which will allow you to have a change from the usual cooked breakfast. The chairs in front allow visitors to relax and survey the majestic seacoast beyond. Ann has served for groups of watercolor painters from the U.S. who have come with master artists to do landscape and seascape painting. It is just that beautiful here, and the Murphys are great hosts.

Cleevaun
Sean and Charlotte Cluskey
Lady's Cross
Dingle, County Kerry
Telephone: 066-9151108; **FAX:** 066-9152228; **E-Mail:** cleevaun@iol.ie
Bedrooms: 9; 8 with private baths, 1 with shared (standard).
Rates: £25-30 p.p. private bath; £22 shared bath; Single £40-50. 10 percent discount for children. **Credit cards:** VISA and MasterCard. **Open:** Mid-March to November. **Children:** Yes, older than 8. **Pets:** Only guide dogs. **Smoking:** No. **Provision for handicapped:** None. **Directions:** Take the roundabout (Rt. 559) in Dingle toward Slea Head Drive. Follow the signs, keeping the water on the left. Go left over the bridge toward Ventry. After about 500 yards, the house is on the left with a fence and beautifully landscaped garden in front surrounding the car park.

Cleevaun is one of our favorites. We have been here for many visits, even before the Cluskeys bought it. We love the panoramic view from the dining room of fields with sheep, Dingle Bay in the distance, and the Eask Tower on the hill protecting the harbor. There is a large ancient burial stone in the field behind the house, as well as some underground tunnels that may have connected some beehive houses. The country pine woodwork of the downstairs corner room, with the green bedcover and drapes, is very attractive, as are the rest of the rooms, all with pine furniture and matching bedspreads. In fact, this lovely house is very nice inside and out, and a good "base camp" from which to explore the Dingle Peninsula, see the Gallarus Oratory, St. Kilmalkedar, and other Christian antiquities. Charlotte Cluskey will cook you a wonderful Full Irish breakfast with many choices of eggs, fruit, yogurt, Irish cheese, pancakes, muffins, scones, good jams, and fresh-brewed coffee, including decaffeinated. She won the 1994 Galtee Breakfast of the Year Award. She has an extensive library in the fireplaced lounge, which describes the history and sights of the Dingle Peninsula and includes loads of books to browse through. This B&B is rated by the British RAC and AA.

Cluain Mhuire House

Mrs. Margaret Noonan
Spa Road
Dingle, County Kerry
Telephone: 066-9151291
Bedrooms: 4, all with private baths, plus extra full baths.
Rates: £18 p.p.; Single £20; 20 percent discount for children under 10.
Vouchers accepted. **Credit cards:** All major ones. **Open:** All year.
Children: Yes. **Pets:** Yes. **Smoking:** No. **Provision for handicapped:**
None. **Directions:** At the roundabout in Dingle go right and follow the
sign to Cluain Mhuire, as if going to Connor Pass. It is the second
house after Hillgrove Hotel on the left.

This comfy, cozy B&B is hosted by a lovely lady who will take care
of your every need. Attractive rooms with two doubles or double and
single are available. There are nice lounge chairs and umbrellas in the
front garden, and the house has a beautiful view of fields and mountains. In the living room there is a beautiful, large fireplace made
with colored stone from Minard Castle. The bedrooms are all carpeted and pretty, with TVs, electric blankets, hair dryers, irons, and
tea-making facilities. Mrs. Noonan serves a standard Irish cooked
breakfast with choice of cereals and juice, but yogurts, fruit, fish,
beans, or a cold plate are also served. Hot Barry tea and fresh scones
were rolled out for a nice Irish welcome when we visited Mrs.
Noonan's traditional Irish home. There is a soccer table game in the
dining room and some musical instruments. Take a five-minute walk
into Dingle for shops and restaurants.

The Half Door
Denis and Teresa O'Connor
Mail Road
Dingle, County Kerry
Telephone: 066-51883; **FAX:** 066-51883
Bedrooms: 7, all with private baths.
Rates: £20-25 p.p.; Single £30-35. Dinner à la carte £12-20. **Credit cards:** VISA. **Open:** Mar. to Nov. **Children:** Yes. **Pets:** No. **Smoking:** Restricted; not in bedrooms. **Provision for handicapped:** None.
Directions: It is the first B&B on the right as you enter Dingle on the Tralee Road, set back with pine trees on each side, overlooking the bay. Look for a yellow house with a red door.

   This friendly couple will greet you at the door and welcome you to their pretty, new, three-story bed and breakfast. It is bright yellow with a red door and has a view of Dingle Bay. The rooms are modern, decorated in pastel pink and white with floral drapes and lovely matching rugs and duvets. Baths are spacious, with fully tiled showers. A beautiful bedroom on the first floor has a fireplace and view of the bay. The sitting room has a fireplace and TV. Breakfast is standard Irish Breakfast, with other specialties like smoked salmon on a croissant, bacon, fish cakes, and poached eggs, all preceded by brown bread and a medley of fruit. You can walk to town and shop and visit the many excellent restaurants in Dingle, including our favorite, the Forge, which Teresa can direct you to. Another good one is the Half Door Restaurant, owned by the O'Connors. The best music is at O'Flaherty's Pub. Dingle is supposed to have the most 4-star restaurants in Ireland. Play golf 8 miles away at Ballyferriter, ride horseback at the youth hostel, and play tennis in Dingle. Drive out to Slea Head to see the Blasket Islands and local potters, or visit the beehive houses and ancient stone church just beyond Dingle going west. You'll need explicit directions from your hosts.

The Lighthouse
Mary Murphy
Dingle, County Kerry
Telephone and **FAX:** 066-9151829
Bedrooms: 6, all with private baths.
Rates: £18 p.p., £25 for Single. 50 percent discount for children 20 percent. Vouchers accepted. **Credit cards:** None. **Open:** Mid-February to mid-November. **Children:** Yes. **Pets:** No. **Smoking:** Sitting room only. **Provision for handicapped:** Yes, large bedroom with private bath on ground floor. **Directions:** Take the right at the roundabout in town. Then take a left at the end of Main Street and continue to the top of the hill (about .5 km). As you descend a little, The Lighthouse will be a yellow house with white fencing on your right.

What a joy to stay at this bed and breakfast with the charming hosts Mary and Dennis Murphy. A brief period in Boston inspired this couple's choice of architecture and the use of handsome, naturally furnished woodwork throughout. The dining room has a picture-postcard view of Dingle Bay. Each room is spacious, with comfortable beds and modern tiled baths. The breakfast menu allows many choices, from fresh fruit salad, the standard Irish fry, or eggs and omelets done many ways. After breakfast you can make a short walk to the village shops on Main Street, enjoy the craft village, or visit the fishing fleet as they bring in the day's catch. Just to view the surrounding green hills and checkerboard of stone walls is a thrill. Dingle is very popular, and be advised to book well ahead if you are traveling in the peak summer season. The Murphys welcome families with young children, as they have two of their own. For recreation, there is blue-flag swimming at Ventry, archeological explorations, fishing, horseback riding, or a harbor tour to see "Fungi," the tame porpoise.

Pax House
Joan Brosnon-Wright
Upper John Street
Dingle, County Kerry
Telephone: 66-9151518; **FAX:** 66-9152461; **E-Mail:** paxhouse@iol.ie
Bedrooms: 13, all with private baths.
Rates: £25 p.p. with private bath; Single: £35; 50 percent discount for children. Vouchers accepted for hotel/guesthouse only. **Credit cards:** VISA and MasterCard. **Open:** From March 1 to November 1. **Children:** All ages. **Pets:** No. **Smoking:** Restricted. **Provision for handicapped:** Yes, but not wheelchairs. **Directions:** On entering town from Conor Pass take the first left and continue up John Street for .5 miles. On entering Dingle on N86, pass the racecourse on left, then a red-brick house on the right. Turn right at the Pax House sign.

This beautiful family-run guesthouse has a panoramic view of the bay and harbor. You can view the fishing boats returning with their catches or see "Fungi" the porpoise cavorting in the water. The lounge with fireplace, dining room with view, and bedrooms, some with views, are spacious and nicely decorated in Celtic themes. The bedrooms vary in color, and are blue, cream, or yellow, with off-white curtains with Ohham letters on the side. The baths are beautifully tiled. A large gourmet breakfast is served, with seafood freshly caught in Dingle Bay a specialty, as well as a superb range of meats and cheeses. Joan and Ron are extremely outgoing and have extensive knowledge of the area. They will be able to recommend the best music sessions in town and help plan your visit to the archeological sites on the peninsula, including Slea Head. Other recreational features in the area include fishing, walking and hiking, blue-flag swimming, two equestrian centers, golfing, and pub entertainment.

Ocean Wave

Noreen O'Toole
Glenbeigh
Kenmare, County Kerry
Telephone: 066-9768249; **FAX:** 066-9768412; **E-Mail:** oceanwave@iol.ie
Bedrooms: 6, all with private baths.
Rates: £22.50 p.p.; Single £30. **Credit cards:** Yes. **Open:** March to November. **Children:** Yes, 10 and over. **Pets:** No. **Smoking:** Lounge only. **Provision for handicapped:** None. **Directions:** From Killorglin, go south on N70. The house is 1 km before the town of Glenbeigh on the left. It is about 7 miles south of Killorglin on the Ring of Kerry.

A beautiful, large home set on a hill among flower gardens, Ocean Wave overlooks Dingle Bay and the Dooks Golf Links, with mountains behind it. The delightful bedrooms have some antiques and are decorated in soft apricot and peach, cream and pink, and navy. They have canopy beds, TV, hair dryers, and tea-making facilities. Some have whirlpool baths. The sitting room and dining room have views of the bay, and Noreen's specialties in her breakfast menu boast 10 main dishes. You'll find horseback riding, hill walking, fishing, golf, and sandy beaches nearby. The home has the high rating of AA QQQQ. Be sure to look into Puck Fair, a real treat in Killorglin in the middle of August.

Rockcrest House
Marian and David O'Dwyer
Gortamullen
Kenmare, County Kerry
Telephone: 064-41248; **FAX:** 064-42253; **E-Mail:** dodwy@tinet.ie
Bedrooms: 6, all with private baths.
Rates: £19 p.p.; 33 percent discount for children. Vouchers accepted.
Dinner offered. **Credit cards:** All major ones. **Open:** All year. **Children:**
All ages. **Pets:** Yes. **Smoking:** Yes. **Provision for handicapped:** Yes.
Directions: Heading south just outside Kenmare town center, there is
a sign posted for Rockcrest House off of N71 Killarny Road (on the
outskirts of Kenmare town).

Rockcrest House is an elegant, dormer-style guesthouse on a quiet,
scenic location overlooking the prehistoric site of a dolmen stone circle and the Kenmore River Valley. A beautiful rock garden and stone
wall adorn the entrance to the house. All six rooms are spacious and
nicely decorated in bright colors. They have TVs, hair dryers, and
other facilities. Most have views of the lovely countryside. There is a
thirteenth-century arched bridge, the stone circle, and a holy well, all
within 800 yards of the house. Marian and David O'Dwyer serve a full
Irish Breakfast in their attractive dining room, and dinner is offered
if booked ahead. Babysitting is offered until midnight. Nearby you'll
find golf, horseback riding, walking (including a guided hill walk),
fishing, boat trips, and all watersports on the Kenmare River. The
house is only a five-minute walk from the town of Kenmare, with its
good restaurants and pubs.

Whispering Pines
John and Mary Fitzgerald
Bellheight
Kenmare, County Kerry
Telephone: 064-41194
Bedrooms: 4, all with private baths.
Rates: £20 p.p.; Single £30; 50 percent discount for children under 12.
Vouchers not accepted. **Credit cards:** None. **Open:** March 1 to
November 15. **Children:** Yes, ages 5 and up. **Pets:** No. **Smoking:**
Restricted to outside. **Provision for handicapped:** None. **Directions:**
From the center of Kenmare take Glengarriff Road south. About .5
mile from the center of town, but before the harbor on the right, is
Whispering Pines, pink with white trim.

This pretty 1914 home, decorated inside with beautiful pastel colors,
is a wonderful place to stay. It is located on the edge of town, set behind
a lovely garden. John and Mary give you a warm welcome to their
home. The four spacious and handsomely decorated rooms, all with
private baths, are painted in soft colors with matching borders—one in
black and pink roses, another with peach walls and matching pink
flowered duvets. The home has a comfy, restful feeling. The dining
room is spacious, with separate tables. Breakfast is a hearty Irish cooked
meal with homemade brown bread. Dry cereals are available with fruit
and other provisions for those who want vegetarian or lighter fare.
There is an arched front hall and a nice sitting room with a marble fireplace and TV. A nine-hole golf course and a riding stable are nearby for
reasonable fees. We walked to town one night and watched a *caeli*. A
caeli is a Gaelic amateur-night singalong or dance done in the pubs or
local hotels. Kenmare is a quaint town by the sea, not as busy and full of
tourists as Killarney, yet more preferred by many.

Brookside
Anne and Neilius Moriarty
Gortacollopa, Fossa
Killarney, County Kerry
Telephone: 064-44187
Bedrooms: 6, 5 private baths, 1 room with shared bath; plus a 3-bedroom housekeeping cottage with fireplace.
Rates: £18 p.p.; Single £16.50 p.p., shared bath; 25 percent discount for children. Vouchers accepted. £13 dinner. **Credit cards:** Yes, all major ones. **Open:** March 1 to November 1. **Children:** All ages. **Pets:** No. **Smoking:** No. **Provision for handicapped:** Limited. **Directions:** From Killarney, take N72 (R562), follow the signpost to Hotel Europe. Brookside is two miles further, on right side of road, next to Kerry Die Products.

This handsome bungalow on the outskirts of busy Killarney is in a quiet pastoral area, and features a lovely flower garden in front. Anne and Neilius are very gracious and generous with their time, showing guests the best way to appreciate their wonderful town. Neilius is now the head of Killarney's Chamber of Commerce. The bedrooms are decorated in pastel pinks, peach, and green, with handmade duvets and matching drapes in flowered materials. Some rooms have views of hills with sheep and ponies grazing. Brookside was awarded the Country Rover Irish B&B of the Year in 1993 and 1994. The sitting room with turf fire is a social center of this home where tea is served. Breakfast varies from the full Irish to choices of smoked salmon, beans on toast, scrambled eggs, poached eggs with bacon, cheese and tomato, fruit, yogurt, tea, coffee, and hot chocolate.

This home is four miles from Killarney with its jaunting-car trips, the Gap of Dunloe, boating on the lakes, golf, cycling, pony-trekking, and a bus to the Ring of Kerry. Your stay will be a memorable one, with the Moriartys indulging every convenience.

Carrowmore House
Pat and Kathleen McAuliffe
Knockasarnett
Aghadoe
Killarney, County Kerry
Telephone: 064-33520
Bedrooms: 5, all with private baths.
Rates: £18 p.p.; Single £23. 25 percent discount for children.
Vouchers are accepted. **Credit cards:** None. **Open:** April 1 to October
31. **Children:** All ages. **Pets:** No. **Smoking:** Restricted. **Provision for
handicapped:** None. **Directions:** Take the N22 on the Killarney, Tralee,
Limerick Road. The house is about 2 km from Killarney town.

Set in a tranquil area with a beautiful panoramic view, this bed and
breakfast comes highly recommended by other hosts in our book. The
bedrooms are spacious, done in rust and cream, peach and brown,
pink and blue, and other fashionable colors. All rooms have color-
coordinated carpets, linens, and curtains, with the color scheme con-
tinued in the ensuite bathrooms. Breakfast is the full Irish cooked one
with eggs any style, both puddings, and grilled tomato. Juice and
hot/cold cereals are also served. Save room, though, for the home-
baked bread and sultana scones. For recreation there is horseback riding, golf, swimming, boating, and fishing locally. Pat and Kathleen can
arrange local tours from the Carrowmore House.

Coffey's Loch Lein Guest House
Eithne Coffey
Golf Course Road, Fossa
Killarney, County Kerry
Telephone: 064-31260; **FAX:** 064-36151
Bedrooms: 12, all with private baths.
Rates: £20-25 p.p.; Single £25-30. 50 percent discount for children.
Vouchers accepted. **Credit cards:** VISA, MasterCard, Access. **Open:**
March 12 to November 1. **Children:** All ages. **Pets:** No. **Smoking:**
Restricted. **Provision for handicapped:** Yes. **Directions:** From Killarney
Center take Killorglin Road for 3 miles. Pass Hotel Europe on the
left and Prince of Peace Church. Take the next left on Golf Course
Road. Follow the signs to Coffey's Loch Lein.

This spacious, very comfortable, and neat guesthouse, located just
outside Killarney among beautiful old trees with a large front garden,
is made special by Eithne Coffey with her energetic and humorous
style. It is situated by Killarney's Loch Leana, with the mountains rising
up to the south, a pretty vista from the lounge and dining room. Snow
was on the mountains in May when we were there. All of the rooms
have been tastefully decorated and are very comfortable, with large
private baths. We liked the guesthouse because it is off the main road,
set back, and free from the hustle and bustle of downtown Killarney.
There are many things to do in Killarney, including the nearby golfing, tennis, boating, fishing, hiking, and horseback riding. A Dublin
hiking club was there when we were at the guesthouse. They were
ready to hike the snow-covered MacGillycuddy's Reeks. A delight for
many is the trip up the nearby Gap of Dunloe in a pony trap, and stopping for a pint after at the pub, Kate Kearney's, near the entrance. A
pint before will make the scenery even rosier. This is one of our
favorite guesthouses because of the relaxed atmosphere and the
charm of the Coffeys.

The Grotto
Joan and Jerry Ryan
Fossa
Killarney, County Kerry
Telephone: 064-33283
Bedrooms: 6, all with private baths.
Rates: £18 p.p.; 50 percent discount for children under 12. Vouchers accepted. **Credit cards:** Yes. **Open:** March 1 through mid-November 30. **Children:** All ages. **Pets:** Yes. **Smoking:** Restricted. **Provision for handicapped:** Yes. **Directions:** Take Killorglin Road (R565—Ring of Kerry/Dingle road). The home is just a few yards beyond Castlerosse Hotel and before the entrance to the Golf Club, 2 km west of Killarney.

A pretty garden greets you as you enter the gate to this beautiful modern country home. The spacious bedrooms with dressing tables are done in Laura Ashley style with colors of peach/cream, grey/pink, and blue/grey, each with its own tea/coffee-making facilities. The dining room has separate tables with white tablecloths and flowers. There is a cozy lounge with a TV. Breakfast could be a delicious cooked Irish one with eggs and bacon, or a ham, cheese, and mushroom omelet, or a continental/vegetarian one with cereal, yogurt, cheese, and a variety of fresh fruit. Jerry and Joan are extremely helpful in guiding you to the various tourist sights and activities of Killarney, of which there are many and as diverse as any place in Ireland. Killarney's two championship golf courses and fishing club are situated opposite the Grotto on the Ring of Kerry/Dingle road. Horseback riding and hill and mountain hiking are some of the other features. The Irish Tourist Board Office in the Killarney town hall (Tel.: 064-31633) can provide you with dates and times of special events in this region. This B&B has been recommended by many other B&B owners and travelers in Ireland.

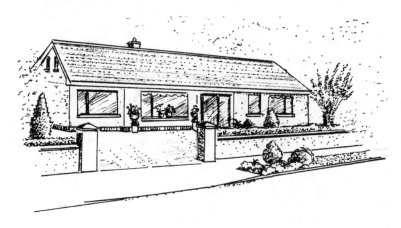

Lisaden
Betty O'Sullivan
97 Countess Grove
(off) Countess Road
Killarney, County Kerry
Telephone: 064-32006
Bedrooms: 5, all en suite, some triples or family rooms.
Rates: £18-20 p.p.; Single £25-28; 50 percent discount for children.
Vouchers accepted. **Credit cards:** Yes, all major ones. **Open:** March 1
to October 31. **Children:** Yes. **Pets:** No. **Smoking:** Restricted to lounge.
Provision for handicapped: None. **Directions:** Signpost on Countess
Road. Call Mrs. O'Sullivan for directions.

This beautiful bungalow was chosen the best town and country
home in Killarney in 1994. It is situated in a quiet area off of the main
road, surrounded by lovely gardens and shrubbery, and allows you to
escape the hustle and bustle of Killarney, which is usually brimful of
tourists. All five rooms have been newly repainted in colorful, pastel
shades of pale pinks and off-whites, with matching curtains and flowered duvets. They are equipped with tea-making facilities and hair dryers. The pretty dining room has individual tables with linen cloths and
a garden view. Breakfast includes full Irish or continental/vegetarian
with fruit, yogurt, and a choice of cereals. You'll enjoy Betty's generous
congeniality. It is only a seven-minute walk to the center of Killarney
town, with its great restaurants and tourist sights. Golf, fishing, and a
national park are nearby.

Lohan's Lodge

Cathy and Mike Lohan
Tralee Road (N22)
Killarney, County Kerry
Telephone: 064-33871; **FAX:** 064-33871
Bedrooms: 5, all with private baths.
Rates: £18.50 to 19.50; ⅓ discount for children. Vouchers accepted.
Credit cards: VISA, MasterCard. **Open:** February 1 to October 31.
Children: Yes, over 6. **Pets:** No. **Smoking:** No. **Provision for handicapped:** None. **Directions:** The house is 3.5 miles from Killarney center, on the left of N22. Going south, the house is 5 miles from Farranfore center.

This home has floor-to-ceiling windows for viewing beautiful gardens and the spectacular countryside beyond. The dining room has formal, separate tables. The very comfortable bedrooms are pastel with floral print. The fabrics are in cream and pink, all with modern showers, color TVs, hair dryers, and tea/coffee makers. The beautiful sitting room is located at the front, with large windows and cathedral ceilings. Cathy and Mike work together on the delicious breakfast, which includes the traditional offerings plus a variety of pancakes, eggs benedict, hash browns, scrambled eggs with salmon, fruit salad, and yogurt or porridge. Visit the lakes of Killarney, the Gap of Dunlae, or bicycle in the National Park to Ross Castle and trails beyond. Find great Irish tradition nightly at the Grand Hostel Pub. Watch Irish dancing here also. Other spots have more eclectic music. We ate at the Laurels and were more than satisfied. Try the Bricin at the bottom of High Street, near Quillan's Store. Killarney Court Hotel has great carvery lunches daily. It is a two-hour drive to Shannon Airport.

Muckross Lodge
Bernadette O'Sullivan
Muckross Road
Killarney, County Kerry
Telephone and **FAX:** 064-32660
Bedrooms: 4, all with private baths.
Rates: £19-21 p.p.; Single £37-40 p.p.; 33 percent discount for children. Vouchers not accepted. **Credit cards:** VISA, MasterCard. **Open:** April to October. **Children:** Yes, 5 and up. **Pets:** No. **Smoking:** No. **Provision for handicapped:** None. **Directions:** From Killarney town, follow signs for National Park and Muckross. Muckross Lodge is near the Eagle Hotel.

This attractive two-story, dormer-style residence is very close to exciting Killarney town and adjacent to Muckross House Museum and Gardens. Bernadette is a warm and welcoming hostess, and you will find her rooms beautifully decorated in blues, pinks, and rusts; they are comfortable, with tea- and coffee-making facilities, television, and hair dryers. In her dining room, she serves a full Irish Breakfast with additional offerings of homemade scones, fresh fruit salad, yogurt, cheese, and freshly served coffee. The beautiful Killarney lakes are nearby, as are traffic-free walking and cycling paths, golf courses, and coaches to the Ring of Kerry. Pony-trekking is also available at the Gap of Dunloe, along with jaunting-car rides from Killarney center to Muckross House. The drivers have a great line of history plus blarney. One guest said Bernadette's hospitality was "superb."

MULBERRY HOUSE - KILLARNEY

Mulberry House
Eileen Tarrant
Rookery Road
Killarney, County Kerry

Telephone: 064-34112; **FAX:** 064-32534; **E-mail:** mulberry@tinet.ie
Bedrooms: 5, all with private baths.
Rates: £19-23. 25 percent discount for children up to 12. Vouchers
accepted. **Credit cards:** Yes, all major ones. **Open:** February 1 to
December 1. **Children:** Yes, all ages. **Pets:** No. **Smoking:** Restricted to
sitting room. **Provision for handicapped:** None. **Directions:** From
roundabout at the beginning of Muckross Road, take an immediate
left onto Countess Road, and then the second right, onto Rookery
Road. You'll see a sign for the house.

Mulberry House is a beautiful home with two stories, a balcony, and
a brick front. The guest lounge is formal, with a fireplace and views
of gardens. Out front you can see mountains and farm animals. The
rooms are elegant and brightly colored, and all have names over the
doors. One has a balcony. All have hair dryers, tea/coffee makers, and
TVs. Breakfast includes the choice of standard Irish or different styles
of eggs, waffles, pancakes, smoked salmon, and fruit and yogurt. The
house backs out into farmland. It is lovely to be in such a quiet and
rural area, and yet be only 10 minutes away from Killarney center
with all of its gift shops and entertainment. There is also horseback
riding, fishing, and hiking. Muckross House, Ross Castle, and the lakes
are big draws.

Ashgrove House
Nancy O'Neil
Ballybunion Road
Listowel, County Kerry
Telephone: 068-23668/21268; **FAX:** 068-21268
Bedrooms: 4, all with private bath.
Rates: £18 p.p.; Single £25. 20 percent discount for children.
Vouchers accepted. **Credit cards:** VISA and MasterCard. **Open:** April
1 to October 31. **Children:** Yes, all ages. **Pets:** No. **Smoking:** In front
lounge. **Provision for handicapped:** None. **Directions:** From Listowel
town take the route to Ballybunion (R553). The house is 1 km from
Listowel, on the right.

A modern home in a country setting, with breakfast served in a
sun room overlooking a garden, is sure to make for a relaxing stay in
this bustling market town with its rich literary traditions and colorful
shop fronts. Nancy can show you up to your comfortable rooms with
orthopedic beds and done in bright, restful tones, and make your
visit a pleasant one. Each room has TV and tea/coffee facilities. Advice
on the area's historical and recreational facilities, as well as amenities
of the area, are offered upon request. The breakfast can be your
choice of a continental one or a full Irish one with fresh homemade
bread and scones with preserves. The world-famous Ballybunion golf
course is within 10 minutes. Also, fishing in the River Feale, a swim in
the Leisure Center, or just a visit to the local cinema or theater (the
Arts and Heritage Center) will encourage you to tarry in scenic and
mystical Listowel for a while.

Ceol Na M'Abhann
Kathleen Stack
Tralee Road
Listowel, County Kerry
Telephone and **FAX:** 068-21345
Bedrooms: 4; 3 with private baths, 1 with shared bath.
Rates: £18 private, £16 shared. Superior room £22. No discount for children. Vouchers accepted. **Credit cards:** VISA and MasterCard.
Open: April to mid-October. **Children:** Yes, over 12 years of age. **Pets:** No. **Smoking:** In veranda only. **Provision for handicapped:** None.
Directions: First and only house on riverbank beside bridge over River Teale on the Listowel-to-Tralee road.

This lovely bed and breakfast received an Irish National Trust award for its appearance and quaintness. It is one of the few thatch-roofed, white cottage B&Bs in all of Ireland, and the only one in Listowel. Its picture-postcard look is memorable. It is situated a half-mile outside Listowel on a riverbank near a beautiful wooded area. Kathleen serves tea and scones upon arrival in her Georgian dining room with fine linens, china, and silver. The bedrooms are modern and bright. A charming sitting room with river view and sun lounge are available to guests. Nearby, there is golf, tennis, pitch and putt, and fishing. The famous Ballybunion golf course, beach, and Shannon car ferry are only about nine miles away.

Fern Rock
Irma Clifford
Tinnahalla
Milltown, County Kerry
Telephone and **FAX:** 066-9761848
Bedrooms: 4, all with private bath.
Rates: £18 p.p. Vouchers accepted. **Credit cards:** None. **Open:** All year except Christmas. **Children:** Speak to owner. **Pets:** No. **Smoking:** No. **Provision for handicapped:** None. **Directions:** Going south from Tralee, it is exactly 3 km south of Milltown and 3 km north of Killorglin on the N70.

Situated on a hill with superb views of the Slieve Mish Mountains and Dingle Bay, this neat-as-a-pin, beautiful, two-story, split-level, modern home is a good base for visiting the Dingle Peninsula, Killorglin, and the Ring of Kerry. Surrounded by large gardens, Fern Rock has lovely bedrooms on both floors, with a magnolia theme and color scheme. It has a luxurious lounge with flowered drapes for guests, as well as private parking. The bedrooms and lounge have views of mountains and the bay. You'll find it quiet and restful here in this rural setting. Irma's breakfasts are typical Irish, with other choices of the popular smoked salmon and scrambled eggs, or baked bass on toast, and yogurt or cheese and fruit, with tea or coffee. Recreation nearby includes a golf course around the corner, fishing, swimming on Inch Beach, and walking. Plus, there are eight championship golf courses within an hour's drive. The Puck Fair in Killorglan, one of the oldest county fairs in Europe, is quite a delight to visit in August. One guest claims Fern Rock is "A-1, the best in Ireland." Some French guests spoke of "perfect artistic harmony, with little rabbits included." And another French guest called it "a palace and the hostess a princess."

Brook Manor Lodge
Vincent and Margaret O'Sullivan
Fenit Road, Spa
Tralee, County Kerry
Telephone: 066-7120406; **FAX:** 066-7127552
Bedrooms: 6, all with private baths.
Rates: £27-35; 50 percent discount for children. Vouchers not accepted. **Credit cards:** VISA, MasterCard. **Open:** All year. **Children:** Yes, all ages. **Pets:** No. **Smoking:** No. **Provision for handicapped:** Yes, one room. **Directions:** From Tralee center, take R551 and follow signs for Ardfert, then turn left at R551/R558 junction onto R558 towards Tralee golf course. The house is 2 km from Tralee on the left.

This large, two-story house is "purpose built" on 3.6 acres. It is just outside of Tralee and offers a view of the Slieve Mish Mountains. You will find the O'Sullivans are friendly and helpful hosts. The sumptuous rooms are tastefully decorated in navy and white, or pink and white, with Victorian lamps, chairs, and mirrors. Many rooms look out onto private gardens, and all provide television, telephone, tea/coffee machines, hair dryers, trouser press, and radio/alarm. The breakfast is served in an elegant dining hall by the fireplace or in an adjoining conservatory. Many combinations from the menu are offered, including locally made pork sausages, Irish smoked salmon with fruit or eggs, baked beans or yogurt, cheese and crackers, and freshly made coffee. Afternoon tea is served by the fire in the relaxing guest lounge. Nearby is horseback riding, golf, sailing, and fishing, and the beaches are only minutes away. There is also the "Siamsa Tire" show in Tralee, and there are award-winning seafood restaurants nearby.

Knockbrack
Helen Lyons
Oakpark Road
Tralee, County Kerry
Telephone: 066-27375
Bedrooms: 3, all with private baths.
Rates: £18 p.p. Single £24. Discount for children. Accepts vouchers.
Credit cards: Yes, all major. **Open:** April 1 to November 30. **Children:**
Yes, over 5. **Pets:** No. **Smoking:** Only in living room. **Provision for hand-icapped:** None. **Directions:** On Listowel Road (Car Ferry) N69, about .5 miles from town center. The house is about 100 meters from McEllical's Garage (Mercedes-Benz agent), on the opposite side of the road.

This new, bright bungalow, located in a residential area, features cheery gardens and pastoral scenes viewed from the living room. Some bedrooms are on the ground floor. The large living room is decorated with mahogany furniture and pink furnishings, and tea- and coffee-making facilities are available during the day. The carpeted bedrooms with orthopedic beds are decorated in pink and green, yellow and blue, and peach and green floral patterns, with matching duvets and drapes. Helen serves a traditional Irish Breakfast with options of hot and cold cereal, fresh fruit, yogurt, and homemade breads and scones with freshly brewed tea or coffee. The back garden of Knockbrack borders on a farm where cows can sometimes be seen grazing. This home is convenient to golf, the National Folk Theater, and the greyhound racetrack. You'll find horseback riding, fishing, and beautiful scenery here, and musical entertainment in the pubs. Listowel is the home of the famous Irish playwright, John B. Keane. You might even meet him in the pub he runs. We have seen his plays in Dublin and Kilkenny.

O'Sheas
Mairead O'Shea
2 Oakpark Drive
Tralee, County Kerry
Telephone and **FAX:** 066-7180123
Bedrooms: 4, all with private baths.
Rates: £18 p.p.; Single £24. Vouchers not accepted. **Credit cards:** None. **Open:** May 1 to September 30. **Children:** No. **Pets:** No. **Smoking:** No. **Provision for handicapped:** None. **Directions:** Turn right at the traffic lights at the railway station, coming from Limerick/Killarney direction. After a 3-minute drive, O'Sheas is on the left side. Look for the sign. From Shannon, take N70 south at Tralee train station, then turn right on N69. The house is a 3-minute drive away.

This young, hospitable, and helpful couple will make for a pleasant stay in the area. Fran's sister Carol was especially appreciative of the care Mrs. O'Shea took to give them advice on traveling over Connor Pass during daylight hours. This traditional modern home is cozy with family pictures and fluffy pillows in the living room. There is a satellite TV and a VCR. The carpeted bedrooms are perfect, with curtains, lamps, and bedcovers matching with a Victorian flair, individually decorated in light blues, pinks, peaches, and creams. All rooms have radios and orthopedic beds. The breakfast is either the traditional Irish cooked breakfast or the continental. The side buffet has hot and cold cereal, yogurt, fruit, and juice. The home is close to downtown restaurants and "Siamsa Tire" (the National Folk Theater of Ireland show). Tralee is a good central place from which to visit the Dingle Peninsula and Killarney. It is convenient to beaches, golf courses, Kerry Airport, and the racetrack. The owners of this B&B run a tour bus company called O'Shea's Travel, which offers group and individual tours around Ireland and in the U.K. They also offer educational tours.

ALSO RECOMMENDED

Dingle, *Bambury's Guest House,* Bernie Bambury, Mail Road. Telephone: 066-51244; FAX: 066-51786. Bedrooms: 12, all with private baths. Modern guesthouse within 2 minutes' walking distance of town. Scenic view of harbor from back rooms. Many amenities. Pretty dining room decorated with three green colors. Very good breakfast menu.

Dingle, *Milltown,* John and Angela Gill, just beyond town, facing the harbor entrance. Telephone: 066-51372; FAX: 006-51095. Bedrooms: 10, all en suite. Comfortable and well located. 4-star rating from the Irish Tourist Board and highly recommended by many guidebooks.

Dingle, *Sos an Iolair,* Mrs. Mary Moriarity, Ballintlea, Ventry. Tel: 066-59827. Bungalow in countryside. Small but comfortable bedroom, en suite or private bath and shower suitable only for people of small build, but separate toilet available at end of corridor. Very caring and welcoming couple. Tea/coffee and cookies available whenever requested. Generous draughts of Irish whiskey supplied before one goes out to local restaurant. Recommended to us by Harry McWilliams of Chalfont St. Peter, Buckinghamshire, England.

Kenmare, *An Bruachan,* Julie O'Connor, Killarney Road. Telephone/Fax: 064-41682. E-Mail: bruachan@iol.ie Bedrooms: 5, all en suite. Friendly and pretty home in mature garden on the N71. Minutes from town center. Riverfront property.

Kenmare, *Hawthorne House,* Trina and Kevin Murphy. Telephone: 064-41035; FAX: 064-41932. Bedrooms: 8, all with private baths. Lovely gardens surrounding, with private car park. Period beds and furniture.

Kenmare, *Mylestone House,* Mrs. Fiona O'Sullivan, Killowen Road. Telephone: 064-41753. Bedrooms: 5, all with private baths. New luxury residence opposite Kenmare Golf Course. Town center 4 minutes away.

Killarney, *Gap View Farm,* Mrs. Mary Kearney, Ballyhar. Telephone: 066-64378. Bedrooms: 6, 4 with private baths. 8 miles from Killarney town. Send for their color brochure. Recommended by our friend Marge Brennan of Gloucester, Mass.

Killarney, *O'Mahony's,* Sheila O'Mahony, Park Road. Telephone: 064-32861. Bedrooms: 6, all en suite. Pleasant home, yellow with white trim, across from Ryan's Hotel. Within walking distance of town center.

Killarney, *St. Anthony's Villa,* Mrs. Mary Connell, Cork Road. Telephone: 064-31534. Bedrooms: 4, 3 with private baths. Especially nice B&B in the Cork Road area. Recommended by many travelers and especially by a top Irish historian, Dr. Edna McGlynn.

Killarney, *Shraheen House,* Maureen Fleming, Cork/Killarney Road. Telephone. 064-31286/37959; FAX: 064-37959. Bedrooms: 6, all en suite. Luxurious home off N22. Satellite TV, tea/coffee facilities, hair dryer in all rooms. Breakfast menu. Open all year except Christmas. 2 km from town. Chosen by many travel guides. Recommended by Carmel O'Halloran of Galway.

Sneem (Ring of Kerry), *Woodvale (Old Convent House),* Mrs. Alice O'Sullivan, Pier Road. Telephone: 064-45181. Bedrooms: 6, all with private baths. All major credit cards. Old-World Tudor house set on own grounds on estuary of Sneem River, overlooked by Direenvourig Mountains.

Tralee, *Seaview House,* Mrs. Bridie Fitzgerald, Main Dingle Road, Annagh, Blennerville. Telephone: 066-21830. Bedrooms: 5, all with private baths. Spacious bungalow in picturesque surroundings, beneath Slieve Mish Mountains. Overlooking Tralee Bay. 4.5 miles to Tralee. Recommended by Vera Feeney of Galway.

COUNTY KILKENNY

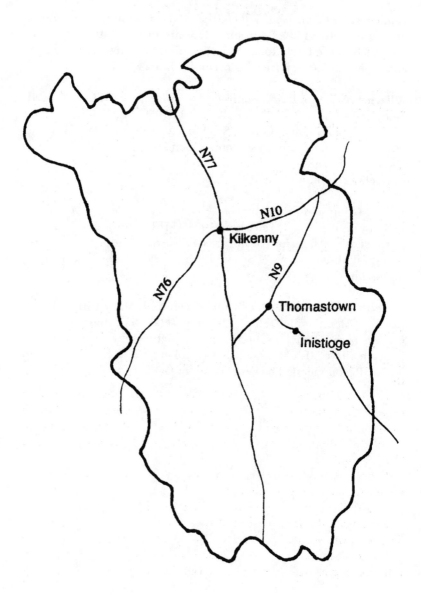

County Kilkenny

County Kilkenny is strategically located between Cork or Tipperary and Dublin, and it's between Waterford and Dublin, which makes it a natural stopping place. It is also only a little over an hour away from Glendalough in the Wicklow Mountains. The countryside is poetically rural, with many sheep farms and the Nore River flowing through the center of the county, adding to its scenic beauty.

Kilkenny town, although holding well to its medieval history, is worldly. It offers fine cultural features such as the Irish National Design Center across from the castle, built to encourage young craftspeople. It has a showroom where crafts can be bought, and upstairs is a restaurant with delicious, creative meals. Also, good Irish plays are put on at the Watergate Theater, and there is a cinema in town. You may want to peruse the art galleries and bookstores.

Imposing thirteenth-century Kilkenny Castle, on the river, is the center of attention in this town. Nicely restored with its two enormous turrets on either end, it covers 49 acres, including a huge public park with playgrounds for children, and attractive gardens. You can tour the castle daily, mid-March to September 30, and on weekends the rest of the year.

Go to the Tourist Information Office at the old Shee Alms House on Rose Inn Street at the bridge and join a tour of the town. With a well-informed guide, you'll take a brisk walk to see the Black Abbey; St. Canice's Cathedral; Kyteler's Inn, which once housed a witch; and "Irish Town."

Kyteler's has a fun restaurant downstairs in cave-like rooms. Get a terrific meal at Edward Langton's at 65 John Street. It has a high glass-ceilinged dining room and has won many awards.

For a beautiful tour out of Kilkenny town, drive south on R700 to Thomastown, Woodstock Forest Park, and Jerpoint Abbey. Visit the grounds of Mount Juliet House, a hotel on 1,400 acres of pastureland with horses grazing. It has an Equestrian Center and Stud Farm.

Continue through the pastoral country to the town of Inistioge, a heavenly village with the town center nestled among hills and a humpy bridge over the river with sheep lying on its banks. Just across from the park is an excellent restaurant for lunch. The fishing is good in this relaxing area. It is also a pretty ride over to Carrick on Suir and Clonmel in Tipperary.

Ashville
Maura Naddy
Kilmacshane
Inistioge, County Kilkenny
Telephone: 056-58460; **FAX:** 056-58418
Bedrooms: 4; 3 with private baths, 1 with shared.
Rates: £18 p.p. private bath; £16 p.p. shared bath; Single £22.50; 50 percent discount for children under 12. Vouchers accepted. **Credit cards:** VISA, Access. **Open:** March 1 to October 31. **Children:** All ages. **Pets:** No. **Smoking:** In lounge only. **Provision for handicapped:** None. **Directions:** From Kilkenny city, the B&B is 15 miles southeast on the Rosslare Road on the right, just north of the town of Inistioge. It is 4 miles south of Thomastown.

This modern grey and white brick bungalow overlooks the beautiful Nore Valley and has gardens for visitors to enjoy. Maura is genial as she serves you her welcoming tea. She says she treats her guests "like family." The rooms are cheerful with their colors of red and white, pink and beige, and green and yellow. The lounge and dining room have a lovely view. A full Irish Breakfast is served and you may have dinner there if you order it ahead. The charming town of Inistioge, where Fran painted one of her favorite scenes of sheep across the river and a pretty arched bridge, is two minutes away, with a very homey restaurant right in the square. There is also Woodstock Forest Park, Jerpoint Abbey, fishing in the Nore River, golf, walking, and swimming very nearby. Horseback ride at Mount Juliet, a gorgeous estate, and of course visit the exciting medieval town of Kilkenny. Visitors can also enjoy nearby pubs and traditional Irish music.

Cnoc Mhuire
Helen and Don Sheehan
Castle Road
Kilkenny Town, County Kilkenny
Telephone and **FAX:** 056-62161
Bedrooms: 4; all with private baths.
Rates: £18-19 p.p.; Single £22; 33 percent discount for children under 12. Vouchers accepted. **Credit cards:** Yes. **Open:** All year, except Christmas. **Children:** Over 6. **Pets:** No. **Smoking:** No. **Provision for handicapped:** Yes. **Directions:** From Kilkenny town center, at the castle take Bennetsbridge Road (R700) to the second B&B sign; go right. The house is the first B&B on the left.

This modern bungalow is run by an enchanting couple, Helen and Don, who really put themselves out to make you comfortable and help you with directions for a good tour of Kilkenny. Their rooms are cozy with peach, pink, and rose colors. All have electric blankets, and the bathrooms are good-sized. There is a separate small lounge with a bay window and TV. The dining room is quite pleasant and there is plenty of tea and coffee in pots with cozies to keep them hot. Don squeezes fresh orange juice every night, and besides the typical Irish Breakfast, you'll be offered lots of homemade scones, yogurt, fresh fruit like grapefruit, and—some days—kippers. It's a great spot as it is just a short walk to town, where you can visit the medieval castle and park with a playground, and walk around the old city of museums, craft shops, and great pubs and restaurants. We attended the Watergate Theater and saw *Sive,* a fine Irish play by John B. Keane. Golf, fishing, and horseback riding are also within 15 minutes' drive. Be sure you visit the Irish National Design Center for good crafts and a wonderful lunch. Visitors can also enjoy playing tennis and walking amongst attractive scenery.

Danville House
Kitty Stallard
New Ross Road
Kilkenny, County Kilkenny
Telephone: 056-21512
Bedrooms: 4; 3 with private baths, 1 with shared.
Rates: £18 p.p.; £16 shared; 10 percent discount for children. **Credit cards:** No. **Open:** April 1 to November 1. **Children:** All ages. **Pets:** No. **Smoking:** No. **Provision for handicapped:** None. **Directions:** Find the ring road south of the city. At the roundabout for New Ross (R700) go south for about 200 yards. The entrance for Danville House is on your right.

This stately 1790s Georgian farmhouse, situated in a peaceful location just outside Kilkenny, will give you a chance to see a 100-acre dairy farm in action. Many antiques adorn the living quarters; one bedroom has a canopy bed (half-tester). Outside there is a large old garden with a swing, and farther back a walled kitchen garden where produce and herbs are grown for the meals. The rooms are spacious and provide views of the lush green farm. The dining room has a pretty chandelier over a large antique mahogany table where breakfast is served, consisting of fresh eggs in your cooked breakfast with homemade breads and plum, marmalade, and raspberry jams. Fishing, golfing, flying, and horseback riding can be arranged nearby. You can do all the sights in Kilkenny while you spend your time outside in a country setting with meadows and tall mature trees. Kitty will set up the miniature croquet set in the backyard for your amusement, or you can tour the cowbarn at milking time, gather the eggs, and observe the inner workings of an Irish farm. It is no wonder that this B&B was a winner of the Galtee Award.

Dunboy Bed and Breakfast
Helen Dunning
10 Parkview Drive, off Freshford Road
Kilkenny, County Kilkenny
Telephone and **FAX:** 066-61460
Bedrooms: 3, all with private bath
Rates: £18 p.p.; Single £20-25. 25 percent discount for children under 12. Vouchers accepted. **Credit cards:** VISA and MasterCard. **Open:** All year except Christmas. **Children:** Yes, all ages. **Pets:** No. **Smoking:** Restricted. **Provision for handicapped:** None. **Directions:** Call hostess for directions.

   This modern bright and cheery home is situated in a quiet cul-de-sac, within walking distance of the city center. One bedroom, decorated in greens and yellow with double and single beds, is located on the ground floor. The other two rooms are upstairs and fully coordinated using wine, green, cream, and pink. The guest lounge is a restful and relaxing room with TV, tea- and coffee-making facilities, and an open fire. Helen enjoys sharing her information folder she has gathered over the years describing history and places of interest. Guests can choose from their breakfast menu of a full Irish Breakfast with farm-fresh eggs, home-baked brown bread, and preserves. Vegetarians are catered for with a selection of cheese, fresh fruit, and yogurts. Recreation in the area includes golf, horseback riding, and fishing. Kilkenny has excellent features such as live theater, historic tours, a medieval castle and abbey, an outstanding Design Center, and a brewery that makes a famous ale. Helen can advise you on Kilkenny's great selection of shops, restaurants, and pubs for traditional Irish music as well.

Hillgrove
Margaret and Tony Drennan
Bennetsbridge Road
Kilkenny, County Kilkenny
Telephone: 056-51453/22890; **FAX:** 056-51453
Bedrooms: 5; all with private baths.
Rates: £18 p.p. private bath; Single £22; 50 percent discount for children under 12. Vouchers accepted. **Credit cards:** None. **Open:** February 1 to November 30. **Children:** All ages. **Pets:** No. **Smoking:** No. **Provision for handicapped:** None. **Directions:** From Kilkenny city, take Bennetsbridge Road (R700) by the castle; the house is 2 miles down on the right, 1 mile from the roundabout.

This lovely ivy-covered house sits on a hill overlooking a patch of beautiful Irish farmland. Margaret and Tony give you a friendly welcome, and their two talented daughters play music and do stepdancing. Margaret has a good flair for decorating—her downstairs room has small-flowered wallpaper and looks out onto the garden; the others are green and pink or peach, two with striped paper; some have antique wardrobes. The Drennans have a handsome Victorian living room with antiques and a TV. Their full Irish Breakfast is augmented by apple jelly and yogurt, with offerings of French toast or pancakes with maple syrup sometimes. You may also have smoked kippers or smoked trout. The dining room, at the front of the house, has a farm view. You can easily reach the town center, with its castle, museums, and abbey; or try some golf, tennis, fishing, or horseback riding very close by.

The Laurels
Teresa and Jack Nolan
College Road
Kilkenny Town, County Kilkenny
Telephone: 056-61501; **FAX:** 056-71334; **E-Mail:** nolant@tinet.ie
Bedrooms: 4, all with private baths.
Rates: £19.50. 20 percent discount for children. Vouchers accepted.
Credit cards: Yes. **Open:** January 1 to December 20. **Children:** Yes, 4
and up. **Pets:** No. **Smoking:** No. **Provision for handicapped:** Yes, one
room. **Directions:** From Kilkenny Castle, turn left at lights at the inter-
section in town center; go up Patrick Street and turn right after Club
House Hotel. Then continue to end of road opposite Hotel Kilkenny.
Take next turning on right again. The Laurels is on the left.

Teresa and Jack(and their boxer dog, Cleo) are ready to give you
a friendly welcome with tea and biscuits and direct you to Kilkenny's
special tourist places, many a few minutes walk from their door. Their
remodeled, historic, and attractive home is a quiet place off the main
road. The lounge looks out on the front lawn through a large picture
window. The excellent beds in the pink, cream, and green rooms are
perfect for a good rest for weary travelers. All have electric blankets,
a TV, and hair dryers. Separate tables are filled in the morning with
the full Irish Breakfast, fruit and yogurt, cheese, eggs as you like, and
homemade brown bread, as well as special pudding or various waffles. It's a breakfast fit for a king! Walk to Kilkenny Castle. Nearby are
championship golf courses. The Nolans are especially good at directing you to historical and cultural features of the region. Fishing and
horseback riding are also nearby.

Newlands Country House
Aileen and Seamus Kennedy
Seven Houses, Danesfort
Kilkenny, County Kilkenny
Telephone: 056-2911; **FAX:** 056-29171; **E-Mail:** Newlands@indigo.ie
Bedrooms: 5, all with private baths.
Rates: £20 to 30 p.p.; Single £20-30. Vouchers accepted. £18 elegant dinner can be ordered 24 hours in advance. **Credit cards:** MasterCard and VISA. **Open:** All year, except Christmas. **Children:** No. **Pets:** No. **Smoking:** Restricted. **Provision for handicapped:** Yes, with help. **Directions:** From Kilkenny drive out Waterford Road (N10) to the roundabout. Continue on N10 for 4 miles and turn right at Harvester Pub. The house is .75 miles down on the right. The sign is on the main road.

Aileen and Seamus say, "nothing is too much trouble for our guests." They will greet you with tea in their handsome navy and pink living room by an open fire, and you will be shown to a lovely, large room, decorated in navy and pink or cerise. All have canopied beds, and some have a whirlpool bath and a refrigerator. Breakfast is served in a stunning dining room, glassed in with light foot windows. There is an elaborate menu offering dishes such as plaice, kippers, lamb's liver, and hash or potato waffles, besides the Irish Breakfast. Outside is another story. Seamus raises turkeys and calves for sale, but their pets are chickens, Donks the donkey, a pony named Fred, ducks, lambs, and Pea the peacock, who struts on top of bales of hay. You will be close to Kilkenny town, with its golf, tennis, and crafts at the Design Center across from the castle. Enjoy beautiful scenery and relaxing walks at this award-winning B&B.

Shillogher House
Michael and Goretti Hennessy
Callan Road (N76)
Kilkenny, County Kilkenny
Telephone: 056-63249/64865; **FAX:** 056-64865
Bedrooms: 5, all with private baths.
Rates: £17-18.50 p.p.; Single £25-35; 20 percent discount for children under 12. Vouchers accepted. **Credit cards:** VISA, Access. **Open:** All year, except December 20 to 27. **Children:** All ages. **Pets:** No. **Smoking:** No. **Provision for handicapped:** None. **Directions:** From Kilkenny City, go 1 km out the Callan Road, past the Hotel Kilkenny.

This fashionable brick house is very new and attractive. Its special feature is the glassed-in conservatory, where you may have tea and chat while enjoying the view of the gardens. The Hennessys will give you a warm welcome, and the house has a friendly atmosphere. The rooms on two floors are modern with grey and pink flowers, peach and navy, or pink and wine colors. An extra bathroom with a tub is tiled in delft blue and white. Tea makers are provided in each room. The dining room is stunning. The large breakfast selection includes the typical Irish Breakfast, baked beans, kippers, fresh plaice, waffles with poached egg and cheese, fresh fruit, cheese board, and yogurt. They are proud of their menu. The B&B is within a few minutes of all the sights of Kilkenny and 1 hour from Cavan. Golf, fishing, and tennis are nearby.

Carrickmourne House
Julie Doyle
New Ross Road
Thomastown, County Kilkenny
Telephone: 056-24124; **FAX:** 056-24124
Bedrooms: 5, all with private baths.
Rates: £18-20 p.p.; Single £23 -25 p.p.; Vouchers accepted. **Credit cards:** VISA, Access, Eurocard. **Open:** All year, except Christmas week. **Children:** 10 years or older. **Pets:** No. **Smoking:** Restricted. **Provision for handicapped:** None. **Directions:** From Thomastown follow the signs to Inistioge/New Ross (R700) for approximately 1 mile. The Carrickmourne House sign is on the left. Take that road up the hill for about 2 km (about 1.25 miles). The driveway is on your left.

This is a gem of a modern home surrounded by beautiful country scenery, on a woodsy hillside above the beautiful Nore Valley. Julie's husband is a custom builder, and it shows. The floors are new pine, all the doors are paneled mahogany, and the spacious bedrooms are really beautifully decorated in pinks and creams, blue and creams, forest greens, and rusts. The lot was selected from the Doyle family farm and trees were planted to complement the natural forest. Guests are invited to relax in the private TV lounge and browse through the local information brochures. Tea- and coffee-making facilities are in every room, as well as TVs. The full Irish Breakfast is first-rate, with freshly squeezed orange or grapefruit juice and the care of preparation setting it apart from the usual. You can visit Jerpoint Abbey; walk, ride, or golf at the famous Mount Juliet sporting estate; visit local gardens; or fish the Nore or Kings Rivers. This is a B&B you feel like visiting more than once.

COUNTY LAOIS

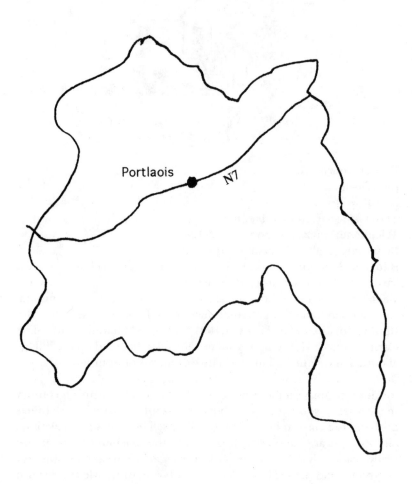

County Laois

County Laois is bordered by Counties Kilkenny, Kildare, Offaly, and Tipperary. It is generally flatland except for the Slieve Bloom Mountains in the northwest. Just four miles east of Portlaois is the Rock of Dunmase, which was the scene of many conflicts after the invasion of the Anglo-Normans. On its summit are the ruins of a castle that was razed by Cromwell's men in 1650. We enjoyed painting watercolors here one sunny day. It is a lovely hike up to the castle ruins and a very gratifying panorama from the top of the surrounding farmlands. We saw Jersey cows grazing nearby and a small, quaint Church of Ireland that is still used as a house of worship. Off the N7 going from Ballydavis north toward Portarlington is a beautiful Palladian-style mansion called Emo Court that is surrounded by beautiful gardens. Call ahead to ask when the mansion is open to the public. Drive through the Glen of O'Regan in the mountains or picnic and hike in the Monicknew Woods, south of Clonaslee. South of N7 on Swan Road is Timahoe, where there is a lovely 96-foot-high Round Tower from the 1100s.

County Kildare, the horseracing county, borders on Counties Dublin, Wicklow, Laois, and Offaly. The world-famous Curragh racecourse is seven miles northwest of the large town of Naas. Other courses are at Naas and Punchestown, east of the Curragh. See and ride the finest horses of Ireland at the Frenchfurze Riding Stables east of Curragh. Visit the Castletown House in Celbridge on the R403; social functions are still held here. The famous Japanese Gardens and National Stud Farm in Tully is a "must" visit. A good full-service restaurant, cafeteria style, is situated here. Also, there are many golf courses. Kildare Town is a beauty, with Brigid's Castle and the Celtic High Cross at Noone. Fish and cruise the canals and visit Mondello Park and the Steam Museum at Straffan.

Chez-Nous
Audrey Canavan
Kilminchy
Portlaois, County Laois
Telephone: 0502-21251
Bedrooms: 4, all with private baths. A large suite for 4-5 people possible.
Rates: £18.50-22; Single £25-30. Vouchers accepted. **Credit cards:** None. **Open:** All year, except at Christmas. **Children:** No. **Pets:** No. **Smoking:** No. **Provision for handicapped:** Restricted to walkers.
Directions: Chez-Nous is 2 miles out from the city center on Portarlington Road, on the left as you leave the city traveling eastward. Travelers are advised to call ahead for directions, as the nearby motorway is under construction.

We stayed at this lovely country home on our way from Dublin to Limerick. We enjoyed it so much we stayed two days and painted watercolors at nearby Dunamaise Castle on the Slieve Bloom Mountains. There is much to see and do in this region: golf, fishing, horseback riding, and walks. The bedrooms are beautifully decorated in cranberry and cream, pink, lavender, terra cotta, and peach, and furnished with canopy beds, which add a touch of grandeur. Rooms are named by color. The living room and hall are fashioned with fine and color-coordinated antiques. The conservatory at the rear where a sumptuous menu is served allows one to view the garden. The breakfast menu was impressive, with the full Irish Breakfast, or fish, pancakes, and/or potato cakes. Exceptional! The table setting when we were there was a beautiful yellow and deep blue. Audrey is very clever at decorating and making you feel welcome.

ALSO RECOMMENDED: COUNTY KILDARE

Athy, *Bellindrum Farm,* Vincent and Mary Gorman, Ballindrum. Telephone: 0507-26294. Bedrooms: 3, all with shared baths, all with H/C. Open April 1 to November 1. Free guided tour of this working dairy and tillage farm. Mrs. Gorman is a receptionist at the Japanese Gardens and National Stud Farm, so you can be advised as to what to see and do at this popular tourist site.

COUNTY LIMERICK

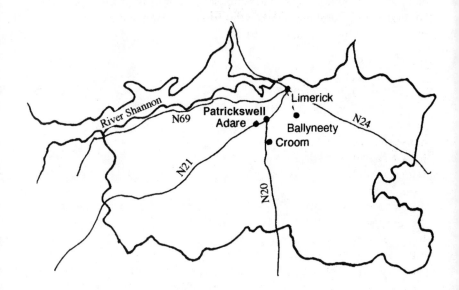

County Limerick

Limerick is a county of rolling farmlands much like Clare and is about the same size as Clare. Although Limerick is the closest large city to Shannon Airport, it's curious that it's in another county. Limerick City is old and charming, with good hotels and a theater. It was a ninth-century Danish town. Take a walk across the bridge to the old castle, or peruse the many antique shops, craft shops, and art galleries. The rooftops of the city make a colorful design when seen from the train station. Visit Limerick University on the city's outskirts and see the medieval treasures in the Hunt Museum there. Visit St. Mary's Cathedral from the twelfth century on Bridge Street and King John's Castle on Castle Street. The Tourist Information Office is in the old Granary on Michael Street. Bunratty Castle and Folk Park are only 10 miles northwest in County Clare.

Adare is a beautiful village about 10 miles southwest of Limerick. It has a row of shops in thatched cottages and a good selection of restaurants. Many people stay here on their first day in the Irish Republic. Adare Manor Hotel is an elaborate Gothic building on one thousand acres of grounds and gardens. Inside, heavy woodcarvings and crystal chandeliers are a sight. Fifty of the rooms have carved fireplaces. The public may walk all around these grounds for a small fee and visit the Ogham Stone in the woods. There is a fenced-in herb garden, and we met two painters there, husband and wife, both working at their easels. About thirty miles west, over the border in County Kerry, you may want to pay a visit to Listowel, where the famous playwright John B. Keane owns and runs a pub. He lives there and is a great storyteller.

Castle View House
The Glavin Family
Clonshire
Adare, County Limerick
Telephone and **FAX:** 061-396394; **E-Mail:** castleview@tinet.ie
Bedrooms: 4; 3 with private baths, 1 with shared.
Rates: £16-18 p.p.; Single £22; Discount for children under 12.
Vouchers accepted. £13 dinner. **Credit cards:** VISA, MasterCard/
Access, AMEX. **Open:** All year. **Children:** Yes. **Pets:** No. **Smoking:** No.
Provision for handicapped: Yes, but not wheelchairs. **Directions:** From
Limerick proceed to Adare on the N20 to Patrickswell, then N21 (the
Killarney Road) out of Adare. Castle View House is the second house
on the left.

   This pretty home is well managed by Colm and Kathleen Glavin
and is in a country setting next to Clonshire Equestrian Centre.
Rooms are neat and fashionably decorated in shades of lemon, peach,
and other pastel colors. There are many amenities such as tea- and coffee-making facilities, electric blankets, hair dryers, and direct-dial telephones. Your breakfast can be ordered from an unusually tasty menu
listing main entrées such as eggs any style and bacon and sausage, or
kippers, toasted cheese, beans and toast, or hot pancakes and maple
syrup. These other items besides eggs make this a nice break from
the usual Irish cooked breakfast. The dining room is cheery and
bright, with a view of the garden. We found our stay very pleasant and
comfortable. The peaceful and quiet country area makes for a nice
respite from the busy village and cities. Golf, badminton, tennis, and
walking tours are available in the charming town of Adare. Shannon
Airport is 35 minutes away. Visitors may enjoy Adare's new heritage
center, as well as castles and ruins.

Murphy's Cross
Ann Abbott
Adare, County Limerick
Telephone and **FAX:** 061-396042
Bedrooms: 5; 2 with private baths, 3 with shared.
Rates: £18 p.p. private bath; £16 p.p. shared bath; Vouchers accepted.
Credit cards: None. **Open:** January 18 to December 15. **Children:** Yes.
Pets: No. **Smoking:** Restricted. **Provision for handicapped:** None.
Directions: The cottage is in Adare on Main Killarney Road, the last house on left at the "T" junction.

This 1840s cottage has the charm of an early Irish home, so it is a little different than the ordinary home. Farm animals greet you in the front yard. It used to be a thatched cottage and it has a huge 10-foot traditional Irish hearth with an old black stove in the dining room. There is a balcony for access to the bedrooms via steep stairs. Some bedrooms have slanted ceilings. The new one at the back is done with a pretty pine ceiling. All in all, the effect is enchanting. A large bathroom with tub and shower serves the shared rooms, which have their own sink. The long table accommodates a large group for an extraordinary breakfast that includes the standard Irish cooked one (choice of eggs), but is nicely augmented by smoked kippers or fresh honeycomb yogurt. Cereals such as muesli or oatmeal (porridge), and fresh fruit in season are also available. Guests have a large cozy sitting room, with fireplace and TV, on the other side of the dining room. Adare is a quaint town you'll surely want to visit. There is a castle, an abbey, the famous Adare Manor Hotel, and numerous great restaurants in all price ranges. Mrs. Abbott will advise you on these and the golfing, tennis, and antique shopping.

Westfield House
Anne Donegan
Ballingarry Road
Adare, County Limerick
Telephone: 061-396539
Bedrooms: 3, all with private bath
Rates: £18 p.p.; 25 percent discount for children; Vouchers accepted.
Credit cards: VISA. **Open:** April 1 to November 1. **Children:** Yes, all
ages. **Pets:** No. **Smoking:** No. **Provision for handicapped:** None.
Directions: Drive through Adare Village. Take first left off N21 onto
Ballingarry Road (R519). Drive for .5 mile. Westfield House is the red-
bricked dormer on the left.

This lovely modern home is situated in a woodland area with beautiful landscaped gardens. Welcoming tea is served upon your arrival.
Rooms are large and bright and decorated annually, currently in pink
and wine, navy blue, and lemon. Guests have a choice of breakfast
from a Ballymaloe menu of delectable treats. Anne guarantees personal attention to your needs. Adare is "Ireland's Prettiest Village."
This is a golfer's haven and good touring base. Shannon airport is only
30 minutes away. Other recreational features are: fishing, horseback
riding, pitch and putt, shooting, archery, and the Heritage Center.

Avondoyle
Evelyn Moore
Ballyclough, Rossbrien
Limerick, County Limerick
Telephone: 061-301590; **FAX:** 061-301501; **E-Mail:** avondoyl@iol.ie
Bedrooms: 4; 2 with private bath, 2 with shared bath.
Rates: £18 p.p. private bath; £16 shared bath. 40 percent discount for
children. Accepts vouchers. **Credit cards:** Yes. VISA, MasterCard.
Open: January 2 to December 20. **Children:** Yes, all ages. **Pets:** No.
Smoking: Yes, limited. **Provision for handicapped:** None. **Directions:**
Turn off N20 at Crescent Shopping Center, 2 miles south of Limerick
City. Follow Rossbrien sign at roundabout after 1 mile. Go straight
through next 2 roundabouts and after .5 miles turn right to Avondoyle.

This large dormer bungalow is located on an acre of mature gardens. It is in a tranquil rural setting in the first three miles outside of Limerick. The guests have their own private entrance hall and a spacious living room. Their savory breakfast menu can be seen on the Web site (http://www.iol.ie). The bedrooms are tastefully decorated in soothing colors and have all conveniences. You'll find 50 places of historic interest from 3000 B.C. within an easy reach of this home. There is an 18-hole golf course in Limerick, many equestrian centers, sea, river, and lake fishing, and excellent Irish music in pubs. When remarking about Avondoyle, a local B&B owner used these words: "Evelyn makes all her guests feel welcome and at ease. She is highly regarded with her professional standards."

Acacia Cottage
Mary Dundon
2 Foxfield, Dooradoyle Road
Dooradoyle
Limerick, County Limerick
Telephone and **FAX:** 061-304757; **E-Mail:** acaciacottage@tinet.ie
Bedrooms: 3, all with private bath.
Rates: £18.50 p.p., Single £25. 20 percent discount for children.
Vouchers accepted. **Credit cards:** VISA, MasterCard, and Access.
Open: All year. **Children:** Yes, all ages. **Pets:** No. **Smoking:** No.
Provision for handicapped: None. **Directions:** 1 km off N20 at round-
about at Crescent Shopping Center in Dooradoyle (south suburb of
Limerick town) go straight through next 2 small roundabouts. Look
for Acacia Cottage on right in Foxfield Development.

This cozy, comfortable, cottage-style family home has a wide variety of comfortable bedrooms done in peach and blue, pink and green,
and blue-green and yellow—all Laura Ashley-style. The breakfast
menu affords guests a choice of chilled juice, hot and cold cereals, and
a main course of six choices, from the full Irish Breakfast to the
"Acacia Cottage" special of scrambled eggs and salmon. Mary pro-
claims her place to "be a haven of comfort and caring service." Acacia
Cottage is 20 minutes from Bunratty and Shannon Airport, and close
to Limerick town. This will allow you to visit historic Limerick, with
St. John's Castle, St. Mary's Cathedral, and the Hunt Museum.
Recreation and entertainment nearby includes golf, horseback riding,
cinema, pubs, restaurants, shopping, and live concerts.

Lurriga Lodge
Lily Woulfe
Patrickswell, County Limerick
Telephone and **FAX:** 061-355411
Bedrooms: 4, all with private bath.
Rates: £18 p.p.; 25 percent discount for children; Vouchers accepted.
Credit cards: VISA and MasterCard. **Open:** April 1 to October 31.
Children: Yes, all ages. **Pets:** Yes. **Smoking:** No. **Provision for handicapped:** Yes, wheelchair accessible. **Directions:** Drive south from Limerick city toward Adare, on the N20/21. At the split of N20/21 is the Lurriga Lodge sign. Then 500 yds. farther south after Patrickswell look again for sign on the right. Lurriga Lodge is 200 meters off main Limerick-Killarney road.

This luxurious, Tudor-style country home with palms and garden, patio, and play area has been drawing rave reviews from guests for many years. Many travelers return year after year. The upper rooms overlook 220 acres of farmlands and woods abundant in wildlife. Pretty rooms with natural wood finishing and meadow-colored and floral-patterned fabrics grace the bedrooms. Antiques, Oriental and African art Michael collected on his globetrotting with British Airways, enhance the common rooms. Breakfast is rated by guests as the best in Ireland, and the homemade scones are prizewinners. Lily and Michael can assist you with your dining plans, visits to local pubs and Irish music, and local attractions such as the thatched cottages in Adare and the Adare Manor hotel. Your kind and gracious hosts will make your stay a memorable one.

ALSO RECOMMENDED

Adare, *Abbey Lodge,* Mrs. Mary Dundon, Kildimo Road. Telephone: 061-396776. Bedrooms: 3, all with private baths. Credit cards accepted. Award-winning breakfasts. Cozy, comfortable home in Adare village; walk to restaurants.

Adare, *Hollywood House,* Peter and Miriam O'Shaughnessy, Croagh, situated 5 km from Adare village. Telephone: 061-396237. Bedrooms: 4, all private baths, 2 in the room or en suite. Open April 1 to November 1. Large 1690s historical farmhouse with beautifully decorated rooms. Regional award winner, 1992. Beautiful setting among tall copper beeches. Tennis courts available. Charming couple.

Ballyneety, *Four Seasons,* Mrs. Mary Conway Ryan, Boherlock. Telephone: 061-351365. Bedrooms: 6, 4 with private baths. Credit cards and vouchers accepted. Open all year except Christmas Day. 7 km southeast of Limerick; 30 minutes to Shannon Airport. Recommended by Judy and Jerry Klinkowitz of Cedar Falls, Iowa.

Croom, *Caherass House,* Eddie O'Donnell. Telephone: 061-397053/397704. Bedrooms: 5, 4 with private baths. All major credit cards. In Croom Village take a right off N20 toward Adare; Caherass House is on right, opposite the Maigue River. Working farm bed and breakfast. Unusual hospitality. Recommended by Christian and Jody Nilsson of York, Maine.

Limerick, *Shemond House,* Raymond and Sheila Devine, Ballyglass, Clonara. Telephone: 061-34367. Bedrooms: 6, 5 with private baths. Modern family-run home. In scenic surroundings, 20 minutes from Shannon Airport and Bunratty Castle. Recommended by Mary McGinty of Ardeevin B&B, Lough Eske, Donegal Town, County Donegal.

County Louth

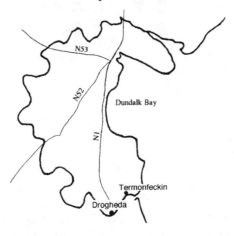

County Louth is very small, about the same size as Dublin, and one of its features is that it borders on County Down in Northern Ireland. It also has the Irish Sea along the whole east coast. The Cooley Peninsula in the north, above Dundalk, is a very special sight to see. Begin at Ballymascanlon, take R173, and do a loop around the point of land, stopping at the quaint village of Gyles Quay, and a little farther, King John's Castle. Some of the green sheep-covered hills in the country-side there remind us of scenes in Dingle.

Dundalk is the largest city in Louth. It is a port and has history back to A.D. 600, and has churches and cathedrals to visit. The salt marshes east of the city are home to one of Ireland's best bird sanctuaries, and you may spot some very unusual species there. North of town, visit the very curious rounded Neolithic mound called Proleek Dolmen, dating to 3000 B.C.

Industrial Drogheda, surrounded by farms, in the south on the Boyne River, claims a large corner of the famous Battle of the Boyne site. This very historical Viking town dates back to A.D. 911. It was once entirely walled in, and you may still view parts of the wall and the lovely medieval St. Laurence's Gate. Visit Monasterboice, with tenth-century High Crosses, and Mellifont Abbey near the Meath border. In the north of Louth, you can drive to Iniskeen in Monaghan, and in the south, you can drive over to see the famed stony tombs at Newgrange in County Meath.

Highfields House Farm

Kitty and Jim McEvoy
Termonfeckin
Drogheda, County Louth
Telephone: 041-9822172
Bedrooms: 3, all with private baths.
Rates: £18 p.p.; Single £20; 50 percent discount for children under 12.
Vouchers not accepted. **Credit cards:** None. **Open:** March 1 to
October 31. **Children:** All ages. **Pets:** No. **Smoking:** No. **Provision for
handicapped:** None. **Directions:** From Drogheda town, take R166 to
Termonfeckin, 5 miles northeast. Go down in a vale and over a humpy
bridge, and just on the left see the pub and Triple House Restaurant.
Highfields House Farm is just past it on the left at the corner, a 2-
story stucco with a stone wall and white gate.

This lovely 1725 farmhouse has been in the McEvoy family since
1928. Termonfeckin is in a quaint and picturesque section of
Drogheda, while the town center is rather dowdy. Kitty and Jim may
greet you in the farmyard; then you will get a cup of tea. We had ours
in the wonderful antique kitchen. The house has a handsome big
entryway and the rooms are all large and nostalgic, with antique beds
and flowered covers in soft colors of lilac, peach and cream, and yellow.
The dining room has a fireplace and a large hand-carved rosewood
sideboard. The huge lounge has a TV and antique furniture, featuring lovely matching Victorian "fainting chairs." Kitty was given an
award by Bord Fáilte for Best Breakfast in the county. Her full Irish
Breakfast includes homemade brown bread with raisins, fresh eggs
from their own red hens, fruit, and white or black pudding. Ask about
the secret room and the tunnels in the fields; Jim loves to tell the history of the house and town. Livestock, grain, turkeys, and goats are
raised on the farm. One mile from the Irish Sea and a sandy beach, this
is a good place to visit the Battle of the Boyne artifacts, the Druid site at
Newgrange, two 18-hole golf courses, pubs, and castles of Drogheda.

Tullyesker Country House
Cepta McDonnell
N1 Road, Monasterboice
Drogheda, County Louth
Telephone: 041-9830430; **FAX:** 041-9832624
Bedrooms: 5, all with private baths.
Rates: £19 p.p. to £24 p.p. for a double room. Vouchers not accepted.
Credit cards: None. **Open:** February 1 to November 30. **Children:**
Yes, 10 or older. **Pets:** No. **Smoking:** No. **Provision for handicapped:**
None. **Directions:** From Drogheda, take N1 north. The B&B is 3 miles
north of Drogheda on N1 at Tullyesker Hill. The house is on the right-
hand side, surrounded by trees.

This marvelous getaway B&B is nested on Tullyesker Hill amid four
acres of gardens with panoramic views of the Boyne Valley. Cepta
McDonnell's luxurious jewel-toned rooms are lavishly appointed with
electric blankets, TVs, hair dryers, toiletries, and tea- and coffee-making facilities. The breakfast menu has more items to choose from than
any other we've seen in Ireland. It includes such unusual items as a
cheese platter with savory biscuits, poached smoked herring with lemon
and grilled tomato, Irish smoked salmon and eggs, chicken liver pâté,
and what they call a "symphony of fruit," a Tullyesker favorite. Besides
these and many different types of eggs, porridge, cereal, and yogurt,
there are homemade scones and bread, Bewley's tea and coffee (including decaf!), and Cadbury's hot chocolate. There are tennis courts and
walks on the property in the gardens or the woodland. Within driving
distance is the 17-foot-high Monasterboice Cross, which has many fig-
ures and ornamental designs carved in stone. And just over the border
in Meath are the Mellifont Abbey, famous Boyne Valley, Hill of Stone,
and fascinating burial mound at Newgrange. The ocean is only a few
miles to the east, and the oldest building in the world is nearby.

COUNTY MAYO

County Mayo

Mayo is another very large county with two lakes, Lough Conn and Lough Mask. From Sligo, you may want to take the R313 out to the Mullet Peninsula to the northwest to explore the unspoiled rolling farmlands with sheep and cattle, and its bogs. There is good fishing on the rocks and from the shore at most coastal areas. The town between two bays, Belmullet, is quite fancy and modernized. Enjoy the views of sweeping, multicolored grasses of the bogs, and the mystical view of Benwee Head with its stark profile. Farther south you may drive out R319 directly to Achill Island for a look at high cliffs and sandy beaches, and there are pubs with music, too.

You may cut down to the classy town of Westport. It has a nice town center with lots of shops, galleries, cafés, and pubs, and it is very proud of its Sailing Centre. There are some breathtaking views of Clew Bay and Croagh Patrick Mountain, with the huge white statue of St. Patrick standing watch at the top. Here St. Patrick made a 40-day fast, and in honor of him, modern-day pilgrims climb this mountain on the last Sunday of each July.

Throughout Mayo there are a good deal of antique and craft shops. Cong, on the southern border, has the ruins of the Royal Abbey of Cong, Ashford Castle, and it was the town where most of the movie *The Quiet Man* was filmed. Knock, a town in the eastern section of Mayo, is known for its Marian Shrine, where an apparition of Our Lady was seen in 1879 at the church of St. John the Baptist. Thousands of pilgrims visit this each year.

Devard
Nora Ward
Westport Road
Castlebar, County Mayo
Telephone and **FAX:** 094-23462
Bedrooms: 5; 4 with private bath (en suite), 1 with separate.
Rates: £18 p.p.; £16 shared bath; Single £21; 50 percent discount for children. Vouchers accepted. **Credit cards:** None. **Open:** January 1 to December 20. **Children:** All ages. **Pets:** No. **Smoking:** Yes. **Provision for handicapped:** Yes, first-floor ramp. **Directions:** Devard is on Westport Road (the N60), 1 km outside town on the left just after Spar convenience store.

This is a really comfortable modern bungalow with a very pleasant hostess in Nora Ward. All the bedrooms are fitted with TV, tea- and coffee-making facilities, electric blankets, and matching bedspreads and curtains, and are spacious. They are done in burgundies, brown, and blue, with cocoa rugs, and peach with white and cream duvets. The baths are also large with bidet, shower, toilet, tiles to the ceiling in pretty coordinated colors, gold fixtures, and parquet floors. Devard is set apart from the usual in style and décor. One room has a beautiful view of the award-winning rose garden. Breakfast is the full Irish cooked breakfast, with white and black puddings, French toast, porridge, yogurt, fruit, etc. But the brewed coffee hit the spot after drinking so much instant for breakfast. We are spoiled; we like ours fresh brewed. There is a handsome marble fireplace in the combination sitting and dining room. But to us the gracious and genuinely warm Nora Ward made this home special. This is a good place to stop while traveling south to Westport from Ballina or Sligo Town. Check out the Breaffy House Hotel for an evening meal. Golf, swimming, tennis, horseback riding, and fishing are some of the area activities.

Lakeview House
Mary and Joseph Moran
Westport Road
Castlebar, County Mayo
Telephone: 094-22374
Bedrooms: 4, all with private bath.
Rates: £18 p.p. 50 percent discount for children. Vouchers accepted.
Credit cards: None. **Open:** March to November. **Children:** Yes, all
ages. **Pets:** No. **Smoking:** No. **Provision for handicapped:** Limited.
Directions: 4 km from Castlebar on the Westport side, on the main N5
route.

This pretty bungalow on spacious grounds has bedrooms all on
the main floor, decorated in beautiful pastel colors. Mary has been
welcoming guests to her home since 1973. The lounge has TV and a
peat fire. Tea and coffee is offered upon arrival. Her breakfasts are
exceptional, with homemade bread and scones. Many of their valued
clients return home to try out Mary's recipes. She has had many repeat
guests for the past 26 years. Her record of thank-you letters documents
this bed and breakfast's high standards. Guests make such comments
as, "I award you four stars and an A+"; "these two wonderful people
[Mary and Joe] deserve the highest accolades for their kindness,
warmth and accommodation"; and "the type of hospitality shown by
the Morans will certainly encourage more American visitors to come
to Ireland." Golf, bowling, swimming, horseback riding, country walks,
bicycle for hire, and mountain climbing are some of the recreations
available.

Silvar
Marion Silke
Ballinrobe Road
Castlebar, County Mayo
Telephone: 094-22096
Bedrooms: 3, all with private baths.
Rates: £24 p.p.; Discount for children. Vouchers not accepted. **Credit cards:** None. **Open:** May to October 31st. **Children:** Baby to teens. **Pets:** No. **Smoking:** Outside in garden. **Provision for handicapped:** None. **Directions:** Silvar is situated on Route N84, 2 km from Castlebar town.

This ultramodern and newly renovated home with beautiful landscaped garden greeting you in the front is hosted by a gracious lady, Marion Silke. She will see to your every needs with a warm welcome and comfortable accommodations decorated in relaxing colors. All rooms have tea-making facilities and satellite TV. She will also arrange for your transport for social outings. There is a large guest lounge and a pleasant dining area. Many guests have recorded their enthusiasm with comments like, "we feel like home," "you fed me like a queen," or, "wonderful Irish hospitality." We are glad to add Silvar into our new list of high-standard B & Bs. Nearby there is angling, bicycles for hire, golf, horseback riding, a gym and leisure complex, a swimming pool, squash courts, and tennis courts. In addition, one may take scenic walks or enjoy the cinema.

Carrabaun House
Angela Gavin
Carrabaun
Westport, County Mayo
Telephone: 098-26196; **FAX:** 098-28466
Bedrooms: 6, all with private baths.
Rates: £18 p.p.; Single £22; Vouchers accepted. **Credit cards:** Yes.
Open: All year except Christmas. **Children:** All ages. **Pets:** No. **Smoking:** No. **Provision for handicapped:** Yes. **Directions:** From Castlebar, you enter on Castlebar Street. Go over the bridge, up Bridge Street, and turn right at the clock. Cross over Shop Street and continue on to Monmument Street. Take a left up Peter Street and continue on Tubber Hill Road. At the back of the hill, turn left on N59 after the railway bridge. After the Maxol gas station, look for the Carrabaun House sign on the left. Enter the driveway through the large white pillars.

This neo-Georgian home, with panoramic views of Croagh Patrick, Clew Bay, Clare Islands, and the rolling green fields and stone walls, sits atop a hill just outside Westport, so you have the peace and quiet of a country setting, yet all the many tourist features of Westport close at hand. We found the entryway and ascending staircase of regal proportions. The equally spacious rooms are all very new and colorfully decorated in lime greens, pinks and reds, and one in periwinkle blue with a delft-blue duvet. All have beautiful matching drapes and white dressing tables. You get a bright and fresh feeling. A new bay window has been added to the guest lounge on the first floor. Ask the Gavins to point out the best walks, golfing, bowling, fishing spots, deep-sea fishing, and other recreational features of Westport. But come morning they will stuff you full of a tasty Irish Breakfast plus choices of puddings, cheeses, fruit, yogurt, etc.

ALSO RECOMMENDED

Charlestown, *Hawthorne House,* Mrs. Josephine Keane, N5. Telephone: 094-54237. Bedrooms: 5, all with shared baths. Lovely and elegantly furnished period house. Charming and courteous innkeeper.

Westport, *Fair Lawns,* Mrs. Sheila Ree, Lecanvey. Telephone: 098-64950. Bedrooms: 4, all with private baths. Vouchers accepted. £11 dinner. Noted for excellent hospitality and cuisine. Recommended by Maeve Walsh of Tubbercurry, County Sligo.

Westport, *Glenderan,* Dermot and Ann O'Flaherty, Rosbeg. Telephone: 098-26585. Bedrooms: 3, 2 with private baths. 1 km outside Westport, 600 m off Louisburg Road.

County Meath

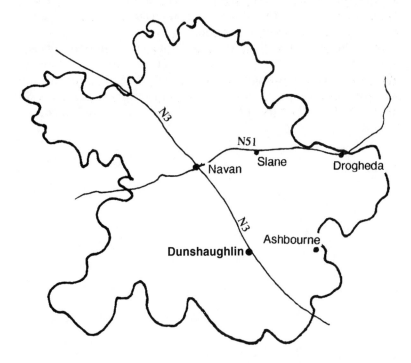

Although County Meath borders on County Dublin, the people are as far from the worldly urban style of Dubliners as Irishmen can be. The mystical spirits of the ancients prevail. In this country made up strictly of farms and small towns, history in the form of Bronze-Age tombs and burial mounds swirls about. The Hill of Tara, where most believe the High Kings of Ireland reigned in the eleventh century, is just south of Navan. Newgrange, a circular tomb made of stones probably about 1500 B.C., is preserved in excellent condition. A large rock positioned at its opening only allows a thin stream of light inside on December 21 each year for 17 minutes. There are curious markings on some of the stones inside. It's quite an experience to stand inside with a guide, with artificial light and other visitors, and ponder its vast age. Newgrange has smaller lines waiting to enter in September and October. In order to get in on December 21, you must put your name on a list that's backed up a few years. They only escort about 10 to 14 in at a time. Even in summer, you should take a look from outside. The mounds of Nowth and Dowth nearby are worth a visit, too.

There are also more Boyne battlefields to visit in the area. Kids of all ages will enjoy the working Newgrange Farm in Slane, where they can touch every kind of soft farm animal imaginable. There are castles, too, at Trim and south of Navan.

A visit to the town of Kells will round out your magical tour. This is where Scottish monks in the ninth century, in St. Columba's Monastery, wrote, illustrated, and preserved *The Book of Kells,* a Latin interpretation of the four Gospels. A copy of it can be seen in St. Columba's Church of Ireland, there in Kells. The original, of course, can be viewed at Trinity College in Dublin.

River Boyne House
Mary Friel
Old Bridge
Drogheda, County Meath
Telephone: 041-9836180
Bedrooms: 3, all private baths.
Rates: £18 p.p. **Credit cards:** VISA and MasterCard. **Open:** March 30 to October 31. **Children:** Yes, all ages. **Pets:** No. **Smoking:** Yes. **Provision for handicapped:** Yes, all rooms on the first floor. **Directions:** Call ahead for directions.

This lovely dormered bungalow with a pretty garden at front is heralded by guests as, "very friendly," "magical," "one of the best we had in Eire," "warmest welcome we ever had in Eire," and "beautiful." What more can one say? Mary has decorated the bedrooms in cream and green, white pine and blue-green, and pink and cream. There is a large sitting room for guests, with tea/coffee facilities and TV. This bed and breakfast is situated on the Boyne Battlefield of 1690. It is near to Newgrange, a huge ancient burial mound that predates Stonehenge. There is golf, fishing, and nature walks, and a beach 10 km away. Drogheda is 3 km away. Mary was nominated for the "Best Family Home of 1997" award. Mary has a breakfast menu printed in four languages—French, German, Italian, and English. She serves an Irish Breakfast with orange juice, choice of cereal, fresh fruit and yogurt, and any type of eggs, plus porridge on request. The dining room with fireplace and separate tables looks out on green fields with cows and sheep grazing there.

Roughgrange Farm
Irene McDonnell
Donore
Drogheda, County Meath
Telephone: 041-9823147
Bedrooms: 3; all with private baths.
Rates: £18 p.p.; Discounts for children negotiable. Vouchers accepted.
Credit cards: VISA. **Open:** March to November. **Children:** All ages.
Pets: No. **Smoking:** No. **Provision for handicapped:** None. **Directions:**
From Drogheda take Donore Village Road on the south side of Boyne
River. In Donore Village, go right toward Dublin Road (N2).
Roughgrange is on your left.

This beautiful seventeenth-century farmhouse B&B is situated in
the most historic of valleys in Ireland. It overlooks the scenic Boyne
Valley and is 1.5 km from Newgrange, Nowth, and Dowth. The large
living and dining rooms are furnished with handsome period
antiques, and with fireplaces to provide warmth and coziness. A full,
sumptuous country breakfast is served on a large antique table.
Homemade scones, brown bread, black and white pudding, tomato,
plus traditional breakfast will get you off to a good start as you visit
some of Ireland's most cherished treasures of antiquity—the Hill of
Tara, Mellifont Abbey, Monasterboice Crosses, Newgrange, or Kells.
Newgrange is a most impressive pre-Celtic tomb. Salmon, trout, and
coarse fishing on 280 acres is free to guests. If you like pastoral scenery
with sheep and cattle, this is the place for you. If you have any energy
left over, golf, swimming, and tennis are within easy reach. The
McDonnells will greet you with a warm welcome and advise you of
the way to get the most out of your visit to Meath.

Gaulstown House
Kathryn M. Delaney
Dunshaughlin, County Meath
Telephone and **FAX:** 01-8259147
Bedrooms: 3, all with private baths. **Rates:** £20 p.p. 20 percent discount for children. Vouchers accepted. Table d'hôte dinner available at £17 p.p. **Credit cards:** VISA and MasterCard. **Open:** April to September. **Children:** Yes, 10 years or older. **Pets:** No. **Smoking:** No. **Provision for handicapped:** None. **Directions:** Exit off N3 at Dunslaughlin, then take the Airport Road (R125) for 2 km. Keep left at the "Y" in the road. House is 400 yards past golf club entrance.

This elegant early-nineteenth-century Georgian farmhouse set in rural parkland will let you relax and enjoy the Meath countryside. Furnished in antiques of the Georgian and Victorian period, this home, with its warm colors, in keeping with the age of the house, will afford you comfort and style in the grand tradition of country living. Tea and coffee facilities are available in rooms. There is a full Irish Breakfast each morning with a choice of menu, and the evening meal features farm-fresh vegetables and their own farm-reared lamb. Kathryn has attended the Ballymaloe Cookery School. The dining room is a rich pink with matching carpet and one large table. The drawing room is particularly sunny, pale yellow with floral curtains and chairs. It features a lovely black fireplace. The farm is a drystock farm and has twice won the Agri Tourism Award and the Family Farm of the Year Award, and been highlighted in many travel guides. Your hosts will be glad to arrange golfing, riding lessons, hunting, and fishing. Places to visit within 30 minutes are: Butterstream Gardens, Grove Gardens, The Hill of Tara, Newgrange, and Mellifont Abbey. There is a Farm Nature Walk right on the property. Dublin city Airport and Ferryport are only 30 minutes away.

Boyne Dale
Paula Casserly
Donaghmore, Slane Road
Navan, County Meath
Telephone and **FAX:** 046-28015
Bedrooms: 4; 3 with private baths, 1 with shared.
Rates: £16 p.p. private bath; Single £21; 20 percent discount for children under 12. Vouchers accepted. **Credit cards:** None. **Open:** April 1 to October 31. **Children:** Up to age 12. **Pets:** None. **Smoking:** No. **Provision for handicapped:** Yes, with help. **Directions:** The house is 2.4 km east of Navan town on the Slane Road (the N51).

This modern bungalow is in the countryside of the famed Boyne Valley, site of the historical Battle of the Boyne. Paula Casserly is bright, enjoyable, and very organized. The rooms—orange, blues and cream, and pink—are pretty, with wide windows overlooking gardens. Hot beverage and hair-drying facilities are in each room, and a restful TV lounge is available for guests. The handsome dining room has a fireplace, separate tables, and a large window with a view. Choose your breakfast from a menu. It is typical Irish with a choice of beans or cheese; ask ahead for yogurt. Horseback riding is ½ mile away. An 18-hole golf course, public swimming pools, snooker, a racecourse, and movies are all nearby. Visit the Dunmore Castle, and September is best to see Newgrange and the Round Tower, 10 minutes away. Other historical monuments are located nearby, including the Newgrange Castle.

ALSO RECOMMENDED

Ashbourne, *Aisling,* Evelyn and Seamus Daly, Baltransa, on Dublin/Derry Road (N2). Telephone: 01-350359/351135. Bedrooms: 9, 6 with private baths. Vouchers accepted. Modern home, 2 km outside Ashbourne. Ideal for Dublin Airport, 17 km away. Recommended by Josephine Martin of Mount Royd country home, Carrigans, County Donegal.

Navan, *Gainstown House,* Mrs. Mary Reilly, Trim Road (2 miles south of Navan). Telephone: 046-21448. Bedrooms: 4, 1 private bath, but H/C in room. Vouchers accepted. Spacious period farm residence, pleasantly decorated, on 200 acres. Fishing, golf, swimming, and horseback riding available locally.

Slane, *Conyngham Arms Hotel,* Mr. Kevin MacKen. Telephone: 041-24155; FAX: 041-24205. Book in U.S. on 800-223-1588, Canada 800-531-6767. Bedrooms: 16. A village inn on main road. The deluxe bedrooms are beautiful. A good bargain for inn accommodations.

Slane, *Hillview,* Mrs. Lily Bagnall, Gernonstown. Telephone: 041-24327. Bedrooms: 5, 3 with private baths. Vouchers accepted. Just a mile west of Slane center off N51, take road on right. Modern home looking out on beautiful Boyne Valley. Well decorated. Very clean and neat.

COUNTY MONAGHAN

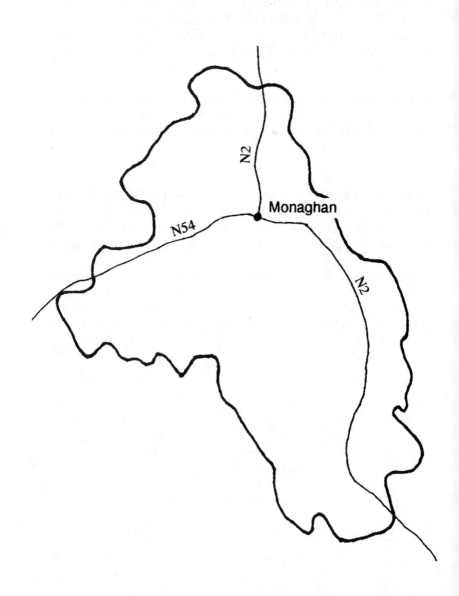

County Monaghan

On entering quiet County Monaghan, you note that there are fewer cars, although the road is wider and the countryside stretches out in wide sweeps of farms. In Carrickmackross you'll find traditional lace, which you can buy at the Carrickmackross Lace Coop. Inishkeen is the birthplace of the celebrated Irish poet Patrick Kavanagh. Monaghan is a good-sized town of fishing fame, and is also known for its County Museum, which was an old market house in 1792. Andy's Restaurant in the center of town has good food and service, reasonable prices, and lots of class. We stopped there for lunch and were very impressed. Rossmere Forest Park, with its beautiful nature walks and lakes, is just to the south of Monaghan town. The town of Clones to the southwest is noted for its Augustinian Abbey of the twelfth century with its 75-foot Round Tower, a tenth-century Celtic carved cross in the town center, and the Clones Lace Centre, where you can buy the lace of the ancient craft passed down through the centuries.

The Cedars
Mary McArdle
Clones Road, Monaghan
County Monaghan
Telephone: 047-82783
Bedrooms: 3; 2 with private baths, 1 with shower in room, toilet in hall.
Rates: £18 p.p.; Single £21.50-24.50; 25 percent discount for children
under 12. Vouchers accepted. **Credit cards:** None. **Open:** January 8
to December 18. **Children:** All ages. **Pets:** Yes. **Smoking:** No. **Provision for handicapped:** None. **Directions:** From Monaghan Town, take
Clones Road (N54, A3); the house is on a hill at the end of a row of
houses on the right, about .5 mile. You'll see a shamrock and a large
sign for Agrihealth Company at the foot of the driveway shared by The
Cedars.

This modern, stone-front, split-level home on a hillside has great
views of the town of Monaghan and the rolling hills or "drumlins" of
the countryside. It was recommended to us by the owner of Andy's
Restaurant in the town center. The bedrooms are attractive, clean, and
neat, and guests have a private entry at the side door. The living room
has a comfortable settee and chairs, TV, and tea-making facilities.
The dining room has a balcony and huge sliding-glass doors for a
grand view of the hills. Besides the typical Irish Breakfast, Mary offers
freshly squeezed orange juice, grapefruit segments and prunes, several cereals including porridge, and percolated coffee. Recreational
features of the area are walking in Forest Park or Beagan Mountains,
fishing, 18-hole golf, horseback riding, and a swimming pool.

Willow Bridge Lodge
Ann Holden
Silver Stream
Armagh Road
Monaghan Town, County Monaghan
Telephone and **FAX:** 47-81054; **E-Mail:** motelbandb@tinet.ie
Bedrooms: 4, 2 with private baths. 2 motel-style suites with full facilities.
Rates: £22.50 p.p. private baths; Single £25; discount for children.
Vouchers not accepted. **Credit cards:** None. **Open:** January 4 to
December 20. **Children:** Yes, all ages. **Pets:** No. **Smoking:** No. **Provision for handicapped:** None. **Directions:** Take Armagh Road (N12)
out of Monaghan Town. Pass army camp on left, a straight stretch of
500 yards. At Willow Bridge Lodge sign turn left, go down the driveway
and over a small bridge; the large bungalow to the left on top of the
hill is Willow Bridge.

This handsome and spacious motel-style bed and breakfast is set
in a beautiful garden with panoramic views. The interior has a creative
blend of red and blue colors and natural wood paneling. All rooms
are furnished with king-sized beds, beautiful natural wood floors, en
suite baths, TVs with satellite and movie channels, hair dryers, and
tea and coffee facilities. There is an inside spacious and attractive
lounge for conversing with other guests, furnished with a large TV and
comfortable leatherette chairs and sofas, and an outside patio where
you can enjoy nature and the fresh air. Monaghan is the crossroads
of Ireland, the main crossing point for ancient Irish kings, where they
crisscrossed to do battle. But today, you can break your journey for a
peaceful and warm welcome by Bill and Ann Holden. A full Irish
Breakfast is served.

COUNTY OFFALY

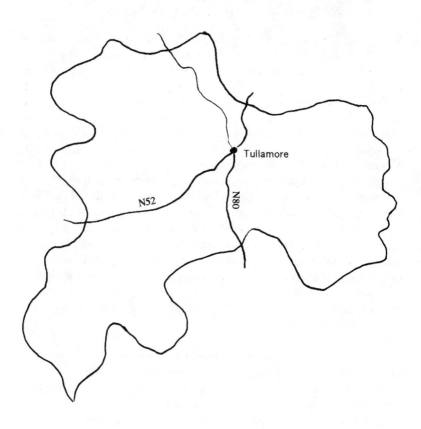

County Offaly

Bordered by Westmeath on the north, Kildare on the east, Laois and Tiperrary on the south, and the River Shannon and Galway on the west, Offaly is centrally located in Ireland but is not far from Dublin. Visit the Birr Castle, with its surrounding gardens and one-hundred-acre demesne. It was originally a fort that bore the hallmark of the Normans, Cromwellians, Jacobites, and Williamites, and survived numerous sieges. See the ruins of Conmacnoise on the left bank of the Shannon, one of the most extensive monastic sites in Ireland, including a cathedral, two roundhouses, churches, a castle, and Celtic crosses. St. Ciaran founded a monastery here in A.D. 545. This settlement derives much of its beauty from being on the Shannon. The Irish Mist factory can be visited in Tullamore, and the Grand Canal that passes through here offers visitors an opportunity for boating and bird-watching. Banagher on the Shannon also offers cruises from its marina, an excellent place to hire a pleasure cruiser. The Slieve Bloom Mountains and the Shannon give Offaly its special character.

Canal View Country House
Bernadette Keyes
Killina Road
Rahan
Tullamore, County Offaly
Telephone: 0506-55868; **FAX:** 0506-55034
Bedrooms: 4; 3 with private baths, 1 with shared.
Rates: Double £18.50, Standard £16.50, Single £22.50-24.50; 33 percent discount for children. Vouchers accepted. £15 dinner. **Credit cards:** All except American Express. **Open:** All year. **Children:** All ages.
Pets: No. **Smoking:** Restricted. **Provision for handicapped:** None.
Directions: From center of Tullamore, take Birr Road (N52) for 2 miles out. Go past the small church in Mullagh Village, then take the next right. You will see the sign here for Canal View. Go 2.5 miles to the third bed and breakfast on the right.

Situated on the banks of the Grand Canal, this modern, lovely home is also a leisure center. Bernadette is very generous and efficient in the way she runs her business, which includes paddleboats and rowboats at no charge for guests. Her rooms are attractive and comfortable. One room is pink with roses, another is gold and brown, and there is one family room decorated with blue and pink flowers. She serves a full Irish Breakfast plus fresh fruit, yogurt, porridge, and potato waffles. Along with fishing on the canal, you can enjoy golf, horseback riding, walking trails, and a guided tour to show the wildlife of the bogs and eskers. Irish music is played at local pubs, and a cinema, dancing, and bingo can be found in Tullamore.

County Roscommon

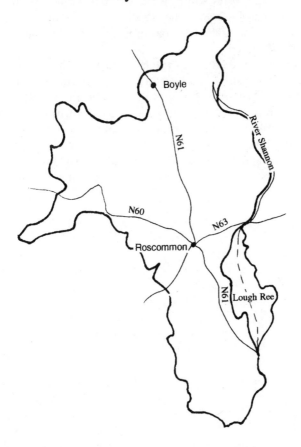

County Roscommon is in the heart of Ireland and is mostly flat plain, making it great farm country. There are just enough boglands, meadows, and low rolling hills dotted with lakes to make it very pleasant to visit. In the north you'll find Lough Key Forest Park, 840 acres with trails for hiking and boats on the lake for renting. There are bog gardens with heather and other small plants to study. Eat at the Lakeshore Restaurant, with picture windows overlooking the water. Very nearby is the town of Boyle, situated between two lakes, with the fascinating thirteenth-century Boyle Abbey in all its ancient splendor. This town and surrounding area is a paradise for walkers and fishermen.

The famous blind harpist Turlough O'Carolan (died 1738), is buried at Kilronan Abbey Cemetery, four miles northeast of Lough Key. At Castlerea, farther south, is the Clonalis House, built in the 1800s, home of the chieftain of the O'Conor Clan. Here you may view O'Carolan's harp, old glassware, paintings, and Gaelic manuscripts. Afternoon tea is served.

In the center of the county is the historical capital, Roscommon, a large town where sheep and cattle raising are the main occupations. Visit the Norman stronghold of Roscommon Castle and the ruins of Roscommon Abbey, with its eight sculptures representing medieval Irish soldiers. Northeast of Roscommon city is Strokestown, with its Gothic arch leading to Strokestown Park House, built in 1660, a captivating place to visit. This town is also the home of Slieve Baun Handcrafts, sold in the markets and shops all over town.

Abbey House
Christina and Martin Mitchell
Boyle, County Roscommon
Telephone: 079-62385
Bedrooms: 6; 5 with private baths, 1 with shared.
Rates: £18 p.p. private bath; £16 p.p. shared bath; Single £22.50-24.50; 33 percent discount for children. Vouchers accepted. **Credit cards:** None.
Open: March 1 to October. **Children:** All ages. **Pets:** No. **Smoking:** Yes.
Provision for handicapped: None. **Directions:** Take N4, Dublin/Sligo Road, to Boyle; the house is .5 km away from town center, on the grounds of Boyle Abbey.

This Georgian house covered with ivy, on lovely grounds between the abbey and a river, is a delight. Martin and Christina work hard at giving guests good personal service and help with touring. You may want to wander through the gardens or walk to the Forest Park, not far away. All rooms are pleasant and the lounge has a TV and an open fire. The Mitchells serve a typical full Irish Breakfast. The house is 110 miles from Dublin, midway between there and Donegal. Boyle is only 20 miles from the famous town of Sligo. Walk four minutes to town, try one of the two nine-hole golf courses locally, or fish the many lakes and rivers of the beautiful surrounding area. The pleasant hosts will give you all sorts of hints on where to go.

COUNTY SLIGO

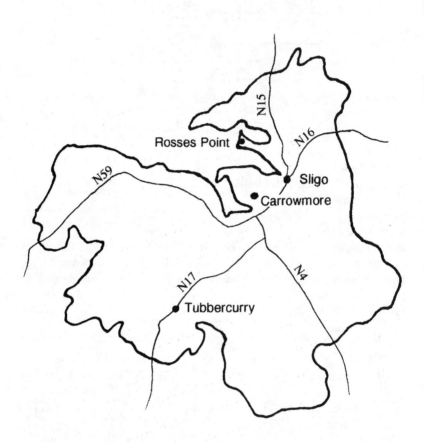

County Sligo

County Sligo is a patchwork of rugged mountains, rolling hills, and sparkling lakes and rivers. The many coves and bays have splendid beaches to enjoy. Starting in the north, coming out of Donegal, you'll reach the wonderful Yeats country right away. You'll see the undulating, moss-green Ben Bulben Mountains and the church spire at Drumcliffe, where W. B. Yeats's father was a minister and where Yeats is buried. The high Celtic cross that he mentions in a poem is here. He called Sligo the "Land of Heart's Desire." Rosses Point and Sandhill are beautiful beaches and the way the sea comes up, you can view mountains, sea, and Drumcliffe all at once. You will be able to visit 60 megalithic mounds and tombs built by Stone-Age man in Carrowmore, outside Sligo town, and in other places in the county. Sligo is a colorful old town with history, good restaurants, art galleries, music, and theater. The Hawk's Well Theatre on Temple Street has good entertainment year-round. Lissadel House and Gardens, built in the 1830s, was the home of the famous Gore-Booth family. The Yeats Memorial Building on High Bridge is a must-see attraction. There is also a Yeats signposted country tour of Sligo beauty spots.

Driving south to Tubbercurry, you'll see the breathtaking Ox Mountains and panoramic Ladies Brae. Tubbercurry is the home of the South Sligo Summer School of Traditional Irish Music and Dance, held every July, where you can learn something about playing the fiddle, pennywhistle, *bodhran* drums, *Uillean* pipes, and set and stepdancing. If you wish to participate please contact Rita Flannery, Tubbercurry, County Sligo, Ireland, or call her at 071-85010. Don't forget to visit Killoran's Restaurant, which has an Irish party every Thursday night from June to September. Everyone gets a chance to churn the butter, taste the "boxty" potato cakes and hot scones, and sing and dance all night.

County Sligo is a great place for horseback riding (pony-trekking), golfing, fishing, cycling, and every watersport you can imagine. You can easily visit Donegal and Leitrim to the north, and County Mayo to the south, with its beautiful Westport and the Croagh Patrick Mountain.

Aisling
Des and Nan Faul
Cairns Hill
Sligo, County Sligo
Telephone and **FAX:** 071-60704
Bedrooms: 5; 3 with private baths, 2 with shared.
Rates: £18 p.p. private bath, £16 p.p. shared bath. Single £5 extra.
Vouchers accepted. **Credit cards:** VISA. **Open:** All year, except December
22-28. **Children:** No. **Pets:** No. **Smoking:** No. **Provision for handicapped:** None. **Directions:** From Dublin-Galway: On N4, turn right at
first set of traffic lights onto Cairns Road. From Donegal, get on N4
and turn left at the traffic lights after the Esso Station. Aisling is the
second bed and breakfast on the left.

The Fauls have a modern bungalow in a peaceful, scenic location
overlooking Sligo Bay in Yeats country. It is a comfortable family home
surrounded by large gardens. The five rooms are decorated in pastel
blues, pinks, and creams, and all have TVs, hair dryers, and electric
blankets. The dining room has a beautiful view of Sligo Bay and the
imposing, rolling, green Ben Bulben Mountains. Nan serves yogurt
and fruit in addition to her full Irish Breakfast. You may visit any of the
several beautiful beaches nearby or walk 20 minutes to Sligo town.
There are golf courses, horseback riding, and cinemas nearby. It's
just a short ride to the church and the huge Celtic cross near Yeats's
grave. Visit the Sports Complex in Sligo, too.

Lissadell
Mary Cadden
Mail Coach Road
Sligo, County Sligo
Telephone: 071-61937
Bedrooms: 3, all with private baths.
Rates: £20 p.p.; Single £25; Vouchers not accepted. **Credit cards:**
None. **Open:** All year, except a few days at Christmas. **Children:** Yes, 12
or older. **Pets:** No. **Smoking:** No. **Provision for handicapped:** None.
Directions: From Sligo town, turn left onto Dublin Road N4, and at
the Silver Swan Hotel turn right. The 2-story house is on the right;
look for the red door.

This brand-new, dormered brick home is very close to Sligo town.
Mary, a pleasant hostess, greets you with tea and scones and will show
you her attractive, neat, and spacious rooms, decorated with ruffled
pine beds covered in pastel flowers of pink or green and white and featuring lovely tiled baths. Her lounge is very comfy, with TV, antiques,
and a white-marble fireplace. Her stately dining room has one long
antique table. All is very trim and neat. There are stained-glass windows on the sides of the front door and some in the attractive dining
room. Besides her full Irish Breakfast, you may choose a continental
breakfast of cereal and scones. You may walk to town or ride a few minutes to Strandhill or Rosses Point Beaches. Visit Lough Gill, with its
boat rides, or the Drumcliffe Mountains and Yeats country just 10 minutes away. Horseback riding is available just 20 minutes away in the
country town of Carrowmore, where you may also see the megalithic
burial mounds.

Stonecroft
Mary Conway
Off Donegal Road N15
Kintogher
Sligo, County Sligo
Telephone: 071-45667; **FAX:** 071-44200
Bedrooms: 5, all with private baths.
Rates: £18 p.p. private bath; £16.50 p.p. shared bath; Single £19.50-21; 20 percent discount for children under 12. Vouchers accepted. **Credit cards:** VISA, MasterCard, and AMEX. **Open:** March 8 to December 8. **Children:** 2 years and older. **Pets:** No. **Smoking:** Restricted. **Provision for handicapped:** Yes. **Directions:** Stonecroft is 3 miles north of Sligo Town, off Donegal Road N15 on the left side.

Mary Conway, a warm, generous hostess, welcomes you with tea or coffee in her peaceful, spacious home. Her living room and two of the guest rooms look out over farmlands to the majestic Ben Bulben Mountains, soft, folded, and moss-green, like the Pali in Hawaii. The famous Drumcliffe church spire can be seen across the road, and over a large sweep of land to the left you can view the beautiful Drumcliffe Bay. Mary will spend time with you, mapping out routes for touring the area, full of history, where Yeats lived and was buried. The rooms, all on the first floor, are attractive with TV and tea- and coffee-making facilities. The matching drapes and quilts are of an unusual modern design in orange and grey or pale green and mulberry. At night, you may eat in the Yeats Tavern, watch TV, and visit with her younger boys, David and Mark, as we did. Breakfast is the typical Irish with added fruited yogurt, fresh fruit, and tantalizing hot, crunchy scones. Rosses Point Beach, golf, country walks, Lough Gill boat trips, surfing, and theater are nearby.

ALSO RECOMMENDED

Sligo/Duncliff, *Rathnashee,* Tess and Sean Haughey, Teesan, Donegal Road. Telephone: 071-43376. Bedrooms: 4, 2 with private baths. Open all year. Scenic location 2 miles from Sligo town center on N15. Very hospitable hosts who can provide information on archeological tours in the region.

Sligo Town, *Tree Tops,* Ronan and Doreen MacEvilly, Cleveragh Road. Telephone: 071-60160/62301. Bedrooms: 5, 4 with private baths. Large and nicely decorated bedrooms. Secluded, lovely home. 5-minute walk to town center.

COUNTY TIPPERARY

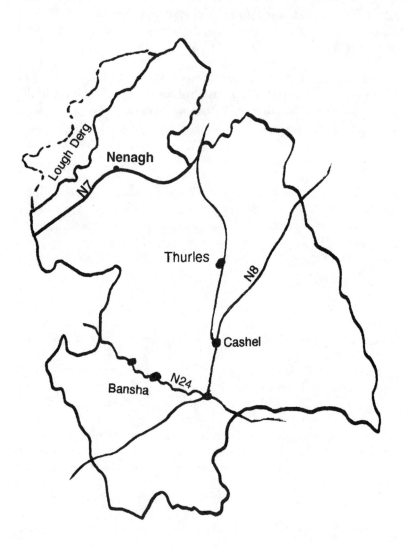

County Tipperary

A drive southeast from Limerick Town will take you across rich farmlands, through Pallasgreen with its excellent Chaser O'Brien pub/restaurant, on to Tipperary Town, a farming center, then to the quaint town of Bansha in a vale that is surrounded by beautiful hills. We liked this little village and spent some time here. There is an Equestrian Center at the beautiful Bansha House, where racehorses are trained, and where one can experience a wonderful horseback ride through the countryside. One should allow time to take the beautiful drive up the Glen of Aherlow and cross over the mountain on the R662, where there is a lookout with a large Christ statue, and turn right on the I119 to Tipperary town. South of Bansha is the town of Cahir with the beautifully restored, fifteenth-century Cahir Castle, where tours are available. To the southeast there are the scenic drives to the market towns of Clonmel and Carrisk-On-Suir, sited in an extremely picturesque region. Stop at Kinsell's pub for a pint and a snack, just outside the West Gate of Clonmel, when you make your southern swing through Tipperary.

Make sure you visit the famous Rock of Cashel, a steep outcrop of limestone, once a fortress where ancient chieftains were crowned and that later became a Gothic cathedral in the thirteenth century, with side chapels. Allow time to have a leisurely visit with a snack and tea at one of the quaint shops near the parking lot before you hike up the road to tour the castle. The area around Cashel is quite pretty and is worthy of an overnight stay. Local shops have the famous Shanagarry tweeds. The Cashel Palace Hotel, a Queen Anne-style building, was once the residence of the archbishops of the Church of Ireland.

Other features of Tipperary are the Kilcooley Abbey, the Abbey of the Holy Cross, and the attractive church at Fethard. Remember the two-day rule. Try to locate a bed and breakfast as a base camp, make side trips from there, and return to your host family in the evening. It's more fun that way.

Ardmayle House
Annette V. Hunt
Cashel, County Tipperary
Telephone: 0504-42399; **FAX:** 0504-42420; **E-Mail:** ardmayle@iol.ie
Bedrooms: 5, all with private baths.
Rates: £19.50 p.p. 33 percent discount for children. Vouchers accepted. **Credit cards:** None. **Open:** April 1 to October 1. **Children:** Yes, all ages. **Pets:** No. **Smoking:** No. **Provision for handicapped:** None. **Directions:** On the north side of town keep left past Rock House (souvenir shop) down the hill. Here take left fork and drive 3 miles. Go through village of Ardmayle and at "T" junction outside of the village turn right. Ardmayle House is the first entrance on the right.

Ardmayle house, family-owned since 1840, is a lovely old Georgian farm home on a 300-acre dairy farm with horses and sheep. It has a rural and tranquil setting among native old trees. The rooms are comfortable and furnished with period antiques. There are two sitting rooms available to guests, one with TV and the other with pool table for young guests. You can fly-fish on the River Suir right on the farm grounds, golf nearby, take country walks, or ride horses at a nearby equestrian center. Annette will assist you in planning visits to historic/tourist sites such as the Rock of Cashel, Holy Cross Abbey, or the Glen of Aherlow.

Dualla House
Martin Mairead and Robert Power
Dualla/Kilkenny Road
Cashel, County Tipperary
Telephone and **FAX:** 062-61487; **E-Mail:** duallanse@tinet.ie
Bedrooms: 4, all with private baths.
Rates: £18-20 p.p. private bath; £15 p.p. shared bath; 33 percent discount for children. Vouchers accepted. **Credit cards:** None. **Open:** February 12 to December 1. **Children:** All ages. **Pets:** Yes. **Smoking:** No. **Provision for handicapped:** None. **Directions:** On R691, signposted near church, travel 4 km from Cashel on the Dualla/Killkenny Road. The Dualla House is 1 km from Dualla Village. The house is on the left with a sign at the gate.

The Dualla House farm and B&B is set in the scenic countryside in the Golden Vale of Tipperary. A Georgian house, it was built in the 1790s by Rody Scully, a local landlord. Going uphill through the entry driveway, you'll see fields full of sheep on either side. Martin Mairead and Robert Power have more than 1,000 ewes, and they breed Suffolk Crosses and Cheviot Crosses. Their rams are mainly Suffolk and North Country. The guest rooms have flowered walls with matching bedcovers, antique beds and furniture, and lovely prints of country scenes on the walls. All have tea-making facilities and grand views of sheep fields. Mairead's delectable breakfasts are comprised of a choice of traditional eggs, sausages, and hams with homemade breads and preserves, a choice of cereals or porridge, fresh fruit, yogurt, and juices. On the property there are farm walks and their colorful, neatly laid-out gardens to enjoy. Nearby you will find tennis, golf, horseback riding, and fishing. With lovely open fireplaces and a drawing room, visitors are sure to enjoy themselves.

Ros Guill House
Evelyn Moloney
Dualla Road (R691)
Cashel, County Tipperary
Telephone: 062-62699; **FAX:** 062-61507
Bedrooms: 5; 3 with private baths, 2 with shared baths.
Rates: £21 p.p. private bath; £18.50 p.p. shared bath; Single £23-26. 20 percent discount for children. Vouchers accepted. **Credit cards:** VISA, Access, MasterCard, and AMEX. **Open:** May 1 to October 20. **Children:** Yes, 7 and older. **Pets:** No. **Smoking:** In lounge only. **Provision for handicapped:** None. **Directions:** First turn right after Tourist Information Office onto Friar Street. Next turn left after church onto R691. The B&B is the first guesthouse on the left, .5 km out.

This elegant country home has been happily serving guests in a professional and friendly manner for the last 28 years. Bedrooms are decorated in colors of pink and cream, burgundy and green, blue, yellow and cream, and jade and peach. All showers are color coordinated with bedrooms, and baths are fully tiled. Each bedroom has tea/coffee facilities, hair dryers, and clock radios. Also, a spacious lounge opens into a large dining room with separate tables with white cloths. Bay windows will allow a spectacular and panoramic view of the famous Rock of Cashel. For breakfast you will be offered a prize-winning menu choice. Evelyn recommends booking ahead during peak season to avoid disappointment. Recreational features in the area are: golfing, horseback riding, tennis, fishing, pitch and putt, and mountain and forest hiking.

Thornbrook House
Mary Kennedy
Dualla Road
Cashel, County Tipperary
Telephone: 062-62388; **FAX:** 062-61480
Bedrooms: 5; 3 with private bath, 2 with shared bath.
Rates: £20 p.p. with private bath; £18 with shared bath; Single £24-28. 20 percent discount for children. Vouchers accepted. **Credit cards:** VISA, MasterCard, and Eurocheque. **Open:** April to November. **Children:** Yes, all ages. **Pets:** No. **Smoking:** No. **Provision for handicapped:** None. **Directions:** On the 691 Dualla/Kilkenny road, north 1 km from the city of Cashel on the right. A sign is posted near church, and there is a sign at the entrance.

Thornbrook House has an excellent reputation for all-around hospitality and accommodations. It is a ranch-type home with beautiful landscaped gardens front and back. Antiques adorn the handsomely decorated dining room and guest lounge, both with fireplaces. Thornbrook is within walking distance of the famous Rock of Cashel castle, and the shops and restaurants of the town. The bedrooms are elegantly decorated and feature tea/coffee-making facilities, hair dryers, and orthopedic beds. An Irish Breakfast is served with a further choice of items du jour plus baked goods fresh out of the oven. There is a garage for bikes and a secure parking area. You will find Mary and Willie experienced in making your visit to the Golden Vale of Tipperary a very pleasant and comfortable one.

Lakeland Lodge
Sheila Darcy
Terryglass, Nenagh
County Tipperary
Telephone: 067-22069; **FAX:** 067-22069
Bedrooms: 3; 2 with private baths, 1 with separate bath.
Rates: £18 p.p.; Single: £24.50. 33 percent discount for children.
Vouchers accepted. **Credit cards:** Yes, all major. **Open:** January 1 to
December 23. **Children:** Yes, all ages. **Pets:** No. **Smoking:** Lounge only.
Directions: Branch off the N7 at Nenagh. Drive north on the N52 to
Borissonkane. Turn left for Terryglass and look for signs or call Mrs.
Darcy. It's about 15 miles north of Nenagh.

Sheila calls Lakeland a "home away from home." The luxurious,
dormered, country house is situated beside beautiful scenic Lough
Derg. The colors that Sheila used in her attractive bedrooms are pink,
peach, and cream. Breakfasts are delicious. Terryglass is a historical village with a castle, churches, and holy wells. Visit their craft shop or
ramble into one of the pubs for great *craic,* or traditional music. This
area is a perfect shopping place for the long ride between Dublin
and Galway or Kerry. You'll find fishing, cycling, boating, horseback
riding, tennis, walking, swimming, water-skiing, and cruises on the
lake.

Inch House
John and Nora Egan
Thurles, County Tipperary
Telephone: 0504-51438/51261; **FAX:** 0504-51754; **E-Mail:** inchhse@lol.ie
Bedrooms: 5, all with private baths.
Rates: £28; Single £33; 20 percent discount for children under 10.
Vouchers not accepted. £23.50 dinner. **Credit cards:** VISA, Access,
MasterCard, Eurocard. **Open:** All year except Christmas week. **Children:** Yes. **Pets:** No. **Smoking:** Not in dining room. **Provision for handicapped:** None. **Directions:** From Thurles, take top right-hand side of
square to Nenagh Road. Drive 4.5 miles, and Inch House is signposted
on the left.

This elegant, 1717 restored Georgian manor house was in the Ryan
family for three hundred years until it was bought by the Egans. The
high ceilings, large windows, and lovely antiques will capture your
admiration. Stained-glass windows look onto a curving stairway to bedrooms that are roomy and have high-back antique beds. The dining
room has classic red and green décor, and there is a restaurant open
to the public for dinners with prime meats, game, and fresh fish
served. The sitting room has a Persian rug, a fireplace, and magnificent plaster ceiling designs. Relax here and read or chat. A full Irish
Breakfast with homemade breads and fresh fruit salad with rhubarb
and strawberries is offered. It is only minutes to the Rock of Cashel,
Glen of Aherlow, Galtee Mountains, and Lough Derg for fishing and
watersports, as well as hunting and horseback riding.

ALSO RECOMMENDED

Bansha, *Bansha Castle Country House,* John and Theresa Russell, off N24 on right coming south into Bansha Village. Telephone: 062-54187; FAX 062-54187. Bedrooms: 6, 4 with private baths. Large handsome mansion restored to original beauty, set on large grassy fields with sheep and horses grazing. Convenient for touring beautiful Glen of Aherlow. Fishing and horseback riding available nearby.

County Waterford

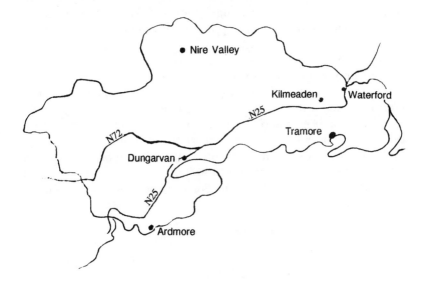

Waterford is a small county in the South most noted for its superb Waterford Crystal Factory in the town of Waterford on the eastern rim. The Visitors' Center's lavish displays and the handling of the public are a bit Disneyesque. We were disappointed that we couldn't take photos of the glassblowers as that was quite fascinating, as well as the delicate and careful etching work. We only saw men working there and wondered where the women artisans were. It is a pleasant enough city to see, with plenty of medieval towers and old walls. Visit the Reginald Tower Museum, the Waterford Heritage Center, and the New Ross Gallery. The Tourist Office is on the quay on the Suir River bordering the northern edge of town. We had a fine and reasonable Irish lunch at the Olde Stand Restaurant at 45 Michael Street. It's a big Victorian place with etched-glass doors and inside are cozy benches and tables and a long, lit-up center buffet and carvery with servers. The choices of light or heavy meals were quite varied.

Curraghmore House is a good visit just outside Portlaw. To the east are the rough and pretty Cheekpoint and Passage East with its car ferry to Arthurstown in Wexford, and its water views, wild goats, and numerous water birds to study. Dunmore East, farther south, has picturesque coves and swimming and snorkeling. Tramore, a tourist town on the ocean, has a 3-mile beach and huge amusement park. North from Waterford town it's a straight shot to Kilkenny and northeast it's only 45 miles to Cashel in Tipperary, with its exciting castle rising out of the rock.

To the west, towards Cork, is one of the most charming towns in Ireland, and that is Ardmore. Here, you'll find a glorious sweep of a beach and on the hill is a very high Norman round tower and Celtic-cross cemetery with fantastic views of the beach and the countryside beyond. It's a nice spot to just sit and meditate. There is a bakery on the west side of the main street that is open in summer, where you'll find "melt-in-your-mouth" hot scones and an adorable garden with tables in the back. Back out on the N25, there are some wonderful dairy farms with views of the ocean. Some are bed and breakfasts listed in this book.

Newtown Farm Guesthouse
Teresa O'Connor
Newtown, Grange
Ardmore, County Waterford
Telephone: 024-94143; **FAX:** 024-94054
Bedrooms: 6, all with private baths.
Rates: £20-25 p.p.; Single £22; Discount for children negotiable.
Vouchers accepted. £13 dinner. **Credit cards:** VISA, MasterCard,
Access, Eurocard. **Open:** All year. **Children:** All ages. **Pets:** In shed.
Smoking: No. **Provision for handicapped:** Yes. **Directions:** From
Ardmore, take the N25 east and turn south at Fleming's Pub. The
farmhouse is ¼ mile on left.

This stunning modern house on a dairy farm in lovely country surroundings has views on all sides. Teresa is very friendly and energetic.
She uses a lot of pink flowers in her room colors, as well as blue and
green floral designs. In the back there are farm animals, ducks, and
guinea hens for children to visit. The O'Connors also have their own
tennis court on the property. The lounge is cozy, with a peat fire, and
the dining room has a pink theme. In her Irish Breakfast, Teresa offers
a choice of eggs, beans on toast, and a buffet with juice, fresh fruit,
and cereals. There is swimming, golf, tennis, and pony-trekking in
the area. A children's pony is available. The farm is also close to the
sea, handy for fishing. You may easily visit the towns of Ardmore, with
its Norman Tower, and medieval Youghal.

Summerhill Farmhouse
Sheila Budd
Kinsalebeg
Ardmore, County Waterford
Telephone: 024-92682
Bedrooms: 6; 5 with private baths, 1 with shared.
Rates: £18 p.p.; Single £21-22.50. 33 percent discount for children under 12. Vouchers accepted. **Credit cards:** VISA, MasterCard. **Open:** March 1 to December 1. **Children:** Yes, all ages. **Pets:** No. **Smoking:** No. **Provision for handicapped:** Yes. **Directions:** On the N25 going east, watch for the Summerhill sign on the left, about 2-3 km after the bridge crossing the Blackwater River outside Youghal. Coming west on the N25, it is 1.5 km after Grange on the right.

The Budd family will greet you with the warmest welcome you can get in this part of Ireland. This modern farmhouse, with a new lounge with cathedral ceiling and big bay-window view of the Atlantic Ocean beyond the green pasture, is extraordinary. The superb breakfasts are served in the modern dining room with separate tables, and the dinners are equally scrumptious. We enjoyed watching the cows coming up the meadow and the cats being fed the fresh milk. It's a happy family where Sheila manages the bed and breakfast inside and her husband tends the livestock outside. However, it wasn't always that way; as newlyweds they worked side by side doing the chores. You'll love the comfortable bedrooms and the side trips: the beach at Ardmore, the medieval walled city of Youghal, and the Blackwater for fishing. Or just relax with a good book in the very beautiful conservatory with a fireplace and pretty blue velvet chairs. Other special bonuses are the pony cart rides around the farm and the miniature golf course by the barn.

Glencree
Rena Power
The Sweep
Kilmeaden, County Waterford
Telephone: 051-384240
Bedrooms: 5; All with private baths.
Rates: £18 p.p. private bath; £15 p.p. shared bath; Single £22; 20 percent discount for children under 12. Vouchers accepted. **Credit cards:** None. **Open:** March 1 to October 31. **Children:** All ages. **Pets:** No. **Smoking:** Restricted. **Provision for handicapped:** None. **Directions:** From Dungarvan, traveling east on the N25, pass the Waterford Coop, go 500 yards farther to the Texaco station, take a sharp right, go a few hundred yards, and take a right at the signpost for Glencree; the stone-wall entrance is on the right.

Glencree means "heart of the glen," and it is a lovely modern home with a very kind and happy family running it. If you arrive late, Mr. Power will join you for tea and a happy chat until Rena returns from her walk and joins you. You can't help noticing the crystal chandeliers in the hall and the lounge, which is very roomy. They get CNN News on their TV. The rooms are comfy with flowered duvets in pink, rose, blue, white and orange, and green and champagne. One room has a sheepskin rug. A section of the lounge serves as the dining room, where Rena will serve you an Irish Breakfast varied with choice of eggs, French toast, cheese, yogurt, and cereal. There is one big table and one small one. They are only 8 minutes from the Waterford Crystal Factory. Beaches are only 15 minutes away and so is horseback riding, golf, and greyhound racing. (One English guest staying at Glencree told us he raised racing greyhounds and had them housed in kennels in Waterford. He loved his dogs and visited them as often as he could.)

Cliff House
Pat and Hilary O'Sullivan
Cliff Road
Tramore, County Waterford
Telephone and **Fax:** 051-381997; **E-Mail:** cliffhouse@tramore.net
Bedrooms: 6, all with private bath.
Rates: £20 p.p., 20 percent discount for children. Vouchers accepted.
Credit cards: VISA, MasterCard, and Access. **Open:** February 1 to
November 31. **Children:** Yes, 6 and up. **Pets:** No. **Smoking:** No.
Provision for handicapped: None. **Directions:** Sign posted in
Tramore, off R675, the coast road from Waterford to Dungarvan.
Drive through the town of Tramore, then turn left at the Ritz Pub to
Cliff Road.

The Cliff House is a luxurious bed and breakfast located at Cliff
Road, with a panoramic view of Tramore Bay. All six bedrooms, including three family suites, are decorated to a very high standard in beautiful pastel colors and include TV, clock radios, and hair dryers. An
extensive breakfast menu offers more than 10 choices. There is a
beautiful, sunny conservatory with a breathtaking view of Tramore
Bay. The Cliff House is highly acclaimed in many travel guides.
Recreational facilities and activities nearby include swimming, sailing, tennis, golf, fishing, walking, horseback riding, and an indoor
leisure center called Splashworld. Waterford Crystal is only 10 minutes
away.

Cloneen
Neil and Maria Skedd
Love Lane
Tramore, County Waterford
Telephone and **FAX:** 051-381264
Bedrooms: 4, all with private baths.
Rates: £18 p.p.; Single £20; 50 percent discount for children.
Vouchers accepted. £12 dinner. **Credit cards:** VISA and MasterCard.
Open: March to November. **Children:** All ages. **Pets:** No. **Smoking:**
Restricted. **Provision for handicapped:** Yes. **Directions:** Stay on the
main Waterford-Tramore Road. Go up steep hill, keep coast on your
left. Take next left to Love Lane.

This pretty white bungalow, on one acre, is surrounded by rose trel-
lises and gardens and has secure parking. Tramore is a lovely country
section of Waterford, not far from the ocean. Maria gives you the traditional Irish Breakfast with a choice of cereals, scrambled or poached
eggs, fresh fruit, and yogurt. Tea and coffee facilities are located in the
comfortable rooms. This home is close to golf courses, tennis courts,
and scenic walks to the beautiful, golden beaches with many seaside
attractions, including a 50-acre amusement park. You can rent a bike
in town and discover miles of quiet country roads. The famous
Waterford Crystal factory and store is a short drive away. Splashworld,
a swimming facility and fitness center, is located on Tramore Beach,
with modern features for all ages to enjoy.

Glenorney
Marie Murphy
Newtown
Tramore, County Waterford
Telephone: 052-381056; **FAX:** 051-381103; **E-Mail:** glenmore@iol.ie
Bedrooms: 6, all with private baths.
Rates: £21 p.p., Single £23-25. 20 percent discount for children.
Vouchers accepted. **Credit cards:** Yes. **Open:** February 1 to November
30. **Children:** Yes. **Pets:** No. **Smoking:** No. **Provision for handicapped:**
Yes. **Directions:** Opposite Tramore Golf Club on the coast road (R 675).

This is a spacious and luxurious home with spectacular views of
Tramore Bay. Pretty bedrooms are done in pastel shades with peaches,
pinks, and greens, and one room in blue and yellow. The lounge and
dining room is done in pink and green. An extraordinary home-
cooked breakfast menu is served. You have a choice of fruit, cereal,
and the Irish cooked breakfast, but you also have a choice of hot kippers with tomatoes, special French toast, baked beans, or pancakes
with maple syrup. After this sumptuous breakfast you can tackle
nearby Splashworld to use up some of the extra energy. The Murphys
will suggest other recreational options, as they pride themselves on
attending to every detail so that your stay is enjoyable and relaxing.
Marie would like you to think of the Glenorney as your home away
from home.

Seaview Lodge
Frances and Cyril Darcy
Seaview Park
Tramore, County Waterford
Telephone and **FAX:** 051-381122
Bedrooms: 5, all with private baths.
Rates: £18-19 p.p.; Single £23. 20 percent discount for children under 12. Vouchers accepted. **Credit cards:** Yes. **Open:** April to November. **Children:** Yes, over 5 years. **Pets:** No. **Smoking:** No. **Provision for handicapped:** Yes. **Directions:** Follow the R675 from Waterford to Tramore. Travel 6 miles to the Maxol Station. Take the first right at the signpost to Seaview Lodge. Coming from Cork, take the N25. After Kilmeaden Village, take the R682 to the right to Tramore. At the next small roundabout you will see Seaview Lodge.

This ranch-style bungalow with a spectacular view of the Atlantic Ocean and extensive gardens has two family bedrooms and three doubles or twins. The rooms are fully equipped with TVs, tea and coffee makers, and hair dryers. The Darcys offer a special menu that includes pancakes, omelets, and smoked kippers or the full Irish Breakfast that is served while overlooking the sea. Nearby is golf, fishing, and nighttime entertainment. You are seven minutes from the Waterford Crystal factory. Mrs. Darcy is an exceptional hostess in every regard. Investigate the sandy beach of Tramore, or motor to Dungarvan and see some beautiful seascapes. Mrs. Darcy will advise you on how to proceed and what to see. Splashworld is nearby, as well as Irish music for visitor entertainment.

Annvill House
Phyllis O'Reilly
The Orchard, Kingsmeadow
Waterford, County Waterford
Telephone and **FAX:** 051-373617
Bedrooms: 5, all with private baths.
Rates: £18 p.p.; Single £27; Vouchers accepted. **Credit cards:** None.
Open: January 1 to December 20. **Children:** No. **Pets:** No. **Smoking:**
No. **Provision for handicapped:** None. **Directions:** From Cork, take a
left just after the Crystal Factory, go to the roundabout, make a left
turn, go 1 block and left again; the house is the first on the left, at
the corner of Ashe Street.

This attractive, modern, two-story home is very near the Crystal
Factory. Phyllis will bring you tea or coffee on arrival in her pleasant
lounge with a TV. If you wish, she has a video/film available of the
factory, plus a three-hour touring film of Ireland. Her rooms are good-
sized, with some brass beds and flowered quilts in purple, yellow, or
brown. In her dining room you'll see a glass display case, lit up, with
treasures of Waterford crystal collected and received as gifts over the
years. Besides the standard Irish Breakfast, she likes to serve potato
waffles, the frozen kind. In the area, there is indoor bowling, a walking
tour of the city, and Irish *caeli* dancing. Visit the singing pub, Mullan's.
Also, golf, swimming beaches, horseback riding facilities, and indoor
bowling are nearby.

ALSO RECOMMENDED

Ballymacarbry, *Hanora's Country Cottage,* Seamus and Mary Wall, Nire Valley Ballymacarbry. Telephone: 052-36134. FAX: 052-36540. Bedrooms: 5, all with private baths. Evening meals à la carte. Beautifully redecorated ancestral home in peaceful setting. Superb meals. Golf nearby. Near Ballymacarbry, south of Clonmel. Very scenic region to tour!

Dungarvan, *Seaview,* Mrs. Nora Fahey, Windgap Pulla, Youghal Road, Dungarvan West. Telephone: 058-41583. Bedrooms: 5, 3 with private baths. Lovely bungalow perched on the hill alongside N25 as the highway descends into city, with sweeping view of Dungarvan Bay.

Waterford, *Dunroven,* Breda Power, Ballinaneeshagh, Cork Road. Telephone: 051-374743. Bedrooms: 6, all en suite. Townhouse on the Cork Road or N25. Open all year, except Christmas. Non-smoking house. TV and tea/coffee facilities in rooms. Recommended by Carmel O'Halloran of Galway.

COUNTY WESTMEATH

County Westmeath

County Westmeath in the Lakelands area is a perfect place to stay to see the Midlands of Ireland. It is a small county with Lough Ennel and Lough Owel near Mullingar in the center, and it has the great Lough Ree along its western edge, which is part of the River Shannon waterway going to the north and south. This is a good county for country walks and bicycling. There is fishing and boating in the lakes and golf in Mullingar, Athlone, Moate, and Birr. You'll find County Westmeath is made up mostly of farmlands, and Mullingar is called the "cattle capital" of Ireland. Much cattle trading is done here, also. In Mullingar, visit the beautiful carved-stone Christ the King Cathedral, and just 5 km south of town be sure to see the Belvedere House Gardens, with its enticing view of the islands of Lough Ennel from its terraced and walled gardens. You'll enjoy the 1790s pub in town called Canten Casey's. On the road from Mullingar to Kells there is a dairy and pig farm called the Ben Breeze Open Farm that children will adore. There are splendid birds to see there also.

North of Mullingar, at Castlepollard, are the Tullynally Castle and Gardens, where the earls of Langford lived, and the Fore Abbey and St. Fechin's tenth-century church in the town of Fore. To the southeast, Athlone is a popular town, being on the N6, the much-traveled road between Galway and Dublin. It stands between Lough Ree and the River Shannon and the views are lovely. Here is where the famous Irish tenor John McCormack was born; and here is where the Irish retreated after the Battle of the Boyne. Visit the handsome Norman thirteenth-century Athlone Castle and the Athlone Crystal showroom. Due east of Athlone is the town of Moate, with its golf and horseback riding. Farther east you may explore the interesting and historical Kilbeggan Distillery and Museum. Other houses with lovely gardens to visit are Emo Court, Birr Castle, Clonalis House at Castlerea, and Abbeyleix at Woodland Gardens.

Hounslow House
Eithne Healy
Fore
Castlepollard, County Westmeath
Telephone: 044-61144; **FAX:** 044-61847; **E-Mail:** eithnehealy@tinet.ie
Bedrooms: 5; 4 with private bath, 1 with shared bath.
Rates: £18 p.p. private bath, £16 shared; Single £5 extra. 50 percent discount for children. £1 dinner. Vouchers accepted. **Credit cards:** MasterCard and VISA. **Open:** All year. **Children:** Yes, all ages. **Pets:** No. **Smoking:** No. **Provision for handicapped:** None. **Directions:** Take Dublin N4 to Mullingar, then on to Castlepollard. Then take the L49 to Fore Village, 4 miles north of Castlepollard, and 6 miles south of Oldcastle. Follow signs from Village of Fore, 1.5 km out.

We don't have many farms in our book, but we have selected a few where you can see a working farm in action, and get a taste of Irish farming. We enjoy them a lot and hope you will too. This lovely 200-year-old farmhouse is located on wooded heights in one hundred acres overlooking the beautiful valley of Fore, and its historic abbey. The farm has horses and beef cows. Two bedrooms have wooden floors decorated with pretty curtains, matching duvet covers, and pillowcases. Three bedrooms have wall-to-wall carpets, and are equally color coordinated. Tea or coffee is offered for a real farm welcome on your arrival. There are many amenities: babysitting, hair dryers in the rooms, tea/coffee facilities in bedrooms, computers, table tennis, and pool tables in the games room. You can visit Tullynally Castle and Lough Lene, and Loughcrew cairns nearby. An 18-hole golf course is also nearby.

Hilltop Country House
Sean and Dympna Casey
Delvin Road (N52), Rathconnell
Mullingar, County Westmeath
Telephone: 044-48958; **FAX:** 044-48013
Bedrooms: 5, all with private baths.
Rates: £20 p.p.; Single £25. Vouchers accepted. **Credit cards:** None.
Open: January 7 to December 20. **Children:** Negotiable. **Pets:** No.
Smoking: Restricted. **Provision for handicapped:** One room is suitable. **Directions:** Hilltop is 2 miles from Mullingar. From Dublin, take second exit off N4 to Mullingar bypass road (not town center) N52/Delvin Road, traveling from Dublin to Sligo.

This lovely, modern, split-level bungalow, situated in the Lakeland District, is a haven of peace and tranquility. The house has a long porch across the front, and terraced gardens. All rooms, comfortably decorated in a mix of antiques and modern furniture, have TVs and original watercolors. The colors are pink and cocoa, rose and white, or pastel flowered. Some rooms have country views or garden views. The splendid gardens, front and back, have a wide variety of trees, shrubs, and flowers. The traditional Irish Breakfast Dympna serves includes a choice of cereals, fresh fruits and compotes, fresh orange juice, and special requests. There is a tea and coffee buffet in the corridor. This house is ideally located as a base for visiting many historical sights such as Christ the King Cathedral and the Military and Historical Museum, or Columb Barracks. There is golf, fishing, and horseback riding available locally. The interior of Canten Casey's Pub, in town, has been kept the same as when it began in the 1790s.

Lough Owel Lodge
Aideen Ginnell
Cullion
Mullingar, County Westmeath
Telephone: 044-48714; **FAX:** 044-4877; **E-Mail:** aginnell@hotmail.com
Web site: http://www.angelfire.com/tx/aginnell
Bedrooms: 5, all with private baths.
Rates: £19-22 p.p.; Single £25-28. 33 percent discount for children.
Vouchers accepted. £14 dinner. **Credit cards:** VISA and MasterCard.
Open: March 17 to November 1. **Children:** Yes. **Pets:** Yes. **Smoking:**
Yes. **Provision for handicapped:** None. **Directions:** On the N4 from
Dublin towards Sligo after passing the third exit for Mullingar, Lough
Owel Lodge is signposted to your left. The lodge is about 1 km past
that, just as Lough Owel comes into view.

Upon entering the tree-lined avenue you will experience an
unusual country feeling as you approach this exceptional farm bed
and breakfast that offers everything from an antique-appointed dining
room to elegant bedrooms done with other beautiful period furnishings. Two rooms have gorgeous fourposter beds. The décor takes you
back to an early day. Each uniquely furnished bedroom is named after
a lake in this "Lakelands District." The name carries with it a mythical
story that Aideen can describe. For more details check out the excellent Web site above. Though a working dry stock farm with horses
and cats, this lodge still has all the amenities for a long stay. Excellent
trout fishing on the lake with hired boat, engine, and gillie (guide)
can be arranged by the hostess. A hard tennis court is available to
guests, with racquets provided, or for indoor sport, there is ping-pong,
table tennis, or billiards in the game room. Down the lake at the end
of the farm there is a sailing club. Relax here as you stroll down the
lane after dinner on a fine evening.

ALSO RECOMMENDED

Athlone, *Harbour House,* Mrs. Bernadette Keegan, Ballykeeran (1.5 km off N55). Telephone: 0902-85063. Bedrooms: 6, all with private baths. Vouchers accepted. All major credit cards. Golf, fishing, sailing on Lough Ree, horseback riding.

Moate, *Temple,* Declan and Bernadette Fagan, Horseleap (4 miles east of Moate on N6). Telephone and FAX: 0506-35118. Bedrooms: 4, all with private baths. VISA, MasterCard. Beautiful Victorian farmhouse with lovely garden in parkland setting.

COUNTY WEXFORD

County Wexford

Wexford is the southeasternmost county and has a strong tie to England, with its ferries crossing from Rosslare harbor. Ferries also cross from here to LeHavre and Cherbourg, France. Wexford City was a major Viking trading center and is full of medieval buildings. It is quite sophisticated and very proud of its arts and culture centers. They have an Opera Festival for a week every October and enjoy presenting unfamiliar operas. During that week, they have art shows and musical features all over town, a whole program to suit all kinds of people. You should visit Johnstown Castle, just south of the city. At Raven Point, across the harbor, is the Wexford Wildlife Reserve.

To the north is Enniscorthy, which has a Strawberry Fair Festival each year at the end of June. You may fish the Slaney River and visit the castle, museum, and famous potters of the area. From Wexford, right on the Irish Sea, drive west to historical New Ross over rolling green hills and farmlands. New Ross is on the River Barrow and has great fishing. The John F. Kennedy Arboretum is a lovely place to visit in this town.

The southwest area has many waterways, and at Arthurstown you may take a quaint car ferry across to Passage East in Waterford. Ride down to view the beautiful lighthouse at Hook Head. Two features you can enjoy as a tourist throughout County Wexford are great golf courses and horseback riding.

Ballinkeele House
John and Margaret Maher
Ballymurn
Enniscorthy, County Wexford
Telephone: 053-38105; **FAX:** 053-38468; **E-Mail:** balnkeel@indigo.ie
Bedrooms: 5, all with private baths.
Rates: £35-45 p.p.; Single £10 more; discount for children. Vouchers not accepted. £25 dinner. **Credit cards:** VISA, MasterCard/Access, Barclay. **Open:** March 1 to November 12. **Children:** All ages. **Pets:** No. **Smoking:** Restricted. **Provision for handicapped:** None. **Directions:** N11 north to Oilgate Village and turn right at signpost. From Enniscorthy, take N11 south to Oilgate village, turn left at signpost. Follow signs to Ballymurn, turn left at sign; it's the second gate on the left.

   This ancestral home of the Maher family is grey Wicklow granite, built in 1840 by John's great-grandfather in the Georgian style. It is set amidst 360 acres of woodlands and farmland and is stylish and elegant, with high ceilings and very large rooms. Soft Oriental rugs grace the front entrance hall and old family oils and original antique furniture are in all rooms. Some beds are fourposter with canopies, and all rooms have farmland views. It has not changed over the years and still has the air of a country manor. Besides the full Irish Breakfast, you'll get yogurt, pancakes, homemade soda bread, and jams. A formal gourmet dinner is served in the beautiful dining room with a set menu. The entrées are 4-star, haute cuisine and must be booked early on day of arrival. The dinner is followed by coffee and tea in the two drawing rooms on handmade tables. There is croquet and an all-weather tennis court at Ballinkeele, and there are good walks on the grounds and fishing nearby. The town is 10 km away. It is not far from the coast or the tourist attractions of Wexford City.

Woodlands Farmhouse
Philomena O'Sullivan
Killinierin
Gorey, County Wexford
Telephone: 0402-37125; **FAX:** 0402-37133
Bedrooms: 6, all with private baths.
Rates: £25 p.p.; 25 percent discount for children. Vouchers accepted.
£12 to £16 dinner. £9 high tea. **Credit cards:** Yes. **Open:** April 1 to
November 1. **Children:** Yes. **Pets:** No. **Smoking:** Lounge only. **Provision
for handicapped:** None. **Directions:** From Gorey, take N11 North for
3 miles to the signpost for Woodlands on left. Take the road in to
Killinierin for 3 km. House is on left with sign (1 km from Killinierin).

This is a beautiful, white, stucco, 1847 period farmhouse with a
fascinating bit of history that Philomena will eventually tell you if you
have the time for a good story. The hostess has a wonderful sense of
humor and is very helpful too. The house is tucked away from hustle
and bustle. The rooms are decorated in peach and pink with fine
taste, and all have view of gardens or panoramic countryside views;
three of the rooms have balconies. The sitting room is handsomely situated with many antiques, and the dining room has green flowered
drapes and pink tablecloths, as well as large windows with views of
prize gardens. Philomena serves a full Irish Breakfast with choices
from the menu. Tea and scones are always served upon your arrival.
There is a pool table, and there are tennis courts (with rackets supplied) on the property, along with a few cattle and a horse. Pony rides
are offered to the children. Killinierin is an interesting town to visit,
and there is a local pub 10 minutes away. There are also singing
lounges, horseback riding, fishing, and dancing in the area. Side-trips
can be made to beautiful Wicklow and Wexford town. The owners
will babysit. Try their three- or five-course farm-fresh, home-cooked
dinners. Your stay should be wonderful.

Cypress House Farm
Nancy and James Wall
Newbawn, County Wexford
Telephone: 051-428335
Bedrooms: 4, all with private baths.
Rates: £18 p.p.; Vouchers accepted. **Credit cards:** None. **Open:** February 1 to November 30. **Children:** No. **Pets:** No. **Smoking:** No. **Provision for handicapped:** None. **Directions:** From Wexford, take the N25 for 12 miles, follow the signs to Newbawn, and look for a *brown* signpost on the left. Stay to the left toward Newbawn for 2 miles and follow the brown signs for Cypress House Farm.

This 1920s two-story farmhouse has a pretty wooden door at its entry. The large windows give you beautiful views of country farm-lands. On these 130 acres, the Walls grow grain and hay. James and Nancy are very friendly and James showed us around the big yard where they have a new tennis court with a walking path around it, and a croquet field. The oversized living room has original paintings and we enjoyed tea and delicious scones by a fire in the fireplace. The rooms have good views and are bright and very nicely decorated in ivory, pinks, and greens. Some have Embroidery Anglais; one has a satin coverlet. A new bedroom has a balcony, and there is a new con-servatory in the back, as well as garden walks. The dining room has antique furniture and here you will be served the full Irish Breakfast, which we hope includes those scones. There is a tennis court on the property and ponies for children. There are equestrian centers, forest walks, golf, fishing, and boating on the River Barrow within six or seven miles. The town of New Ross has many tourist attractions. A pub and a restaurant are five minutes away.

Oakwood House
Susan Halpin
Montgarret
New Ross, County Wexford
Telephone and **FAX:** 051-425494
Bedrooms: 4, all with private bath.
Rates: £18 p.p.; Single £24; 10 percent discount for children. Vouchers accepted. **Credit cards:** VISA, Eurocard, American Express. **Open:** April to November. **Children:** Yes, 5 and upwards. **Pets:** No. **Smoking:** No. **Provision for handicapped:** None. **Directions:** Approximately 1 km outside New Ross on Ring Road N30. About 2 km off New Ross/Rosslare Road N25. Close to Statoil filling station.

This dormer home is situated in open countryside and was purposely built for bed and breakfast guests, with excellent views of the Barrow River and with surrounding landscaped gardens. Bedrooms are decorated in peach, lemon, and pink colors. An 18-hole golf course, a par-3 golf course, and the John F. Kennedy homestead are located nearby, as well as a heated swimming pool, a snooker hall, and the Riverside Keep-fit Center. Daily cruises are featured on the River Gallaly, with tea and dinner provided. Susan previously ran the B&B "Woodlands," at New Bawn.

Ardruadh
Jim and Colette Cahill
Spawell Road
Wexford, County Wexford
Telephone and **FAX:** 053-23194
Bedrooms: 6, all with private baths.
Rates: £20-25 p.p.; Single £25-30; 25 percent discount for children.
Vouchers not accepted. **Credit cards:** VISA, MasterCard/Access.
Open: All year, except 1 week at Christmas. **Children:** Ages 5 and up.
Pets: No. **Smoking:** Restricted. **Provision for handicapped:** None.
Directions: From Wexford City, follow the N25 to Spawell Road and go
right. The house is directly on your left; go into the yard and park in
the back, opposite County Hall.

This fascinating building was built in 1893 by an Irish timber merchant who saw a house he liked in Norway and had the plans, stones,
and wood sent back to Ireland. It has many gables and a handsome
wooden arch design over the front doorway. Original doors and windows are paraná pine. Of the rooms, one has two big bay windows
looking out to the Slaney River with colors of pink, green, and hot
fuchsia in lacy trims. Colors used in other rooms are peach, pastel
blues, and green. The Cahills are very cordial. The oversized sitting
room has a French ornate couch, a baby grand piano, and other lovely
antiques. It also has an open fireplace. The red and white dining room
has a view of the river. Offerings are full Irish, choices of eggs, tomatoes, mushrooms, muesli, and grapefruit. You'll find tennis, golf, boating, fishing, horse racing and riding, opera, theater, and movies
nearby. Also, see the Bird Sanctuary, Johnstown Castle, Heritage Park,
and art museums. Rosslare Ferry is 12 miles away.

Clonard House
Kathleen Hayes
Clonard Great
Wexford, County Wexford
Telephone and **FAX:** 053-43141; **E-Mail:** clonardhouse@indigo.ie
Bedrooms: 9, all with private baths. There is one extra bathroom with bathtub.
Rates: £20 p.p.; Single £25. 20 percent discount for children. Vouchers accepted. £14 dinner. **Credit cards:** VISA and MasterCard.
Open: March 17 to November 1. **Children:** All ages. **Pets:** No.
Provision for handicapped: None. **Directions:** On the Wexford Ring Road, go to the R733/ N25 roundabout. Take R733 south and first road on left, which is Farm Road. The Clonard House is signposted.

Clonard was built in 1783 by an Irishman, William Hutton, who played a role in the First Rebellion of 1798. This luxurious Georgian farmhouse has a very friendly host and hostess. Their daughter, Avril, served us delicious Irish coffee on arrival, and they were very generous with suggestions of where to eat in Wexford. This is a working dairy farm of 60 cows, and it is enjoyable to see them line up morning and night to be milked in the barn. Some of the charming rooms have fourposter beds, some have a far-away view of Wexford Bay, and others face various parts of the farm estate. A full Irish Breakfast is served with a choice of smoked salmon and scrambled eggs or buffet. There is a castle view on the property where Cromwell lived. See the Heritage Park nearby or visit the old cultural seaport of Wexford. There are many good restaurants in town. Also available are: golf, sandy beaches, horseback riding, bird-watching, fishing, and boat trips.

O'Brien's Auburn House
David and Mary O'Brien
2 Auburn Terrace
Redmond Road
Wexford Town, County Wexford
Telephone and **FAX:** 053-23605
Bedrooms: 5; 4 with private baths, 1 with shared.
Rates: £18-25 p.p.; Single £21-23; Up to 50 percent discount for children under 12. Vouchers not accepted. **Credit cards:** VISA, MasterCard. **Open:** All year, except December 22 to January 1. **Children:** All ages. **Pets:** No. **Smoking:** Restricted. **Provision for handicapped:** None. **Directions:** Take the N25 to Dunnes Stores in Wexford. After Dunnes and in front of the railway station, take the first left to Redmond Road, a street parallel to the river. About 50 yards down and across from the cinema, it is the second red brick house on left.

This charming Victorian, red brick 1891 house was elegantly restored in 1991 to the highest standards by the O'Briens. Mary and David take pride in looking after their guests. We liked the high ceilings, large rooms, and Edwardian décor. All of the bedrooms now have TVs and tea- and coffee-making facilities. The Opera Festival was on when we were there, and a couple from England described how they had researched all the B&Bs in Wexford and picked this one. Soft pastels are used in long drapes, quilts, and rugs to give bedrooms a stately touch. Large baths with showers remind us of continental pensions. The young couple are a delight and anxious to please. Their breakfast is served in a large dining room through glass doors off the fireplaced lounge. The breakfast is the full Irish one, but cereals, yogurts, cheeses, and a choice of eggs are available for vegetarians. Amenities within short distances are the blue-flag beaches, golf, horseback riding, swimming, golfing, bird sanctuary, scenic and historic walks, Heritage Park, and Johnstown Castle. The house has a private car park.

ALSO RECOMMENDED

Enniscorthy, *Oakville Lodge,* Mrs. Attracta Doyle, Mountfinn Lane, Ballycarney. Telephone: 054-88626. Bedrooms: 5, 3 with private baths. Vouchers accepted. VISA accepted. Country location overlooking Slaney River Valley. Individual porches outside of three rooms to view pretty landscaped garden. It also has an attractive conservatory.

New Ross, *Rosville House,* Philomena Gallagher, off N25, 1 km from New Ross on the Wexford Road. Telephone 051-421798. Bedrooms: 5, 4 with private baths. Modern bungalow in Knockmullen set on the hillside overlooking Barrow River Valley. Nice border of roses in front. Car park in rear. Sunny breakfast room when we were there. Pleasant hostess.

COUNTY WICKLOW

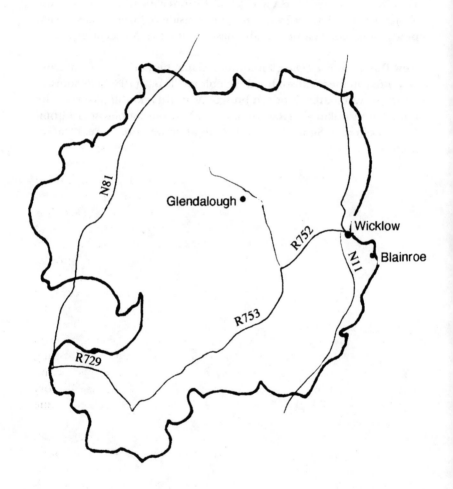

County Wicklow

County Wicklow is unique and notable, especially for its starring feature of the wooded Glendalough Mountains and Valley, and the seventh- to fourteenth-century ruins of St. Kevin's Monastery. With its chapel, cathedral, round tower, and fine old Celtic crosses laid out over acres of greenery, it is awe-inspiring. Its new Visitor Center informs you of the whole history with films, models, and pictures.

The other special feature of this county is its location so central to Dublin, Kilkenny, and the coast. It also contains the direct route to County Wexford in the south. Wicklow town, right on the Irish Sea, has ruins and castles of its own in addition to good beaches. South of Wicklow and Glendalough, at Avondale Forest Park, is a peaceful place called "Meeting of the Waters," named for a poem of Thomas Moore, where you may hear traditional Irish music every day in season. Here you may visit Avondale House, the home of the great Irish patriot, Charles Parnell. Visit the extensive Powerscourt Gardens, the pride of Wicklow.

In the same area is the town of Avoca, home of Avoca Handwoven Woolen Goods. At the Craft Shop, you may watch a weaver working at his or her loom. Working further south you'll enjoy the boats and quays of the fishing town of Arklow. Visit the Arklow Pottery Factory and Craft Shop. Take a walk on Brittas Bay Beach and visit the Maritime Museum.

In the northwest corner of the county is the tiny town of Russborough on a lake that proudly displays the Russborough House, an elaborate baroque, granite house, built in the 1740s, which has paintings by famous European artists. Ashford, to the north of Wicklow town, is known for its lovely Mount Usher Gardens, abloom with azaleas and rhododendrons in the spring. Traveling northeast, you'll want to take the marvelous refreshing hilltop walk along Bray Head, with its panoramic ocean views.

Greenfields
Conor Moloney
Blainroe, County Wicklow
Telephone: 0404-68309
Bedrooms: 5, all with private baths.
Rates: £17 p.p.; Single £20; 25 percent discount for children. Vouchers not accepted. **Credit cards:** VISA and MasterCard. **Open:** January 1 to December 31. **Children:** Yes, all ages. **Pets:** No. **Smoking:** Yes. **Provision for handicapped:** None. **Directions:** Go 5 miles out on coast road (Dunbar Road), south of Wicklow town. Greenfields is the first house on left after Blainroe Golf Club.

This beautiful ranch-style bungalow stands on one and a half acres, with a spring pond in the garden, in a gorgeous setting with views of the ocean. There is a nice sunny guest lounge where tea or coffee is served. The rooms are beautifully decorated in blues and greens, pinks, or blue and white. Guests may also use the sun room facing the Irish sea, or the game room with pool table. There is an extensive breakfast menu served in their handsome dining room; breakfast includes the full Irish Breakfast plus cheeses, yogurts, both puddings, peppered mackerel, and smoked kippers. Go to the beach or sun in the garden, play golf at the championship course next door, go horseback riding 10 km away, take walks downtown, and by all means go hear the traditional Irish music played daily at the "Meeting of the Waters" near Avondale, 8 miles south of town. Avondale is the home of the famous Irish patriot, Charles Parnell. Donald Hunt, author of *To the Greenfields Beyond,* has stayed here.

Carmel's
Carmel Hawkins
Annamoe
Glendalough, County Wicklow
Telephone and **FAX:** 0404-45297
Bedrooms: 4, all with private baths.
Rates: £18 p.p. private bath; Single £27; 25 percent discount for children. Vouchers not accepted. **Credit cards:** None. **Open:** March 1 to October 31. **Children:** All ages. **Pets:** No. **Smoking:** No. **Provision for handicapped:** Yes. **Directions:** From Dublin, take the N11 to the signpost for Glendalough, go to Laragh Village, take a left to Annamoe, and follow the fingerpost sign to Carmel's or ask at any shop in Annamoe.

This home is family run and has been extended to make rooms for the B&B. The Hawkinses are known for their hospitality and congeniality. Set in the heart of the breathtaking Wicklow Mountains, this B&B will give you a break from the hustle and bustle of cities. All the rooms are pretty, clean, neat, and tastefully decorated. Fresh flowers adorn them and for that homey feeling, Carmel has electric blankets and hair dryers for each room. The lounge has been extended and has a TV. In the dining room you will be given a real Irish Breakfast, along with different ideas like fresh fruit salad, home-baked muffins, and cheeses of different countries. The B&B is only one hour to the ferry to England, one and a half hours to Dublin City or Dublin Airport, and 17 miles to Bray Head. It is close to Avoca, home of *Ballykissangel,* and only 7 miles to the well-known mountains and woods of the splendid Glendalough, with its monastic ruins in the valley, ancient chapel, round tower, and numbers of Celtic crosses. Some of the ruins date back to the seventh century, when St. Kevin founded the monastery. You will not want to miss this awesome sight, with its informative Visitor Center. Visit the famed Powercourt gardens and Blessington lakes nearby.

Rosita
Rita Byrne
Dunbur Park
Wicklow Town, County Wicklow
Telephone: 0404-67059
Bedrooms: 4, all with private baths.
Rates: £27 private, £18 shared; Single £22; 20 percent discount for children. Vouchers accepted. **Credit cards:** None. **Open:** March to November. **Children:** Yes. **Pets:** No. **Smoking:** No. **Provision for handicapped:** None. **Directions:** Drive through town center toward Summerhill, on to Dunbur Road. At the pedestrian crossing, turn right into Dunbur Park; it's the last bungalow on right.

A warm welcome greets you at this friendly modern Georgian bungalow overlooking Wicklow Bay, where Rita and her husband George have been hosting B&B guests for over 20 years. This is a popular place with many Irish travelers, many of whom return each year. It is surrounded by a lovely garden. The garden motif continues into the home with pink and green, pale blue and lemon, pink and white, and pink and grey lovely, flowered bedrooms. The lounge has a large TV where tea, coffee, and hot scones with homemade jam are served. The dining room has separate tables with nice mahogany furniture looking out onto the patio and garden. A full Irish Breakfast is served, along with additional items such as cheeses, yogurts, fresh fruit, porridge, and cereals. Here you will be treated as family. Rita notes that the old restored Gaol is worth a visit. It takes you back to 1700/1800. Other recreational features are: golf, tennis, horseback riding, fishing, and snooker.

Silver Sands
Lyla Doyle
Dunbur Road
Wicklow, County Wicklow
Telephone: 0404-68243
Bedrooms: 5; 4 with private baths, 1 with shared.
Rates: £18.50 p.p. private bath; £16.50 p.p. shared bath; Single £21-23;
50 percent discount for children under 12. Vouchers accepted. **Credit
cards:** None. **Open:** All year, except 4 days at Christmas. **Children:** All
ages. **Pets:** No. **Smoking:** Restricted. **Provision for handicapped:**
None. **Directions:** From Wicklow town center, take the coast road
(Dunbar Road) 3.5 km out of town. The house is on the right.

Silver Sands is a bungalow with a front garden that overlooks the
Irish Sea and Sugarloaf Mountains. You can see all the way from Bray
Head in the north to Wicklow Head Golf Course in the south. Lyla's
rooms are very attractive, with pink roses, pink and wine designs,
green, and an unusual black and rose coverlet in one room. Rooms en
suite have TVs and coffee-making facilities. All rooms have tea-making
facilities. The dining room in front has spectacular ocean views, and
the lounge is quite comfortable. Breakfast extras are choice of eggs,
fruits, yogurts, and herring. There are cliff walks and a walk to the harbor across the street from the house that goes by the Black Castle
ruins. Beaches and fishing are very nearby. Golf is across the street and
horseback riding is four minutes away in Ashford. Lyla suggested (and
we tried) the Grand Hotel for dinner and it was reasonable and very
good.

ALSO RECOMMENDED

Bray, *Rosslyn House,* Peggy Kelly. On Killarney Road just south up the street from Bray Town Hall. Telephone: 01-2860993; FAX: 01-2862419. 3 Bedrooms, 2 with private baths. Elegant Victorian in quiet location, within walking distance of restaurants, pubs, and shops. Private car park. Convenient to DART.

Coolgreaney, *Ballykilty Farmhouse,* Mrs. A Nuzum. From Arklow, take Coolgreaney Road at the roundabout and follow the same road for three miles. Ballykilty is the yellow farmhouse on the right. Telephone: 0402-37111. Beautiful, peaceful garden surrounds house. Old-fashioned fireplace in dining room. Won Farmhouse of the Year Award. Working dairy farm with other farm animals in rear pasture. Mrs. Nuzum is a pleasant and accommodating host.

Northern Ireland

NORTHERN IRELAND

Introduction to Northern Ireland

BACKGROUND

One cannot really speak of Northern Ireland as being separate from the Republic. There are so many traditions, common heritages, and histories that bind these countries and people together. Currently, there is a genuine, common hope for peace and future prosperity on both sides of the border. We are encouraged by recent developments that reveal that the Unionists and the Republicans in the North are moving ahead to build a lasting peace.

One need not be afraid. Northern Ireland is presently very peaceful, with a few isolated incidents, none of which threatened life or limb. The people are exceptionally warm, friendly, and helpful. You should not hesitate to visit Ulster. It is perfectly safe! It's like an Irish country with a British mix of customs, currency, and culture—a hybrid of sorts. This gives Northern Ireland its own interesting charm. You will be impressed by the romantic beauty of the Glens of Antrim, where the mountains roll down to the sea, which hides crescent-shaped sandy swimming beaches and spectacular vistas. At one bed and breakfast on a hill above Cushendall we could look across the Irish Sea and see the Mull of Kintyre, part of Scotland—15 miles away!

One should be cautious of generalizing about the Northern Irish. You find here two predominant groups: the Irish Catholics, a minority in Ulster; and the Scots and English, who are most numerous. The Scots brought their Protestant religion with them, which in most cases is rooted in Presbyterianism. The English traditionally belong to the Church of England, which is Episcopalian. This religious difference was thought by many to be at the heart of the conflict in Northern Ireland, but there have been some convincing arguments that a criminal element has benefited from the troubles through drug dealing and gunrunning. The United States has strongly supported programs in both Eire and the North to curb the radicals on both sides by offering economic assistance to create jobs, especially in Belfast and

Londonderry. One is struck by the irony of seeing the beautiful Ulster cities and countryside and imagining this place as a battleground.

We recommend the book cited in our "Introduction to Ireland" at the beginning of this book, Edmund Curtis's *A History of Ireland,* if you wish to explore the roots of this problem in more depth. His is one of the most popular and authoritative historical accounts up through 1922. It will help you to understand the difficulties the Irish face in achieving a lasting peace.

We found the operators of B&Bs in the North to be more conservative and cautious. While all were very friendly, we don't know if their reluctance to be in our book was due to their business acumen or because of the troubles they have endured since the early 1970s. We must explain that when we asked the hosts if they wanted to be in the book after we had inspected the premises, it took a lot more explaining than it did in the Republic of Ireland. We attribute some of this to the rapid changes occurring in people's lives in Northern Ireland. Northern Ireland does not have a *national* Town and Country Homes Association like the Republic of Ireland does. Tourism is organized more by region and county. When we were in Londonderry last June, the Northern Ireland Tourist Board branch office was out of copies of a helpful booklet describing coastal B&Bs, the Town & Seaside House Association's "Be Our Special Guest," which mainly covers Down, Antrim, and Londonderry. The flood of tourists has been somewhat overwhelming.

We deeply appreciate the help from the Northern Ireland Tourist Board representatives in New York, Belfast, and Londonderry. We encourage you to avail yourself of their booking service. We found the staff in Belfast extremely courteous and welcoming. At their city or regional centers, maps, county guides, and event calendars are free. Also quality gifts, slide sets, audiotapes, and the like are available for a nominal price. For information in the U.S. call 1 (800) 326-0036 in New York; in Canada, 1 (416) 925-6368 in Toronto. There is an office in Dublin at 16 Nassau Street, near the Blarney Woolen Mill shop. The Belfast office, which we found very useful, is at 59 North Street; Telephone: 01232-246609. Park in the major car park nearby and walk there. People will be happy to direct you.

PRACTICAL MATTERS

We urge you to review our general advice on travel in the "Introduction to Ireland" at the beginning of the book. We won't repeat it here. These tips and advice apply as well to traveling in

Northern Ireland. We have followed the same procedure and used the same standards in the North for the selection of B&Bs. Let us point out a few of the differences you can expect when you cross the border and give you some tips and advice to make your trip a great success.

Money and Changing Currency

Changing money can be a hassle, but it needn't be if you obtain American Express traveler's checks made out in pounds sterling. Most American Automobile Association offices have these for members free of charge at a reasonable exchange rate. By doing this you avoid running to a bank to exchange dollar traveler's checks and finding them closed. Our advice is if you are going to tour both the South and the North, use both dollar traveler's checks in the South and sterling checks in the North. You won't be able to buy traveler's checks in Irish pounds (or punts) in the U.S.

Rental Cars

Some car rental companies do not allow you to take their car from the Republic of Ireland across the border. Check this out with your travel agent or your car rental company. Again remember MasterCard only provides you with collision insurance for 15 days overseas if you waive the insurance offered by the rental company. VISA Gold covers you for 30 days, a definite advantage if you are contemplating longer trips. Also, as in the South, you drive on the opposite side of the road than you do in the U.S. Don't worry; it is easy and you will catch onto it in one day. We also find that automatic shifting is very helpful in reducing driving fatigue and in increasing ease of driving.

Booking Ahead

It is advisable to call ahead to book your next B&B stay. Most hosts will have recommendations for other B&Bs and might even call ahead for you. You can purchase a CALLCARD (or Phonecard) as in the South. These are not interchangeable with those in the Republic of Ireland. You have to buy a Northern one at the post office or some convenience stores. The rooms are priced per person unless otherwise noted. A single person will usually pay a higher rate. Currently many B&Bs are fully booked in the peak season. In June 1995, we couldn't find one room in Belfast within a reasonable price range. Northern Ireland has become a very popular tourist destination, so getting rooms in the better B&Bs like the ones in this book can be very difficult. That's why we urge you to make reservations ahead if you can.

Rooms

Almost all of the other routines in B&Bs in Northern Ireland are the same as in the Republic of Ireland. You will see the abbreviation H&C in some listings. It means that there is a vanity or sink with a mirror in the room with hot and cold water. This allows you to wash up and brush your teeth without going to a shared bath. We bring light bathrobes and slippers for the shared bath when we occupy a standard room. These accommodations are generally cheaper than the rooms with a private bath. Frank likes the bigger mirror and sink in the shared bath when shaving, plus some shared baths have much larger showers or tub/showers than the baths en suite. We found the standards of both town and country homes and farm B&Bs in Northern Ireland to be excellent. We can't wait to go back to stay at some we could only visit for our usual interview and inspection. The rates are about the same, varying with the exchange rate of the English pound sterling instead of the Irish punt.

County Antrim

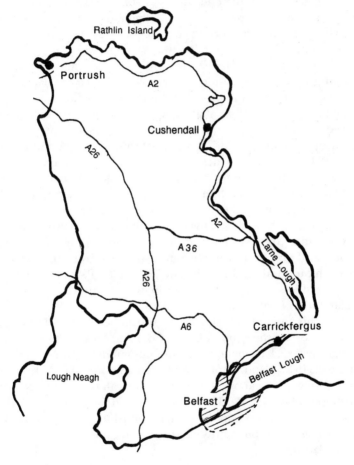

Antrim, on the northeast coast of Ulster, has majestic mountains that sweep down across grassy, green farm fields to the sea's edge, where rugged cliffs, white sandy beaches, and picturesque fishing villages form the boundary to the salty sea. The patchwork-quilt pattern of many shades of green and the man-made rock walls and farm fields complement the rest of the natural beauty and rivals those great vistas we have seen in the southwest of the Republic of Ireland and those in Cape Breton, Nova Scotia, or Hawaii. There are nine scenic glens to explore. Ulster's coastal outline on a map looks like a mirror image of the coast of Scotland—a mere 15 miles away. It is here that you will also find many of Scottish ancestry; these are descendants of the Scots who migrated to Northern Ireland in hopes of finding a better life.

You can start at either end of the Antrim coast road and motor east from Portstewart or northwest from the Norman town of Carrickfergus and follow the rugged coast, up and down the high mountains and then down to the water's edge, with a nice swimming beach at Cushendall. The beaches are safe, clean, and uncrowded— ideal for a day at the seaside. Many towns have seaside paths for hiking. The small ports will provide fishing trips and day cruises. Rathlin Island is a bird sanctuary that draws birders from all over the world to see the razorbill colonies and other rare species. You can book a boat trip to Rathlin Island at Ballycastle and even stay at the island's sole B&B, the Rathlin Guest House. Horseback riding, golf, forest parks and farm museums, and many other recreational activities are available. In addition to the unique experience of exploring castles and ancient tombs and churches, we particularly enjoyed the twelfth-century castle at Carrickfergus on the Belfast Lough, where full-sized mannequins dressed in armor or period garb adorn the walls and rooms and give more dimension to the visit. You can also see the Slemish Mountain at Broughshane, where St. Patrick is reputed to have herded swine as a slave after he was captured and brought to Ireland from England in the fifth century.

Legends abound in Irish history. Antrim has the Giant's Causeway, with its story of the giant Finn MacCool and his walk to Scotland on the unusual rock formation that continues under the sea and rises out of the sea in Scotland. Another fun visit is a walk on the Carrick-a Rede Rope Bridge, high above the beach and ocean below, located 5 miles northwest of Ballycastle. There is Waterworld for the kids at Portrush, and for us older folks, in the village of Bushmills, the Old Bushmill Distillery to liven your spirits. As you can see, there is much to do and see in Antrim.

Beech Grove
Dettie and Jack Barron
412 Upper Rd., Trooper's Lane
Carrickfergus, County Antrim BT38 8PW
Telephone: 01960-363304
Bedrooms: 6; 3 with private baths, 3 with shared.
Rates: £17.50, both singles and doubles; £16 shared bath; £9.50 dinner. 50 percent discount for children. Vouchers accepted. **Credit cards:** None. **Open:** All year. **Children:** All ages. **Pets:** Yes. **Smoking:** Yes. **Provision for handicapped:** None. **Directions:** From Belfast, travel north for 10 miles on A2. Just left of the security wall is Trooper's Lane; follow that until you are 3 miles south of Carrickfergus. Take a right after the four lanes start. B&B is on left.

Beech Grove is a 1790s farmhouse just outside the famed town of Carrickfergus. It has wonderful views to the front of Belfast Lough, where ships from Liverpool and the Seacat from Scotland can be seen. Jack still keeps numerous chickens and will proudly show them to you; children can explore the large garden. The seven rooms are clean and tastefully decorated in soft colors. Our room had a double and a single bed with wide pink-and-white striped coverlets, a TV, a bureau with a mirror, and extra tables (which are sometimes hard to find in Ireland). All have tea services and views of farmlands and the lake. Dettie Barron serves a lovely Irish Breakfast with choice of eggs and all kinds of breads and jams. Her table settings and dishes are attractive. Belfast, with its historic buildings, arts, drama, and museums, isn't far away to the south. You may enjoy the Carrick castle in Carrickfergus, with mannequins dressed as knights and ladies on horseback, the Ulster Walk in the countryside, ferries, fishing, golf, and horseback riding. In town the children will especially enjoy the Knight's Ride, an attraction that tells the history of the area. Knockagh monument can be seen from the farm.

Culbidagh House
Roisin and Charlie Hamill
115 Red Bay Rd.
Cushendall, County Antrim BT44 0SH
Telephone: 012667-71312
Bedrooms: 3; 2 with private baths, 1 private not en suite, 1 additional shower.
Rates: £16; 50 percent discount for children under 12. Vouchers are accepted. **Credit cards:** None. **Open:** April 1 to October 30. **Children:** All ages. **Pets:** Outside only. **Smoking:** No. **Provision for handicapped:** Yes. **Directions:** Take the coast road (A8) to Cushendall. As you come into town, look for the Culbidagh House sign on the left, just after the park on the right. Turn left and you will see Red Bay Boats, Ltd., on your right. Follow this street up to the top and turn left on Kilnadore Road. Go about ½ mile; the street turns sharply right up the hill and becomes Red Bay Road. The Hamills' home is on your right, about ½ mile farther.

This home has one of the most spectacular views in all of Northern Ireland. It is snuggled high on the hillside and overlooks sweeping green fields dotted with cows and grazing sheep, the town, and the Irish Sea far below. You can see the mountains of Scotland off in the northeast. All rooms have been redecorated in soft colors. One large room offers two double beds; another a double and single, what the Irish call a family room; and a third is at the front with table and chairs and a spectacular view. Charming Roisin and Charles work together to prepare your breakfast at a table in front of the bay windows with the panoramic view. They offer a delicious Irish Breakfast with choices of eggs, ham, sausage, fresh fruit, cereal, juice, and coffee or tea.

Although there is golf, fishing, boating, and other watersports at the beach and park, we chose to hike along the Cliff Walk to the left of the beach and do some photography. The swimming was tempting, as Ireland was experiencing a heat wave when we were there. Fran got up early one morning and attempted to scale the green-covered mountaintop off to one side of the property. She made it through several sheep pastures and above until even the house looked small in the distance below. The photos she took of fields, mist, and the sea below are prize-winners. The evening's entertainment is watching the sunset and the mountains change color to red and rosy pink. It stays light until almost 10:30 P.M. during the summer because the North Pole is tilted toward the sun, but the temperature stays in the balmy high 70s or 80s.

✦

Maddybenny Farm House (and Riding Centre)
Rosemary White
Off Loguestown Road
Portrush, County Antrim
Telephone and **FAX:** 02165-823394
Bedrooms: 3, all with private baths, 6 self-catering cottages (4-star rated by NITB).
Rates: £25-27.50 p.p bed and breakfast. Vouchers not accepted. 40 percent discount for children; write to Rosemary for details on cottage rentals. **Credit cards:** VISA and MasterCard. **Open:** All year except Christmas and New Year's. **Children:** Yes, all ages. **Pets:** No. **Smoking:** Yes, except dining room. **Provision for handicapped:** None. **Directions:** Coming south from Portrush follow sign at Magherabuoy Hotel crossroads; from Coleraine north follow signs on A29 at Magherabuoy road and Loguestown road roundabout.

This award-winning home has been recommended to us by many friends in Ireland. It is a Plantation Period farmhouse built before 1650 by the Earl of Antrim and completely renovated and furnished in fine family antiques. The breakfasts have won the All Ireland "Galtee Best Farmhouse Breakfast" award in 1989, 1992, and 1994. Before you turn in, Rosemary White asks that you read the menu and write down your order before you leave for the evening. This will be your ticket to a gourmet and delicious breakfast by the Cordon Bleu cook. For example, the porridge can be taken with Drambuie, honey, and cream. From there you select 12 main dishes. Bedrooms are large and all en suite, with color TV, each capable of sleeping four people. Other amenities include: hospitality trays in rooms, refrigerator use in the hall for keeping your drinks and picnic things, pay phone in the hall, iron and ironing boards, and hair dryers and hot brushes. You also have full use of the cross-country and riding facilities and game room with snooker table. Mrs. White can direct you to local gourmet restaurants, the Giant's Causeway, seven golf courses, beaches, and other tourist sites.

ALSO RECOMMENDED

Ballymena, *Caireal Manor Guest House,* Pat O'Neil, 90 Glenravel Road, Martinstown, BT43 6QQ. Telephone: 021667-58344/58465/58221. 5-star luxury guesthouse with all the amenities, fully licensed restaurant and bar. Recommended by Charles O'Connor, Glastonbury, CT.

Belfast, *Oakhill Country House,* May Noble, 59 Dunmurry Lane, BT17 9JR. Telephone: 0232-610658. FAX: 0232-621566. Bedrooms: 4, 3 en suite. Luxury country home 4 miles from Belfast. Amazing gardens and extraordinarily charming interior. Large baths. No pets. Breakfast served in the conservatory during the summer months.

Cushendall, *Cullentra House,* Olive McAuley, 16 Cloughs Road, BT 44 0SP. Telephone/Fax: 021667-71762. Ulster Tourist Development Assoc. award winner. Nestled amidst breathtaking scenery of the Antrim Coast and Glens.

Dundonald, *The Cottage,* Mrs. Elizabeth Muldoon, 377 Comber St., Belfast, BT16 0XB. Telephone: 0247-878189. Bedrooms: 3, all with shared bath. Bedrooms are small but this is a home remodeled from a 1740s cottage. Delightful with lots of character and attractively landscaped. 3 miles east of Belfast on the A20.

Portrush, *Royal Court Hotel,* 233 Ballybogy Rd., Ballymagarry. Off A2 where you turn to Ballymoney a few miles east of Portrush. Telephone: 01265-822236. A luxury hotel under new management, where we enjoyed many meals while in the area. Ultra-luxurious doubles with canopy bed and tiled baths, some with views of the ocean. There is an ocean-facing suite with 2 bedrooms and living room with large TV plus dining room that could be used for conferences. Nice for a family seeking luxury hotel accommodations in this popular resort. Meals were great but service was slow when we were there. The doubles are a good value as far as hotel prices go.

Portrush, *White Rocks,* Mrs. E. Allen, Prop., 105 Dunluce Rd., BT56 8NB. Telephone: 01265-823407. Bedrooms: 5, 2 en suite. Open all year. Faces the dunes and ocean. Quiet chalet bungalow.

COUNTY ARMAGH

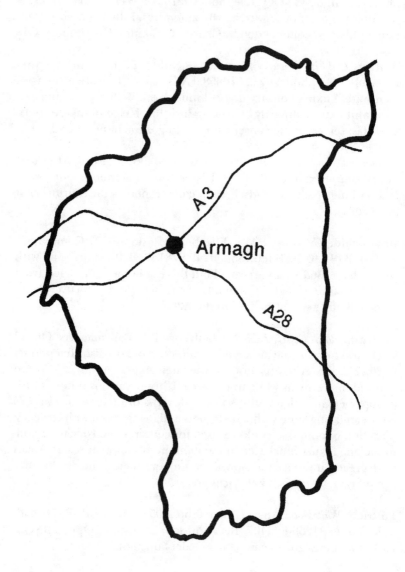

County Armagh

Armagh, the smallest of Northern Ireland counties, reaches from Louth in the south to Lough Neagh and Tyrone in the north and is bordered by Monoghan to the west. Again, gentle hills and quiet farms abide. Saint Patrick called the county, "my sweet hill."

The capitol city of Armagh is the most venerated of Irish cities, and the Roman Catholic Cathedral and the Protestant Church of Ireland Cathedral have been sitting on hills, facing each other, since the mid-1800s. This is where Ulster kings reigned hundreds of years ago and where the great Brian Boru is buried. You'll find this a sophisticated, comfortable old city with many trees, fine Georgian brick houses, iron gates and lampposts, and a wide green mall for walking and games. There is a fusiliers museum on the mall.

Visit the great Observatory, built by Archbishop Robinson, Saint Patrick's Trian, the Palace Stables, and historic houses such as the Argory and the Ardress House. Two miles southwest of Armagh, see the raised, circular Navan Fort, and Celtic crosses. Farther south, towards Newry on the A25, is a 1700s thatched manor house, Derrymore, with a large park of 48 acres for you to visit.

Northeast of Armagh Town in the Bramley apple-growing country, the sweet aroma of apple blossoms fills the air in May. At the end of October, a celebration of Apple Harvest is held, with hundreds of spicy, warm apple pies, freshly baked and served with thick cream. Summers in Armagh bring sheep dog trials, terrier races, and gun-dog scurries.

In Armagh, a popular game is "Road Bowls," where men compete throwing a metal ball down country roads to see how far it will go. Armagh men often win the Irish Championships, which are held at different places each year, all over the North and South of Ireland. On one of our visits to Blarney, the road to our B&B was closed for the playoffs of Road Bowls.

Redbrick Country House
Moreen Stephenson
Corbrackey Lane
Portadown, County Armagh BT62 1PQ
Telephone: 01762-335268
Bedrooms: 7; 3 with private bath, 4 with shared.
Rates: £17 p.p. Vouchers not accepted. **Credit cards:** None. **Open:**
All year. **Children:** Yes, all ages. **Pets:** No. **Smoking:** Restricted.
Provision for handicapped: None. **Directions:** First-time visitors will be
met by appointment.

This modern country home is set in quiet, secluded, rolling farmland and is centrally located so you can drive to any part of the
province in less than two hours. Moreen, a friendly hostess, will help
you plan your trip and enjoy the area. The bedrooms are delightfully
decorated and comfortable. A full Irish Breakfast is served in the
country kitchen. Tea and coffee welcome you on arrival. This bed
and breakfast is close to golf, watersports, shooting, and Lough
Neagh, and the Armagh Heritage Centre. Moreen prides herself on
the warm welcome and the family atmosphere.

ALSO RECOMMENDED

Armagh Town, *Deans Hill,* Jill Armstrong, College Hill, BT61 9DF. Telephone: 01861-524923. Bedrooms: 3, 2 en suite. A nice Victorian country house built in 1772, adorned with period pieces, fourposter bed in one and open fireplace in twin-bedded room.

COUNTY DOWN

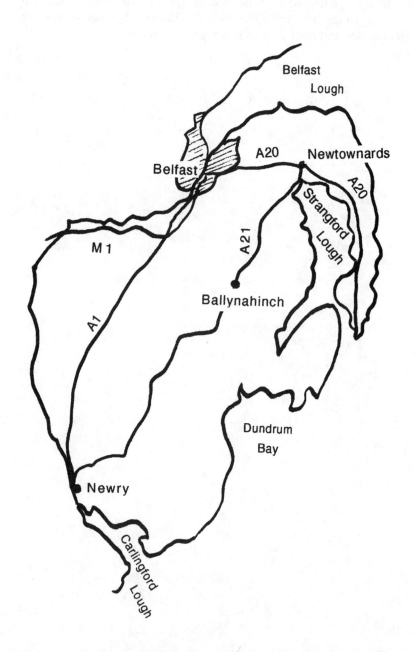

County Down

County Down borders on the Republic of Ireland, where people get their first glimpse of the North coming from Dublin and eastern areas. It presents wonderful first views of rolling green hills, wooden fences, and wide roads. Newry, the first pretty town you'll visit, has an excellent little tourist bureau right in the Town Hall at the bridge in the town's center. Here you can also visit the Newry Arts Centre and Museum. At the head of Carlingford Lough, Newry is mostly a farm town, and you'll see the grazing sheep and cows very soon after you leave the town center. To the southeast, the stately purple Mourne Mountains can be seen for miles.

If you head for the seaside, you'll take the A2, or the coast road, to lovely Kilkeel, where you can enjoy the beaches, watch fishing boats, and visit Green's Castle. Going north to Newcastle, you'll pass Donard Cave and Maggie's Leap. In the port of Newcastle, walk the promenade or go swimming, boating, or pony-trekking along the beach. You can camp at Tollymore Forest Park, where there is a great wildlife reserve.

Downpatrick is a fascinating area, with the cathedral overlooking the Quoile River, and the stone grave of Saint Patrick. This is where Saint Patrick lived out his last days in A.D. 46. You may want to visit the ruins of Saint Tassach's Church near Saul, where he took his last Holy Communion. Cross over to Portaferry and the peninsula of beauty along Strangford Lough. Greyabbey has not only the famed Grey Abbey, but it is also an "antique heaven." Farther north, visit the charming Mount Stewart House and acres of gardens on the way to Newtownards. Strangford Lough, which opens out to the sea, is so large it would be called a bay in America. These towns along the water's edge have gorgeous beaches and views.

From Newtownards you're only a half-hour from Belfast, if you drive during the midday. Here you'll find an astonishing city with many Victorian buildings that hearken back to the days of linen-making and shipbuilding. There are some boarded-up windows, but you'd hardly notice that fighting and guns used to be the order of the day.

They've done some lavish reconstruction of the downtown area, with many streets closed off to all traffic but shopping buses. Well-known storefronts of classy design line these streets, and it's safe to walk anywhere since peace has been established. Visit the huge, glittering multistoried shopping mall called Castlecourt Centre that is off Royal Avenue. The wonderful Northern Irish Tourist Bureau, situated in the town center at 59 North Street, will give you help in all directions. Sheila Cameron and Maureen Campbell were especially tireless and very generous with their attention to us. Their phone number is 01232 or 0-800-317153 (credit cards only).

Not far away, at the end of High Street, is the famed Albert Memorial Clock Tower and the Anglican St. Anne's Cathedral. We enjoyed a delicious and reasonable lunch at the handsome Deer's Head Pub, across from the Tourist Board. Other good pubs are White's Tavern, built in 1630, and the famous Victorian Crown Liquor Saloon at 46 Great Victoria Street. One B&B owner sent us for an excellent Italian meal at Gigolo's Restaurant at 23 Donegal Pass Road. Not only does the charming owner come out of the kitchen to explain his splendid recipes, but at night he'll serenade you with Italian arias. Visit the rococo Grand Opera House, on Great Victoria Street, with all of its gold trim. Here they hold plays, musical operas, and a children's theater. The Lyric Theater also has plays and music. In November, the Belfast Arts Festival at Queen's University has hundreds of cultural events. Don't pass up a tour of the grand old City Hall with its lovely marble inside. Of course, you'll want to see the beautiful Botanic Gardens.

If you were to continue north on the A24 from Downpatrick, you'd reach the historic town of Ballynahinch, with its wide streets. It was the scene of a battle in 1798, where seven thousand United Irishmen died trying to take the city. Go southwest from this town to see Northern Ireland's best known Neolithic dolmen, the Legananny, with its large delicately balanced stones.

Bushymead Country House
Mrs. Sally Murphy
86 Drumaness Rd.
Ballynahinch, County Down BT24 8LT
Telephone and **FAX:** 01238-561171
Bedrooms: 8, all with private baths.
Rates: £15-20 p.p.; Single £5 less; discount for children. Vouchers accepted. £8-12 dinner. **Credit cards:** Yes, all major. **Open:** Mid-January to mid-December. **Children:** All ages. **Pets:** Yes. **Smoking:** No. **Provision for handicapped:** Yes, but not wheelchairs. **Directions:** South of Belfast on the A24, continue south from Ballynahinch Square for about 2 miles toward Drumaness and Newcastle. Bushymead is on the left. Coming from Drumaness on A24, look for the Bushymead sign on your right, about 2 miles before Ballynahinch Square.

This lovely and luxurious country home, surrounded by pretty gardens and set in the heart of Down, has received high recommendations from travelers all over the world. It is at the gateway to Newcastle and the Mourne Mountains. All rooms are colorfully decorated, with the décor highlighted in period-style furnishings, some with antique fireplaces and beds with partial canopies. All rooms have tea- and coffee-making facilities. Some have color TVs. An attractive, separate guest lounge is available for friendly chats. Breakfast is a tasty full Irish one, and meals are available all day. Golf, horseback riding, fishing, museums, and forest parks are nearby, so this would make an excellent base camp for exploring County Down. They recently won the award of "Best for Guests."

Edenvale House
Diane and Gordon Whyte
130 Portaferry Rd.
Newtownards, County Down BT22 2AH
Telephone: 01247-814881; **FAX:** 01247-826192
Bedrooms: 3 with private baths.
Rates: £25; Single £30. Vouchers not accepted. **Credit cards:** Yes, VISA and MasterCard. **Open:** January 2 to December 18. **Children:** All ages. **Pets:** Yes. **Smoking:** Restricted to sunroom. **Provision for handicapped:** Only if they can manage stairs. **Directions:** It is on the east side of Strangford Lough, about 2 miles south of the town of Newtonards and the Flying Club on the Belfast-Portaferry Road (A20). Before the stone pillar entrance, there is a large "Butterlump Rock" on the beach to your right and a row of cottages on your left. The small Edenvale House sign at the entrance on the left is easy to miss. It is before Mount Stewart Garden. *A note of caution:* This is a dangerous entrance when leaving; enter the road slowly.

This elegant 1780 Georgian house, furnished with antiques, fresh flowers, and open log fires, is a part of a seven-acre farm, and Diane and Gordon Whyte keep six horses but not for riding. Stables are available *free* for horses or dogs. Mrs. Whyte gave us a friendly full Irish welcome with a tea and delicious strawberry tarts on the patio outside the sunroom. From here we had a perfect view across the lough to the Mourne Mountains. Their two dogs, Badger and Nip—one large, one small—will greet you as well. The three rooms in this beautifully renovated home are all carpeted and feature large, tastefully decorated baths. Antiques grace all of the rooms. One has a large, canopied, king-sized bed with soft green and pink décor; another is pale blue and yellow. The living room is roomy and the country kitchen with hanging herbs is sunny and inviting. This B&B looks like something out of *House Beautiful* or *Home and Garden* magazines. Their breakfast of hot homemade breads, fried potato bread, and hot fruit compote with cream, along with the traditional Irish Breakfast, will not be forgotten. Places to visit in the area are the world-famous Mount Stewart Garden and Estate, antique shops in Greyabbey, and Castle Espie Wildlife Centre. For the sports-minded, there is sailing, windsurfing, riding, and bird-watching.

ALSO RECOMMENDED

Ardglass, *The Strand Farm,* Mrs. Mary Donovan, 231 Arglass Rd., BT30 7UL. Telephone: 0396-841446. Bedrooms: 2. Open all year. Secluded farmhouse in peaceful surroundings. Home baking. Children's pony and trap.

Bangor, *Hebron House,* The Maddock family, 59 Queens Parade, BT20 3BH. Telephone: 01247-463126. Bedrooms: 3. A Victorian listed home overlooking Bangor Marina. Open all year. Recommended by our friend, Helen Callanan, a B&B owner from Dun Laoghaire.

Belfast, *The Old Rectory,* Mary Callan, 148 Malone Road, BT9 5LH. A luxury B&B remodeled from an 1896 parish home. Handy to city center.

Belfast, *Camera House,* Paul and Angela Drumm, 44 Wellington Park, BT9 6DP. Telephone: 01232-660026. Bedrooms: 11, all with baths and TVs. No credit cards. Lovely red-bricked Victorian-style house near city center. Highly recommended.

Groomsport, *Tanner Cottage,* Mrs. L. Walker, 5 Main Street. Telephone: 0247-46534. Bedrooms: 2, both en suite. Open all year. A lovely home, east of Bangor. Many amenities.

Kilkeel, *Kilmorey Arms Hotel,* Prop: Mrs. McMurray, 41-43 Greencastle Street. Telephone: 016937-622220 or 62801. Bedrooms: 26, all en suite. Discount for seniors. Evening meal available. Delightful small inn with homey atmosphere. Worth the extra money. Nice cocktail lounge and public bar, worthy of a pint or two if passing through Kilkeel, or if you're thirsty from a walk in the Mournes.

Newry, *Ashton House,* Mrs. Bridget Heaney, 37 Omeath Rd., Fathom Line BT35 8QW. Telephone: 01693-62120. Bedrooms: 8, all en suite. Pretty eighteenth-century home situated on 22 acres of farmland overlooking Newry canal on the main scenic route to Carlingford and the Cooley Mountains.

Newry, *Hillside Guesthouse,* Jackie McNally, 1 Rock Road, Tamore, Newry, Co. Down BT34 1PL Telephone: 01693-65484. Bedrooms: 6; 3 with private bath. £18+

County Fermanagh

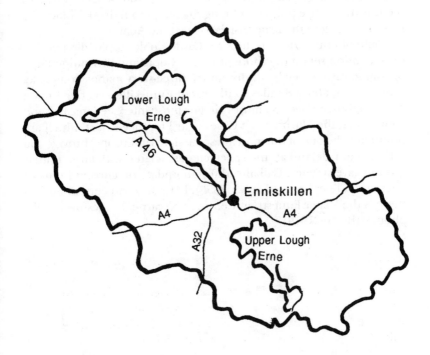

County Fermanagh is a region of rolling hills and farms, but Lough Erne and its upper and lower loughs with their enchanting and historic islands dominate the region. And where the lake and inland waterway appear pinched off in the middle stands the ancient town of Enniskillen. Plan to spend some time here and revel in the beauty of the lakes and mystical and enchanting quality of the ancient tales. Many a struggle for control of this strategic town was fought here. In those medieval times when there was peace, you can almost imagine the lords and ladies gathering at Enniskillen Castle for dinner and poetry reading after the men returned from the hunt.

This restored castle keep and barracks is a must for its display of past life in this region, its natural history, regimental museum, and a room dedicated to the life and work of a famous porcelain artist from Enniskillen. Also, while at the castle, be sure to view the excellent videos on the second floor of the museum that tell the story of Enniskillen past and present and the romantic stories of the Maguires who fought for and against the British. The Buttermarket is now a craft center where you can buy lace, knitwear, and Belleek china. To see this distinctive porcelain being made, go to Belleek Village, 25 miles away, where the Erne rushes to meet the Atlantic.

South of Enniskillen on the A4 is Castle Coole, a splendid neoclassical mansion set on the shore of Lough Coole and surrounded by a parkland. Also the eighteenth-century, three-story manor home, Florence Court, about 8 miles southwest of Enniskillen via the A4 and A32, is another place you must visit. For those interested in caves and cool places, the Marble Arch Caves near Florence Court, which are reported to be one of the most awesome sights in Europe, provide you with a boat ride and all the spectacles associated with large underground cave systems. Call ahead for an update on current hours of operation (Telephone: 01365-348855). For horse and equestrian fans there is the Ulster Equestrian Centre at Necarne, Irvinestown (Telephone: 013656-21919).

Lackaboy Farm
Mrs. Derrick Noble
Tempo Road
Enniskillen, County Fermanagh BT74 6EB
Telephone: 01365-322488
Bedrooms: 7; 4 with private baths, 3 with shared.
Rates: £15 p.p. private bath; £14 p.p. shared bath; Single £18; discount
for children. Vouchers accepted. £10 dinner (4 courses). **Credit cards:**
VISA, Access, and AMEX. **Open:** All year, except Christmas. **Children:**
All ages; babysitting available. **Pets:** No. **Smoking:** No. **Provision for
handicapped:** Yes. **Directions:** Take the B80 out of Enniskillen. Go
about one mile. You'll see the guesthouse sign. Turn left and follow
Tempo Road for a few hundred yards. Past a paddock and opposite
the Fermanagh Agricultural Centre, you will see Lackaboy Farm on
the left. It has a low, white-walled entrance that leads to the white, two-
storied farmhouse.

Lackaboy Farm guesthouse is part of a dairy farm with 45 Fresian
cows. Using a century-old foundation, the Nobles rebuilt the house
in keeping with the character of the original home. It is notable for
its Amish-like simplicity, neatness, and charm. The seven rooms are all
of good size and attractive, with flowered duvets and views of the farm
and surrounding hills. All have H&C. For breakfast Mrs. Noble has a
trolley of cereals, fruit, and cheese, along with her traditional Irish
Breakfast and her brewed coffee. She offers a scrumptious four-course
dinner if you book ahead. At the Agricultural Centre across the street,
livestock auctions and horse shows are held. This farm is just outside

historic Enniskillen, which serves as a connecting channel for the upper and lower parts of Lough Erne. Golf courses are nearby. As we walked alongside the lough in the castle park one evening after having a delicious meal at Mulligan's (33-35 Darling St.), we saw holiday seekers cruising in their rented yachts and young people practicing in their racing shells for an upcoming tournament. Ducks were swimming among the bulrushes. This was a beautiful scene that begged to be painted. This farm was recommended to us as a special place by many Northern Irish who like to come here for a week at a time.

ALSO RECOMMENDED

Enniskillen, *Ashwood Guest House,* Mrs Beryl Harris, Sligo Road. Telephone: 0365-323019. Bedrooms: 7, 4 doubles (2 en suite), 3 family or triples (2 en suite). Award-winning modern country house. Mrs. Harris is a Cordon Bleu-certified cook. Driving range and golf course next door. Near Marble Arch caves. 2 miles out of town on A4. Favorite of Northern Irish and many others.

COUNTY LONDONDERRY

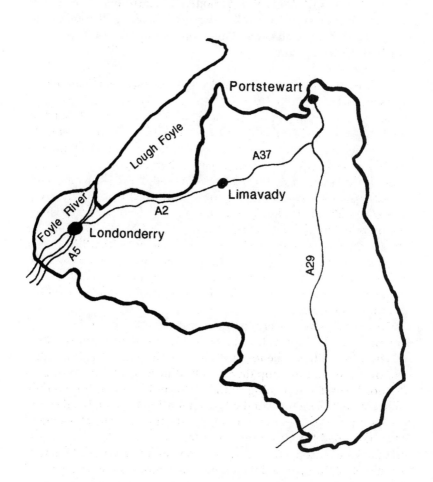

County Londonderry

St. Columb came out of Donegal 1,400 years ago and founded his first monastery in the oak grove ("Doire" in Gaelic), a gift from his cousin, Prince of Ailech. It was a holy place. The saint said that "the angels of God sang in the glades of Derry and every leaf held its angel."

Londonderry is the second-largest city in Northern Ireland and borders on Donegal. This beautiful city, with its massive medieval walls and four gates perched on the banks of Lough Foyle presents a wonderful opportunity for a walking tour of the 1633 Gothic Cathedral of St. Columb, the ornate Victorian Guildhall, and the many shops and pubs. We enjoyed our pub grub pints at J & T McGinleys (24 Foyle Street), after we toured the city. It is an excellent pub with character and history, formerly owned by a tea merchant. We did not see or hear of any troubles in Derry while we were in Northern Ireland, so one should not be fearful of fully enjoying the sights and sounds of this historic and scenic city.

The countryside of Derry spreads over a flat plain from the city to Limavady and Coleraine. If you take the A2 north on the west side of Limavady you will be able to complete a scenic loop of the Roe Valley and over the mountaintop drive of Mt. Bineveneagh, beginning on the north coast and turning south at Downhill, or continue on the coastal A2 to Coleraine, past the Mussenden Temple built by an eccentric bishop of Derry as testimony of his affection for Mrs. Mussenden. The main road from Coleraine to Limavady on the A37 is equally breathtaking in its panoramic view of the valley to the west. Limavady is where Jane Ross penned the tune of the famous "Londonderry Air" ("Danny Boy"), which she heard a passing fiddler play. Another attraction is the Roe Valley Country Park, two miles south of Limavady via the B192. A restored old linen mill and hydroelectric station built in 1896 are on the grounds with a museum. Activities at the park include canoeing, fishing, picnicking, and rock climbing. The most northeastern town in Londonderry is Portstewart, which is astride the Magilligan Strand. The longest beach in Ireland, the Magilligan Strand is formed where the Bann River empties into the Atlantic.

Ballyhenry House
Rosemary Kane
172 Seacoast Rd.
Limavady, County Londonderry BT49 9EF
Telephone: 015047-22657
Bedrooms: 4; 2 with private, 2 with shared baths.
Rates: £17 p.p.; Single £20; discount for children. Vouchers accepted.
Dinner offered for £12. **Credit cards:** None. **Open:** All year, except
Christmas. **Children:** All ages. **Pets:** Outside. **Smoking:** In lounge only.
Provision for handicapped: Partial. **Directions:** Take the A2 from
Coleraine to Limavady. As you leave Limavady headed toward
Londonderry Town, you will cross the Roe River Bridge. At the end
of the bridge and at the light turn right or north onto the B69. 3.3
miles toward Downhill, you will see the colorful sign for the farm on
the left. From Derry, turn left at the light at the end of the Roe River
Bridge. The directions remain the same as above.

Ballyhenry House is a lovely, airy, 1890 farmhouse, built by the Kane
family. It has a large, catchy, bright-colored sign featuring a farmer
with a scythe. The Kane family raises seed wheat and barley and has
more than 100 sheep and 50 cattle on this 1901 farm. The four bedrooms are spacious and sunny and have great pastoral views. One of
the rooms was bright yellow and the one where we stayed had soothing lavender-and-blue wallpaper with matching bedspreads and wall-
to-wall rugs. One room has original floors and is done in denim blue
and yellow. All have sinks in the rooms and shared baths. One new
large family room has a balcony. Rosemary Kane serves an Irish
Breakfast with choice of fresh fruit in season, porridge, yogurt, cereal,

and teas and coffee. The house sits on a flat plain in clear view of the steep Binevenagh Mountain. Mrs. Kane sent us on a short car ride up the 384-meter mountain, which we took in late evening after dinner, for a grand view of the mountains of Donegal, Lough Foyle to the west, and the sea to the north. We spent a long time up there watching some young men haying in the dimming light of sunset, around 10:30 P.M. An enchanting and romantic sight! It's a fascinating area when you realize there is nothing else between you and the North Pole but the Hebrides and a few scattered islands. There is also golf, horseback riding, fishing, a Roe Valley Country Park for picnicking, birdwatching, walks, pony-trekking, and hang gliding in the area. It is only five to seven miles from the beach. A bird sanctuary and a museum, as well as the bustling town of Limavady, are nearby. Also, the many attractions of the large city of Londonderry are not far away. The Giant's Causeway is only ¾ of an hour away by car.

Elagh Hall
Elizabeth Buchanan
Buncrana Road
Londonderry Town, County Londonderry BT48 8LU
Telephone: 01504-263116
Bedrooms: 3; 2 with private baths, 1 with shared.
Rates: £16 p.p. private bath; £17 p.p. shared bath; 50 percent discount for children. Vouchers accepted. **Credit cards:** None. **Open:** From April to October 31. **Children:** All ages. **Pets:** No. **Smoking:** No. **Provision for handicapped:** None. **Directions:** From Londonderry, take Buricrava Road (A2) about 1.5 miles, then turn right at Elagh Road (first right after BP Station).

This 1795 farmhouse is set on one hundred acres of rich farmland where the owners raise mostly sheep and cattle. This was the manse for the Burt Presbyterian Church, just across the border in Donegal. It was purchased by John Buchanan's father in 1948 and it has been in the family ever since. The house is handsomely decorated with antique furniture and all of the rooms have views of either Grianan Castle or the Donegal Hills. Elizabeth offers a full Irish Breakfast, and her specialties are homemade jams (raspberry, strawberry, and black-currant from berries grown in her own garden). The house has an Old-World atmosphere, like a step back in time. You wake up in the morning to lovely fresh air, singing birds, and sheep bleating in meadows below. Templemore Sports Complex is one mile away; there are two golf courses; fishing, horseback riding, and beautiful sandy beaches are nearby. The Buchanans highly recommend Harry's Restaurant, which is not far from Elegh Hall.

ALSO RECOMMENDED

Coleraine, *Blackheath House,* Mrs. Erwin, 112 Killeague Rd. BT51 4HH. Telephone: 01265-868433. Bedrooms: 5, all en suite. Evening meal available. Lovely country home set in rural surroundings 7 miles south of Coleraine. Washing facilities.

Coleraine, *Camus House,* Mrs. Josephine King, 27 Curragh Rd. BT51 3RY. Telephone: 01265-2982. Bedrooms: 3 (none with bath), 1 is a triple. Joey will make you feel welcome in this quaint 1685 home. It has won House-Country awards.

Londonderry Town, *Number 10,* Grace and Gerry McGoldrick, No. 10 Crawford Square BT48 7HR. Telephone: 01504-26500. Bedrooms: 3, all en suite. Family-run, modernized 1890 Victorian town house. Quiet neighborhood, good location to see many sites of the city.

Londonderry Town, *Robin Hill,* Malcolm and Gemma Muir, 103 Chapel Road, Waterside BT47 2BG. Telephone: 01504-342776. Bedrooms: 8, 6 en suite. A Presbyterian manse built in 1879, located on a large lot with panoramic views of the city, River Foyle, and the Donegal Hills.

Portstewart, *Ashleigh House,* Margaret Gordon, Station Road BT55 7PU. Telephone: 01265-834452. Bedrooms: 6, all en suite. Lovely modern home with pretty garden and beautiful rooms.

COUNTY TYRONE

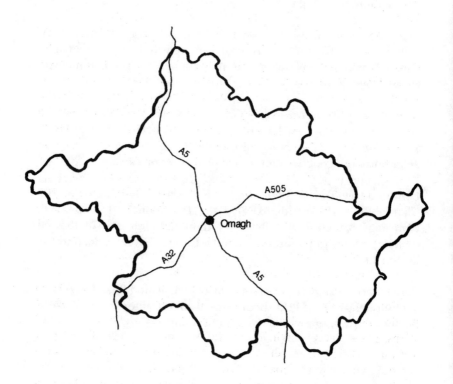

County Tyrone

When we first drove up to County Tyrone from Monaghan, we were struck by the pretty green rolling hills and neat farmlands with fertile valleys. Farther north there are the majestic Sperrin Mountains, which are excellent for walks through fields with grazing sheep, yellowed in the mild winter by whin or gorse (juniper). Dyeing boiled eggs in whin to color them yellow is an Easter custom.

At Strabane you can see some special Tyrone countryside if you drive southeast on the B47 through the Sperrin Mountains to Draperstown, south on the B162 to Cookstown, and then west to Omagh on the A505—stop at a pub or two along the way to quench your thirst. Farther north from Omagh is Gortin, with the Sperrin Heritage Center, where there are gold-mining and natural history exhibits, a craft shop, and a café. One of our favorite stops (where you will want to spend at least a half-day) is the Ulster-American Folk Park. Its main theme is the history of the eighteenth- and nineteenth-century Ulster emigration to North America. Original homes, one from the ancestors of the Mellon family (who endowed the park), are arranged in tree-lined paths, and each one tells in chronological order the story of the Ulster Irish in America, the covered wagons, the sod prairie houses—even a large ship that you can board to see the appalling conditions endured by the emigrants en route to America. It is very creative and educational as well as great fun. A café is there at the entrance for teas and light meals.

Neolithic sites include the Beaghmore stone circles at Cookstown, which were uncovered only 40 years ago, and the chambered cairn of Knockmany at the top of a steep wooded hill north of Clogher. At Ardboe there is an 18-foot Celtic cross. Another Celtic feature is the fourteenth-century Gaelic stronghold in West Tyrone: Harry Avery's Castle. The ancestral home of Woodrow Wilson is at Strabane, and his farm is still kept open by the Wilsons, who will show callers around the house. We almost lost count of the number of American presidents with Ulster roots or ancestors. Antrim has five alone!

Greenmount Lodge Country House
Louie Reid
58 Greenmount Rd.
Gortaclare
Omagh, County Tyrone BT79 0YE
Telephone: 01662-841325; **FAX:** 01662-840019
Bedrooms: 8, all en suite.
Rates: £19 p.p.; Single £11-14. 50 percent discount for children.
£12.50 and up dinner. **Credit cards:** Yes. **Open:** January to December.
Children: All ages. **Pets:** Outside. **Smoking:** No. **Provision for handi-capped:** Yes, the best accommodations in the area (NITB Category 1 classification). **Directions:** Off of the A5 (or Omagh to Ballygawley Road), about 8 miles south of Omagh town or 7 miles from Ballygawley. Turn right after the Carrick Keel/Pub toward Beagh. The sign for Greenmount is on the left after the 4-way intersection. The house is one mile farther on the left.

This lovely Grade-A farm bed and breakfast, really a historical coun-try estate, is set in the tranquility of 150 acres of beautiful scenery. West Tyrone is a surprising mixture of bleak, brownish boglands with whale-back hills that are separated by fertile valleys and rich pastures. Award-winning Greenmount Lodge has luxury accommodations that draw rave reviews from many guests from different countries. One guest wrote, "The host and hostess make us feel as though we are their sole guests." Their guestbook sings out "Excellent" in many languages. The guest rooms are fashionably decorated and the beds are comfortable. Bathtubs have been added to some rooms. There is a guest laundry room. The full Irish Breakfast is begun with a buffet table of "starters" of various cereals, oats, fresh fruits, juices, and yogurts. Fish and vegetarian dishes are also available on request. The Reids can accommodate most dietary requirements. The "sweet table" on weekends is reputed to be the best in Ireland. Having hosted guests for 25 years, the Reids will provide you with warm hospitality, good food, and a relaxing atmosphere. As they are on the northwest passage, this will make an ideal "base camp" for exploring the many parks, castles, museums, and natural and historical features of the region. They give 10 percent off cash payments and a good discount for booking direct with credit cards. Play tennis on their new court, golf, fish, or go game shooting nearby. There are great walks near lakes and you can visit the Ulster American Folk Park. We enjoyed it.

Self-Catering

This new section introduces travelers to the world of self-catering lodgings, which, as the name implies, means we (the innkeepers) supply the utensils, you do the cooking; we supply the bedding, you make the beds and keep house. The operators of most self-catering accommodations will show you the property, show you how to operate the equipment and appliances, take readings on the gas and/or oil for heating and cooking, and orient you to the neighborhood service, and then bid you adieu until you leave. A deposit is taken at the booking or reservation, and the agent or owner will meet you at the door or guide you to the place. Be sure they leave their home phone number so you can ask them questions as they arise.

Our experience is that this is a great, cost-effective alternative for traveling families. You can save money over staying in a bed and breakfast, guesthouse, or hotel, and it gives you freedom and flexibility over when you do things. You are not tied down with someone else's schedule. You also get to experience Ireland like a native, shopping in grocery stores, going to dry cleaning, getting a haircut, and the like. For kids, they have the outlet of their own home, the privacy of their own bedroom, and the fun of walking to neighborhood shops.

This section will identify recommended places, some of which the authors or friends have stayed at. We have selected accommodations in places where you might want to stay for at least a week, at the top tourist spots. In selecting a place, the demeanor of the host is important, and you will have to judge what kind of person you are dealing with. But you usually can tell after a few phone calls how hospitable they are. This is an important consideration in booking self-catering. Weekly rates are quoted; the low rate is off-season, the high rate is peak season—July and August. The number of bedrooms and how many they sleep might not agree since a couch or cot might be counted. Utilities are extra. In the off-season, the rate can usually be negotiated. The location of the accommodation is listed first in bold, and the address of the owner and agent is given, which will be some-where else. The first telephone number will be the owners'; the second may be an association number or booking service.

REPUBLIC OF IRELAND

Dublin City and County

Clontarf, Mrs. Nan Lowe, 207 Sutton Place, Sutton, Dublin 13. Telephone/Fax: 01-8203866, 01-6057777. 2-bedroom, superbly situated modern townhouse, 3-star, adjacent to Clontarf Castle. Sleeps 4. £290 June-October. Rest of year on request. We recommend this townhouse as it is in a lovely and upscale part of suburban Dublin, close to public transport and good restaurants. You can walk to Drawbridge Pub in Castle for lunch.

Clontarf, Mrs. Maeve McKenna, 6 Seacourt, Seafield Road East, Clontarf, Dublin 3. Telephone: 01-8330185 or 01-6057777. FAX: 01-6957787. Same 3-star townhouse complex as above, only larger, with 3 bedrooms. Sleeps 6. £320-370.

Dun Laoghaire, Mrs. Elizabeth Davies, 11 Glenageary Road, Dun Laoghaire, County Dublin. Telephone/Fax: 01-2841674. 3 bedrooms, 2-star house, sleeps 5. £250 peak season.

Glasnevin, Mr. Eamon Walsh, 48 Castle Crescent, Ashbourne, County Meath. Telephone: 01-8350952/01-6057777. FAX: 01-6057787. 3-bedroom, 1-star house, sleeps 7. £250-270. Located in North County Dublin.

Rathcoole, Mrs. Brid Fitzpatrick, Shamrock Lodge, Castlewarden, Straffen, County Kildare. Telephone: 01-4588327/6057777. 4 bedrooms, 3-star detached house. Sleeps 6. Suburb south of Dublin City Center. Very nice owner, good access to Wicklow and Kildare. £225-325.

Templeogue, David Brophy, 12 Nutley Lane, Dublin 4. Telephone: 01-269-1309/01-6057777. FAX: 01-6057787. 3 bedrooms. Sleeps 6. Modern semi-detached house. South Dublin suburb. £170-275.

Southeast

Ballon, Mary Jordan, Milltown, Kilbride, Ballon, County Carlow. Farmhouse on tillage farm near owner's residence. Nature's paradise. Telephone: 0503-59136/051-852444. FAX: 0503-59136/051-877388. 3 bedrooms. Sleeps 7. £140-230.

Inistioge, Margaret Dunne, St. Columb's Presbytery, Kilmacshane, Inistioge, County Kilkenny. Telephone: 056-58550/051-852444. FAX: 051-877388. 2 bedrooms. Sleeps 5. Eighteenth-century coach house. 4-star. Beautiful setting in Nore River Valley. £190-275.

Kilkenny, Joan and Kevin Mahon, The Gables, Archersgrove, Kilkenny, County Kilkenny. Telephone: 056-61869/051-852444. FAX: 956-51788. Winner of Agritourism award. Restored eighteenth-century house on deer farm. 3 bedrooms. Sleeps 5. 3-star. £225-270. Off-season rates by request.

Tramore, Mrs. A. Alyward, 25 Newgrove Avenue, Sandymount, County Dublin 4. Telephone: 01-2692463. Restored Georgian terraced house in town center. 4 bedrooms. Sleeps 6. 4-star. Close to beach. Many activities and attractions for the family. Separate dining, kitchen, and sitting area. £225-395.

Southwest

Bantry, Mary Coakley, Snave, Bantry, County Cork. Telephone: 027-50902. 4 bedrooms, 3 en suite. Sleeps 8. Bungalow in scenic location overlooking Bantry Bay, 5 min. walk to sea. 3-star. £100-400.

Kinsale, Clare O'Donovan, Laurel Wood House, Ballinhassig, County Cork. Telephone 021-885103/021-273251. FAX: 021-885103. 2 bedrooms. Sleeps 4. House within 5 min. of picturesque Kinsale. £165-325.

Kinsale, Carol Kennedy, Sea Antone, 10 Park View, Victoria Road, Cork City, County Cork. Telephone: 021-963513/021-273251. FAX: 021-273504. 4 bedrooms. Sleeps 7. Modern 2-story, semi-detached house. 5 min. from Kinsale Center. Private garden and patio and off-street parking. Fully furnished. £175-375.

Dingle, John Street, Curtain Call, Dingle, County Kerry. Telephone: 066-51989. 3 bedrooms. Sleeps 6. Upstairs apartment in the heart of Dingle, superbly furnished. 4-star. Accessible to excellent restaurants and pubs. £280-380.

Dingle, Teresa Devane, 20 Meadowlands, Oakpark, Tralee, County Kerry. Telephone: 066-26169 (after 6 PM). 4 bedrooms. Sleeps 8. 3-star, 2-story house overlooking Ventry Harbor and beach. £220-320, rest of year by request.

Killarney (Farranfore), John and Mary O'Connell, Curraleigh, Dripsey, County Cork. Telephone: 021-873396/021-273251. FAX: 021-273504. 3 bedrooms. Sleeps 6. 150-year-old, modernized, 2-story farmhouse. 14 km outside Killarney. £200-350.

Killarney, Helen Foran, Ard Na Griene, Tralee Road, Killarney, County Kerry. Telephone: 064-31778/021-273251. FAX: 021-27504. 4 bedrooms. Sleeps 8 comfortably. Detached modern house with garden. Fully furnished in all regards. Wonderfully accommodating owner. Just outside Killarney off Tralee road in country setting. £150-400.

Shannon

Ballybunion, John O'Connor, Main Street, Ballybunion, County Kerry. Telephone: 068-27112/061-361362. FAX: 068-27787. 3 bedrooms. Sleeps 5. New centrally located townhouse in a sunny, south-facing courtyard. Near beach and golf courses. 4-star. £200-495.

Doolin, Breda Cullinan, Ballyvara, Doolin, County Clare. Telephone 065-74349/061-362689. FAX: 061-361362. 2 bedrooms. Sleeps 4. Traditional thatched cottage on Main Cliff of Moher Road. 1 km from Doolin. Renowned for its traditional music and seafood. 1-star. £120-280.

Lahinch, Janet Cornellan, Kilcolumb, Cahercalla, Ennis, County Clare. Telephone: 065-20442/061-362689. FAX: 065-20481. 3 bedrooms. Sleeps 6. 4-star. Beautifully decorated semi-detached house, near beach and golf courses. £350-450, rest of year on request.

Ireland West—Galway

Clifden, Maureen O'Malley, Hillside Lodge, Sky Road, County Galway. Telephone: 095-21463/091-567673. FAX 091-565201. 3 bedrooms, 1 en suite. Sleeps 8. Modern, large, self-contained. 3-star. Apartment adjacent to B&B, on scenic Sky Road. Large sitting room with open fire. £220-360.

Galway (Sea Road), George Clancy, Crescent Close, Sea Road, Galway, County Galway. Telephone: 091-587338/091-567673. FAX: 091-565201. 3 bedrooms. Sleeps 5. 3-star apartments. In Salthill, beach within walking distance, close to Galway city and amenities. £210-325.

Galway West—Mayo

Westport, Jacqueline and Frank Brady, Newtown House, Partry, Claremorris, County Mayo. Telephone: 092-43009/091-567673. FAX: 091-565201. 3 bedrooms. Sleeps 5. New, modern, 2-story, 3-star house. Within walking distance to town. Close to beach, golf, and fishing. Many features. £170-330.

Northwest—Donegal

Donegal Town, Brian Espey, Summerhill, Donegal Town, County Donegal. Telephone: 073-21327. 3 bedrooms. Sleeps 5. Semi-detached house 4 km from Donegal Town. Magnificent views of Donegal Bay, islands, and mountains. Beach .5 mile. 2-star. £100-220.

NORTHERN IRELAND

(Rates in pounds sterling)

Antrim

Cushendun, Anne Blaney, 114 Tromra Road, Cushendum, County Antrim. BT44 0ST. Telephone/Fax: 021667-61221. E-Mail: mullarts@1dpt.demon.co.uk. 4-star. Located between Cushendall and Cushendun on Antrim Coast. Converted church into three award-winning apartments. Two sleep 2, and one sleeps 5. £200-375.

Portrush, Rosemary White, 18 Maddybenny Park, Portrush, County Antrim. BT52 2 PT. Telephone/Fax: 01265-823394. 6 mews cottages. Sleeps 6/8. Pretty equestrian center on the coast. 4-star. £200-400.

Down

Newcastle, D. Maginn, Tory Bush Cottages, 79 Tullyree Rd., Bryansford, Newcastle, County Down. Telephone: 013967-24348. 8 traditional cottages. Sleeps 5. 3-star. Situated in middle Mourne Mountains, 4 miles from coastal resort of Newcastle. Many recreational features nearby. Beautiful vistas. £250-410.

Fermanagh

Enniskillen, C. McManus, Teemore, Derrylin, County Fermanagh. BT92 9BL. Telephone/Fax: 013657-48493. 6 bungalows. Sleeps 3/6. On the Shannon-Erne canal link. 3-star. Day-cruisers can be rented to explore the pleasures of the waterway and to explore neighboring villages. £200-360.

Index

LODGINGS

(County in parentheses)

NORTHERN IRELAND CITIES AND TOWNS

LODGINGS
(County in parentheses)

SELF-CATERING
REPUBLIC OF IRELAND
DUBLIN AND COUNTY

Southeast Region

Southwest Region

Shannon Region

Ireland West-Galway

Galway West-Mayo

NORTHERN IRELAND
(By County)

Antrim

Down

Fermanagh

PLEASE HELP US
TO KEEP OUR STANDARDS HIGH

To help maintain the high reputation of *The Irish Bed &*
Breakfast Book, we ask for your comments about your stay. It will
help us if you return all comment forms in one envelope.

Name of Host _____

Address _____

It was (please circle one):
Absolutely Perfect, Excellent, Good, Adequate, Not Satisfactory.

Do you have any comments that could help your host, on such
things as breakfast, meals, beds, cleanliness, hospitality, or value
for money?

Complete this section. It will be detached before we send your
comments to the host.

YOUR NAME _____

YOUR ADDRESS _____

_____

Please mail this form to Pelican Publishing Co. Inc.,
P.O. Box 3110, Gretna, LA 70054-3110, USA

FOLD HERE. FASTEN LIP ON FRONT WITH CLEAR TAPE.

PLEASE FASTEN SIDES WITH CLEAR TAPE.

PLEASE FASTEN SIDES WITH CLEAR TAPE.

CUT

FOLD HERE

RE: 4th edition, Irish B&B

Place
first class
postage
here

IRISH B&B
Pelican Publishing Company
1000 Burmaster Street
P.O. Box 3110
Gretna, Louisiana 70054

CUT

THIS IS DUBLIN POCKET GUIDE

By Myles Plunkett

This two-in-one guide and removable, waterproof, Tyvek city map are the perfect touring companions to the enigmatic capital of the Emerald Isle.

The birthplace of James Joyce, home of Trinity College and the *Book of Kells,* and location of the Guinness Brewery, Dublin truly has something to offer for everyone.

Directions for three classic walks are provided, and include a tour of Dublin pubs. Excursions outside Dublin are detailed as well, as are places to stay, eat, shop, and be lively. And with the extremely handy removable city map, Dublin is literally at your fingertips . . . or in your pocket.

112 pp. 4¾ x 8¼ 56 color photos 3 b/w photos 1 illus. 5 color maps plus separate city map Index ISBN: 1-56554-683-0

THE SCOTTISH BED AND BREAKFAST BOOK

By June Skinner Sawyers

A Glasgow native shares lodging secrets she has learned on her yearly return visits to her homeland.

June Skinner Sawyers also is the author of *Famous Firsts of Scottish Americans* and *Maverick Guide to Scotland*, both published by Pelican.

256 pp. 5½ x 8½
75 illus. 75 photos Maps Index
ISBN: 1-56554-651-2

THE MAVERICK GUIDE TO SCOTLAND

By June Skinner Sawyers

This increasingly popular tourist destination claims lush highlands, castle ruins, and picturesque lochs within its borders. From bustling Edinburgh, the country's largest city, to the quaint Outer Hebrides, this guide provides all of the information necessary to make any trip to Scotland both easy and enjoyable.

608 pp. 5½ x 8½
54 photos 19 maps Index
ISBN: 1-56554-227-4

GOLFING IN IRELAND
The Most Complete Guide for Adventurous Golfers, 2nd Edition

By Rob Armstrong

Ireland is one of the most popular golf venues for Americans who are eager to sample famous golf courses like Ballybunion and Lahinch.

In the first edition, author Rob Armstrong predicted the Irish golf boom. In his thoroughly revised second edition, he revisits old golf courses and profiles the best new ones, including County Cork's magnificent Old Head Golf Club, already regarded as one of the most exciting new courses in the world.

304 pp. 6 x 9 Photos
Scorecards Appendixes Index
ISBN: 1-56554-726-8

THE BOOK OF IRISH GOLF

By John Redmond

Discover all of the aspects of Irish golf, from the courses and competitors of its early days to the new courses and players who are emerging and adding to its legacy at home and abroad. The author takes the reader back to some of the greatest moments in Irish golf and presents statistics and records that have been set on Irish courses. Stunning photographs of the historic courses as well as many notable competitors are included.

176 pp. 8½ x 11
Color and b/w photos Index
ISBN: 1-56554-327-0

THE AUSTRALIAN BED & BREAKFAST BOOK: 11th Edition

Compiled by J. & J. Thomas

"Some of the comments are quite evocative."

Los Angeles Times

This thoroughly updated guide lists prices, facilities, addresses, illustrations of the various homes, and telephone numbers for making reservations, along with easy-to-follow directions.

**464 pp. 5½ x 8½ Illus. Maps Index 11th ed.
ISBN: 1-56554-734-9**

THE NEW ZEALAND BED & BREAKFAST BOOK: 11th Edition

Compiled by J. & J. Thomas

Kiwis make Yanks feel at home in these B&Bs.
    The definitive guide to bed and breakfasts in New Zealand presents descriptions of more than 1,000 private homes and hotels and their services. This thoroughly expanded, newly updated reference book includes names, addresses, telephone numbers, prices, illustrations of the various homes, and more.

**784 pp. 5½ x 8½ Illus. Maps Index 11th ed.
ISBN: 1-56554-743-8**